Secrets of Successful Women

19 Successful Women Share their Thoughts and Offer Advice on Business, Health, Fitness and Life

Andy Charalambous

Contributors To This Book

FIT EXPERT SERIES

Copyright Information

Secrets Of Successful Women
By
Andy Charalambous

Copyright 2013 Andy Charalambous

All rights reserved. Published in the United States of America. No part of this Book may be reproduced or transmitted in any form or by any means, electronic or mechanical or by an information storage and retrieval system unless given permission to do so by the author.

This Book is a general educational health/fitness related information product.
As an express condition to reading this Book, you understand and agree to the following terms:

The content in this Book is not a substitute for direct, personal, professional medical care and diagnosis. None of the exercises or treatments mentioned in this Book should be performed or otherwise used without clearance from your physician or health care provider.

There may be risks associated with participating in activities mentioned in this book for people in poor health or with pre-existing physical or mental health conditions. If you choose to participate in these risks, you do so of your own free will and accord, knowingly and voluntarily.

Under no circumstances, including, but not limited to, negligence, shall the Author, (Andy Charalambous), be liable for any special or consequential damages that result from the use of, or the inability to use this Book, even if the Author has been advised of the possibility of such damages. Applicable law may not allow the limitation or exclusion of liability or incidental or consequential damages, so the above limitation or exclusion may not apply to you. In no event shall the Author's total liability to you for all damages, losses and causes of action exceed the amount paid by you, if any, for this Book.

You agree to hold the Author of this Book, the Author's owners, agents, co-authors, contributors, affiliates and employees harmless from any and all liability for all claims for damages due to injuries, including attorney fees and costs incurred by you or caused to third parties by you, arising out of the products, services and activities discussed in this Book.

Fact and information are believed to be accurate at the time they were placed in this Book. All data provided in this Book is to be used for information purposes only. Information provided is not all-inclusive and is limited to information that is made available and such information should not be relied upon as all-inclusive or accurate.

IF YOU DO NOT AGREE WITH THESE TERMS AND EXPRESS CONDITIONS, DO NOT READ THIS EBOOK. YOUR USE OF THIS EBOOK, PRODUCTS, SERVICES AND ANY PARTICIPATION IN ACTIVITIES MENTIONED IN THIS EBOOK MEAN THAT YOU ARE AGREEING TO BE LEGALLY BOUND BY THESE TERMS.

Copyright 2013

Recommended Related Books

More Books you may like by Andy Charalambous

Just type 'Andy Charalambous' in the Amazon search bar to see all of his latest books:

Special Thanks

I would like to thank all the women featured in this book.

I am amazed at how honest you all were in answering these personal and inquisitive interview questions.

Let's face it....there were a lot of questions!

However, none of you complained. You focused on getting the job done in order to help others who want to be where you are now.

I actually had fun creating this book and, (as a man), learned so much about what it takes to be happy and successful in all areas of life.

You are an inspiration to all women who are searching for that special something in their lives whether in business, in health and fitness, in relationships or just life in general.

Thank you for being a part of this book project.

Andy

Introduction

Before you get started reading these amazing interviews I would strongly advize you to keep a notepad and pen handy. Better still, use your Kindle highlighter because you are going to learn so much from these women.

Ok, so why did I decide to create this book?

Honestly, I am just totally fascinated by people who go out and achieve their own personal success. Against all odds there are people who just keep driving forward and battle to make their dreams a reality no matter what.

This includes men and women but I think for women the path to success is a little different.

It seems that for years women have been hindered by traditional role models, stereotyped views, and even their own friends and family's attitudes.

Despite these barriers, thousands of women from all walks of life have found the path to their own personal success.

It is a known fact that if you want to turn your life around and be the best you can be you need to surround yourself with those who have already done so.

You need to learn to live and breathe as they have in order to follow the path they have taken and achieve the goals they have achieved.

Ok, so where can you find women such as this who are ahead of the game, effectual, prosperous and effective in all they focus their mind on?
The answer is right here in this book.

I specifically wanted to interview women who I thought would not only be role models for exercise and good health but also for business and many other areas of life.

We all love to hear true accounts of success and in many ways we can learn from these insights.
While putting this book together and reading all the interviews I found myself learning so much about myself and why I am where I am today. These life lessons apply to men too!

What is interesting is that as you read through the interviews you will notice many similarities in how these women live their lives and how they focus on a particular mindset to get them to their destination.

They have applied a common set of characteristics and broke through personal, mental and physical barriers to succeed.

I asked questions about business, personal life, health and fitness, nutrition and much more.

You will be intrigued and inspired by the answers to the many questions I asked these 19 interviewees. I am amazed at how determined these women are to help others who are seeking the inspiration and motivation to push forward and realize their own dreams and personal successes.

In this book you can explore the life strategies these women have used to help them succeed and provide a blueprint you can use to achieve success in your personal and professional life.

If you want to know the secrets of those women who are successful in business, in wealth, in health and fitness, in relationships, in athletic activities, in mental wellbeing and much more then read on!

Table of Contents

Introduction
Interview 1
Page 1
Forbes Riley
Interview 2
Page 23
Lisa Anderson
Interview 3
Page 63
Michelle Brown
Interview 4
Page 88
Dr. JaNee' G. Mobley
Interview 5
Page 110
Iva Franks-Singer
Interview 6
Page 127
Jessica Li
Interview 7
Page 156
Elspeth Polt
Interview 8
Page 180

Dr. Marisa R. Silver
Interview 9
Page 202
Elizabeth Kallam Turner
Interview 10
Page 232
Kellie Davis
Interview 11
Page 243
Teiler Robinson
Interview 12
Page 261
Rhonda Shear
Interview 13
Page 279
Sherry Ann Boudreau
Interview 14
Page 294
Nicole Busch
Interview 15
Page 315
Lori Ann Freemire
Interview 16
Page 340
Madeline Hernandez
Interview 17
Page 362
Alicia Bell
Interview 18

Page 382
Diane Adeler
Interview 19
Page 390
Lisa Moskovitz
Recommended Reads
Would You Be Willing To Leave A Review?
About the Author

INTERVIEW 1
Forbes Riley

Personal Information

Full Name:
Forbes Riley

Age:
53

Location:
St Petersburg

Number of Children:
10 year old boy/girl twins

Profession:
TV Host, CEO SpinGym, author, speaker, actress

Honors & Awards:
National Fitness Hall of Fame 2010, Moxie Award Winner "Best Female Presenter of the Year (2x), "Best Home Home Shopping Presenter", TeleAward Winner, Miss Teenage NY/America

Certifications:
Personal Fitness Trainer IFTA, AFFA; Licensed Massage Therapist, Licensed Hypnotist, Certified NLP Master, Brown Belt Tae Kwon Do

....

General Questions

What are you known for professionally?
As the 2010 National Fitness Hall of Fame inductee I am most known for being a leading authority in the health, fitness and wellness industry. I am most known for selling more than $2 Billion dollars worth of health & fitness products on TV via infomercials and Live Home Shopping (HSN & QVC).

I am most recognized from hosting the Jack LaLanne Power Juicer that aired for 8 years in 80 countries and the Montel Williams HealthMaster Blender for the past 6 years. I am also known for creating the fitness sensation SpinGym – the most unique, innovative and portable fitness product. When I launched it on the Discovery TV series PitchMen I was told it would never work and I was wasting my time – we have gone on to sell more than 600,000 SpinGyms in just 3 years. Professionally I am the health and wellness Martha Stewart!
......

Tell us about how you got into your line of work.
I was an actress on TV and movies (Fox's 24, The Practice, Picket Fences) and a TV host (ESPN's The X-Games, my own daily talk show on TLC –Essentials etc) My daily job however was to promote health and fitness products on home shopping – I have been doing it for more than 20 years. I was overweight and ridiculed most of my life in spite of my "success" and decided that after I figured out my own personal body issues that I could inspire others to get fit, happy and healthy.
......

How long have you been doing what you do?
I began working on stage since my early 20's (I worked on Broadway with Christopher Reeve, Bob Fosse and more) all the while fighting a weight issue. I have acted in more than 30 TV and film projects – so the short answer is my whole life!! I changed direction and began helping others transform their bodies shortly after 9/11 – I had the chance to personally survive the tragedy and have been working on this reinvention of my mission since then.
......

What do you enjoy most about what you do?
Helping others. There is amazing joy watching someone come into their own, gaining confidence, and getting not only the body they've always dreamed of but they life they didn't even know was waiting for them!
......

What are you most passionate about professionally? What most excites you about your work & the contribution you can make?
I am most passionate about building the fitness sensation SpinGym – I have created a product that gets people in wheelchairs easily get cardio, helps women who hate their arms and find embarrassing bingo wings keeping them from enjoying their lives to giving hope to people who can't get to

the gym. I am excited to have struggled as hard as I did and make the journey to health and fitness so much easier for everyone else!
……

What's the single most important reason for your success?
A crazy desire to help others and being in front of the camera – just LOVE what I do!!
……

What do you consider to be your greatest achievement?
Getting SpinGym from a product "no one wanted" to become an international fitness sensation. I own the company 100% and it's all my heart and soul in the creation and execution of this dream.
……

How do you think women have changed over the years? Regarding business, sports and fitness.
There is definitely a large crack in the glass ceiling. In sports women have made amazing strides in competition and our superstars like Serena Williams, Mia Hamm, Gaby Reese – both as athletes and role models. In business it still seems like a struggle to get equal pay, to get noticed for your work not how you look, but we continue to move forward.
……

What is the number one thing you like best about being into fitness?
Truly nothing tastes as good as fit feels. Most of my life I struggle with an extra 30 pounds and it was just frustrating – I tried all the popular fad diets – would lose the weight and gain back even more – finally understanding the truth about food, nutrition, exercise, and balance has changed EVERYTHING about me as a person. I am more confident, I enjoy clothes, I enjoy being a mom – and at 53 with 10 year old twins that

could have been a struggle – but I am stronger, fitter and healthier than most of the other 4th grade moms – and they are younger than me!
……

Is there anything wrong with wanting to portray women athletes, actors, etc as feminine and physically attractive?
I love looking at strong fit bodies but I am not a fan of women who overdo it. Female body builders can push that masculine line a bit too far with the desire for big sculpted bodies. I am a fan of athletic, agile, fit, and toned bodies. Feminine and attractive are admirable qualities for women – we should enjoy them and of course use them to our benefit ☺
……

How do you deal with cravings for junk foods, sweets and salty food?
That is what has changed as I've gotten older. I have better balanced nutrition – eat more raw, organic foods, use spices and have noticed that I don't have the crazy cravings I had in my 20's and 30's. I don't believe in junk food as I value my energy – would you put water in your car's gas tank and expect it to run at top quality! I do enjoy my chocolate and some sweet – but everything in moderation. When you eat clean 80 percent of the time – you can indulge 20 percent and still stay on target!
……

Describe a typical day for you, starting from the moment you wake up in the morning.
Kiss my twins and get them ready for school – prepare all of us a nutritious lunch with protein veggies etc – start our day with a power packed protein smoothie. Get in a quick workout – always SpinGym (at least 3 times a day for 5 minutes minimum) – then there is NO typical day – some days on I'm set shooting a TV show or live on HSN – some days I have photo shoots, video workouts, magazine interviews – then

there's writing, email, facebook and phone calls – did I mention there's no typical day.

Health & Fitness Questions

What sports do you participated in for fun?
I love to ski, scuba dive, play tennis, go hiking, biking, roller skating with the kids, volleyball on the beach, swimming – everything except golf – I plan to learn when I slow down in my 70's.
......

Please describe your normal diet. What do you eat in a typical day to stay in shape?
Avocado, chicken, lettuce, watermelon, lemons, ginger, sweet potato, wonderful new energy drink called Celsius, pineapple, coconut water, green beans, all kinds of seafood, hummus, tomatoes, celery, carrots, beets, garlic, olives, spinach and kale.
......

What is the most challenging thing you deal with about consistently staying in top shape?
Balancing working out with work and life – that's why I'm such a fan of my on the go SpinGym workouts.
......

What type of exercises do you include in your routine to stay in shape?
SpinGym EVERYDAY – 5 minutes to 30 minutes 3 to 4 times a day – has toned my arms, abs, core and I'm the smallest dress size I have EVER been: http://BuySpinGym.com
......

A total beginner is about 35 pounds overweight. She doesn't really know where to start. What tips can you give her to follow the right track?
 1. Keep a journal – when you get honest with what you eat – everything changes – you know more about good eating than your realize – and I just launched a new

motivating journal called e.a.t. – a journal for what you eat and for what's eating you
2. Start your day with a shot of apple cider vinegar followed by a big glass of water with lemon.
3. SpinGym 3 times a day for ONLY 5 minutes at a time – boost your stubborn, sluggish metabolism. You will double your heart rate in less than a minute and start to become a fat burning machine not a fat storing machine.
4. Drink a healthy green super food drink and get your ph back in balance.

Find a buddy – accountability is very motivating! I recommend joining my community at www.fitwithforbes.com - I have 20 hours of education tips on food, nutrition, diet, exercise and so much more – you need good information – not fads!
……

What tips do you recommend for eating out at restaurants to make sure we don't gain too much weight/fat?
Easy – there's ALWAYS great food at a restaurant but:
1. Don't let them put the bread on the table
2. Ask for water, when they try to push pre-dinner cocktails
3. Order dressing on the side, same with any sauces – YOU need to portion it out – the chef is not there to keep you skinning
4. Ask for broiled fish, chicken or meat – nothing fried –

Let your dessert be a hot cup of green tea!
……

What are your top tips for developing toned and defined arms? Specific exercises, diet advice, etc.
For arms – there's only 1 thing I recommend – www.SpinGym.com tightens tones fast and deeper than resistance bands or dumbbells – my DVD routines are designed to sculpt not bulk!

......

What are your top tips for losing unwanted body fat? Specific exercises, diet advice, etc.
Amp up your metabolism – with clean eating and short burst exercises throughout the day.
......

What are your top tips for staying motivated on a fitness plan?
Follow www.FitwithForbes.com -- why – because I offer mental motivation – physical is only a small part, but cracking the mindset of what is holding you back is the key to all your success in life.
......

What is your training routine like? Please include a few details.
Honestly the best is to turn on the music (in my house, iPod) and just DANCE!
......

What is the best way to get started in your industry?
I am professional TV host who also markets on TV. To get to my position you need to train in speech, presenting, improve, and perhaps a bit of acting – I run a workshop 2 times a year in Tampa to coach people who dream of hosting on HSN/QVC, an infomercial, TV shows like EXTRA and ET, newscasters and more.
......

What is the best way towards becoming a personal trainer?
You have to love fitness and people – so many certifications and conventions around the country.
......

Have you suffered any injuries? What injuries?

I torn my left knee's ACL in a skiing accident in the 30's and had replacement surgery – worst year of my life – rehab was insanely painful, constant having to break up scar tissues and learn to us my leg again.
Thanks to SpinGym (which you may have only thought was upper body) I have conditioned my quad and hamstrings better than they have EVER been.
……

Isn't it hard to stay fit? How do you manage that?!
Hard to do anything is a mindset. It's just a part of my happiness to be fit so I workout daily, eat clean, hang out with positive people and stay focused on the dream.
……

Business Questions

What is the most difficult part of starting your business?
Having people believe in you.
……

What do you consider to be success as a business owner or entrepreneur?
Making positive impact on people's lives and having them understand and achieve a new level of happiness. Financially to take care of all those around me from family to employees.
……

What's your least favorite part about being a business owner or entrepreneur?
You are always responsible for everything – the smartest thing you can learn to do is delegate, surround yourself with smart, capable people and trust.
……

What's the biggest thing you struggle with as a business owner or entrepreneur?
Staying focused – as a mom I want to run off and play with the kids, fool around on facebook – it's hard when you're the boss – but I also would NEVER change it!
......

How do you think running a business or being an entrepreneur has made you a better person?
I am more compassionate, patient and committed to helping others.
......

What's unique about the service that you provide?
My company and mission is "whole body" – I don't JUST offer a fitness product but a lifestyle solution.
......

Do you have any of your own branded products? If so, what are they?
SpinGym is the most amazing fitness training product – portable, compact but more effective and toning, tighting and burning calories that almost anything on the market – PLUS you don't have to be in the gym to do it. I also offer amazing transformational coaching that has not only changed people's bodies but inspired them to become millionaires. I take inventors products onto a TV platform from infomercials to home shopping and SO MUCH MORE – my masterminds and coaching are second to none!
......

Mixed Questions

If you could be any character in fiction, who would you be?
Obi Wan Kanobi or James Bond.

What things do you believe differentiates you from your contemporaries?
I am the health and wellness Martha Stewart – with creative innovative products and solutions to make you life better, happier and healthier.

Who has been the biggest influence on your life? What lessons did that person teach you?
Meeting Jack Lalanne and spending more than 8 years working alongside him has been my greatest influence – he was sold health, food and exercise conscious mixed with being a smart entrepreneur and a family man – a hero on every level.

If you could paint a picture of any scenery you've seen before, what would you paint?
The mystery of Lake Powell – amazing mountains with pristine water – it was unearthly looking – another was the 2000 ft sea wall behind the water off of Turks and Caicos – the most beautiful colored water, a rainbow of fish and sea life mixed with plants – like being INSIDE a magical fish tank!

What are some goals you are still trying to accomplish?
To get back on National TV with a studio audience devoted to health and wellness – like Rachel Ray, Dr. Oz and Martha Stewart.

What are the most important lessons you've learned in life?
To dream bigger than you ever imagined and enjoy the results – the Law of Attraction works miracles.

......

What are you proudest of in your life?
That I have healthy, smart, ingenious 10 year old children (twins) They are at an age where they model their parents and it keeps me on my game. They will say the most amazing things but daily my inspiration is as simple as "mommy, I love you – you are the best – can we cuddle!"
......

How do you set your goals?
Start at my memorial and work backwards.
......

What else would you do if you weren't in your current line of work?
Can not even imagine why I would do anything else.
......

Do you believe in the Law of Attraction?
It IS my religion.
......

What would we find in your refrigerator right now?
Almond milk, pineapple, watermelon, ice tea, white wine, broccoli, lettuce, carrots, cucumber, beets, garlic, ginger, onions, frozen grapes, apple cider vinegar.
......

If you had the opportunity to get a message across to a large group of people what would your message be?
Dream it, believe it, achieve it!
......

Where do you see yourself in 5 years?
Everywhere! From TV to magazines, movies, radio and more ☺
......

What are you best at?
Inspiring others.
......

What books do you like to read?
Motivational, inspiring stories, business books and the occasional rag magazine you find in the grocery store – love pop culture and dichotomy.
......

What is your favorite type of music?
The full gamut – music is my lifeblood and the backdrop to my days and nights – from romantic to rock n roll – I stretch to music in the morning – workout to cranking beats, then love to dance at night – from classical to rap and everything in between.
......

Describe your parents, what are they like?
They were married for 40 years – loved me so much, so supportive and I am the luckiest kid ever to have known them.
......

What were your dreams as a child and did you achieve any of them?
To dance with Fred Astaire – and I did as a guest at the 50th annual academy awards in Los Angeles!
......

Tell us a time in your life that was a time you'll never forget?
Working at club med in my 20's – I worked all around the world, scuba dived in amazing places, learn to ski, speak French, create shows – it was so carefree yet FILLED with adventures.
......

What things do you find yourself doing that you said you'd never do?
Taxes.
……

What are some qualities that you value in a person?
Humor, passion, commitment, focus, vision, integrity, compassion, joy.
……

Name 5 of your favorite movies.
Starman, The Year of Living Dangerously, Butch Cassidy and the Sundance kid, Roman Holiday, West Side Story – and 5000 more – I love my movies! Can't forget James Bond flicks, all of Steven Spielberg and Hitchcock! And my favourite: Splatter University because I star in it back in my early 20's – todays it's a classic cult – go figure!
……

What TV shows do you like?
Child of the 60's : Man from Uncle, Betwitched, The Monkees, Partridge Family, and It Takes a Thief Today: Revenge, Desperate Housewives, Falling Skies, 20/20, Dancing with the Stars.
……

What do you enjoy doing on a Sunday afternoon?
Kids, park, rollerskating, movies, jet skiing, bike riding, and every once in a while just sleeping in.
……

You are stranded in the Amazon rain forest. What 3 items would you want to have with you and why?
A really talented tour guide – I failed survival class so he would come in handy. My iphone – great photos, videos and perhaps if I could get a signal I wouldn't be stranded and a SpinGym – go for staying fit and warding off dangerous creature (you can hit them!).

......

Is there anything in particular that you wish you could do over? What is it?
My 5th grade math class – only "B" I ever got!
......

What personality traits in your mind are best suited for your job, career, etc?
Quick wit, gift of gab and a crazy sense of curiosity and mischief.
......

What is your favorite drink?
Fresh brewed iced tea black or green over ice!
......

What is your favorite color?
Hot Pink.
......

Name a movie that touched you in some way.
Sophie's Choice – I am a mom of 2 and the thought that anyone would have to choose would have driven me insane as well – I get physically ill at just the thought of that!
......

When in life have you felt most alone? Why?
At my mom's funeral – my dad has also recently passed away and the thought of being orphaned and missing my best friends for the rest of my life was overwhelming – it has taken years to grieve and every once in a while I will still just cry cause I want my mommy!
......

What would be impossible for you to give up?
The need to get exciting new products in people's hand – I'm relentless but I love it!

……

Why would someone not want to work with you?
Because I work at 110% and demand that of everyone around me – you to be driven and passionate to want to work with me – but I also play hard and love to have fun – if you don't see the magic in life – you won't be able to hang wit me!
……

What activities did you enjoy in school?
Loved being in the theatre, was an A+ student who skipped a year of high school and graduated college in 3 years with 2 degrees.
……

What kind of child were you?
Young.
……

If you could be a superhero, what would you want your superpowers to be?
To be invisible at will.
……

How do you want to be remembered?
As a passionate, energetic role model for women who was also a kickass mom!
……

What is one of your favorite quotes?
Leap and the net will appear. You are the sum of the obstacles you overcome.
……

What chore do you absolutely hate doing?
Laundry.
……

What is your best feature?

My smile – after 8 years of braces – I am proud to show off my teeth – but I just genuinely love life and get great compliments on my smile – it comes from the heart!
......

What was the last experience that made you a stronger person?
On March 20th 2013 I almost died in a NYC hospital 2000 miles from home when a huge kidney stone (my first ever) blocked my tubes, my blood was septic, I had emergency surgery and they weren't sure I would make it – 4 ½ days later – I was out of the woods – but more grateful than ever to see my family and get back to my mission!
......

What makes you uncomfortable, besides these questions?
Sitting on long plane flights – so fidgety and the seats are NEVER that comfortable – I fly 2 to 4 times a month – and the TSA, security, screening – really!!??
......

If you could change something physical about yourself, what would it be and why?
I'd have bright blue eyes like my son!
......

Besides money, what are your favorite ways to compensate people?
SpinGyms – oh you saw that coming – okay – gift cards.
......

When was the last time you tried something new?
We just started raising chickens at home – seriously something new – but loving the fresh eggs – they are blue – you heard of green eggs and ham – I gotcha beat.
......

How would you describe yourself in three words?
Energetic, passionate, relentless.
……

What is one thing you are not?
Male.
……

Do you think crying is a sign of weakness or strength?
Yes.
What makes you angry?
Close mindedness.
……

What makes you laugh?
My children (daily), great comedians (love jokes) and taking life too seriously – it makes me laugh a lot.
……

What are you afraid of?
Aside from these questions never ending – sharks – I live on the water – Tampa Bay is infested with sharks – makes water skiing with kids freaky.
……

What would be the first thing you would do if today was your last day?
Eat a HUGE container of Hagen Daz vanilla ice and kiss my kids till my lips fell off!
……

What's your vision of a perfect society?
Blurry.
……

What's something you check daily?
Facebook – committed to my virtual world – love it – then emails – don't really love them but a necessary evil.

......

Are you an emotional person?
In every way imaginable.
......

What's your own definition of happiness?
Inner peace, knowing everyone in my life is happy/healthy and that I've done something to inspire someone. Happiness is a simple state of enjoying the moment – no worries.
......

Which famous person would you like to interview and which questions would you ask him/her?
Joseph Pilates – the godfather of creative, innovative fitness. How did he come to such profound knowledge of the human body and I'd love to show him just HOW popular his dream became because during his lifetime he could never had imagined such global success – its what gives me hope about what I'm doing!
......

If you could choose to be born with a particular natural skill what skill would it be?
I so wish I could sing~ to stand on a stage in front of 10's of 1000's like Beyonce, JLO, Tina Turner and just entertain with your voice – I just can't carry a tune and do NOT ask me to karaoke!!
......

What advice would you give someone who wanted to do what you do?
Read my book – its way too complicated for here – lots of skill, timing, luck, passion with a dose of not living in the real world!! It's the reason I offer private coaching – I can get someone to achieve THEIR inner greatness and success but like any accomplished world class athlete do NOT expect to do it without a coach.
......

While you are watching TV in your home a penguin walks through the door wearing a sheriff's hat and badge. What does he say?
Stop drinking those double tequila margaritas because you're seeing a penguin in a sheriff's hat and badge.
......

Do you have any secrets you want to share with the few of us reading this? We won't say anything....promise!
Then it wouldn't be a secret then would it! But here goes – in my 20's I delivered singing and stripping telegrams – true story!
......

Are there any words of wisdom you'd like to pass along to us?
Dare to dream~ and dream bigger than you imagine possible!
......

Did you enjoy answering these questions? On a scale from 1 – 10. 1= I hated it. 10= I really enjoyed it.
11.

......

About Forbes

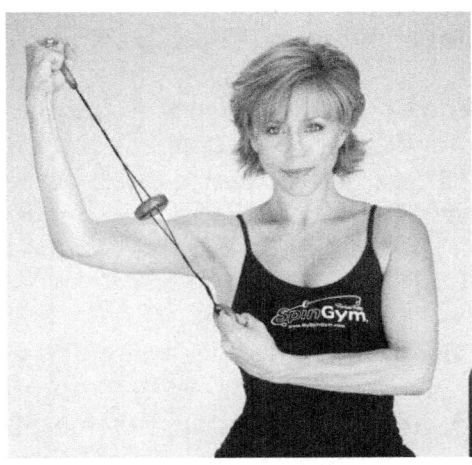

National Fitness Hall of Fame inductee 2010 Forbes Riley is an award-winning TV host, author, highly sought-after spokesperson, motivational keynote speaker, and life coach to celebrities and CEOs.

She has helped millions take positive action in their own lives by sharing her passion for and unshakeable belief in the impact a healthy lifestyle can make in your life.

Forbes has gained international celebrity due to her highly successful, globally broadcasted infomercials for the Jack Lalanne Juicer and the Living Well Healthmaster Blender, both of which have grossed into the hundreds of millions of dollars.

One of today's most accomplished entrepreneurs, she has been highlighted by Forbes magazine as a megabrand CEO for her SpinGym® alongside Silly Bandz, Skullcandy and Carol's Daughter. E! has produced a TV special profiling each of these hot new products and their talented creators, filmed Got Rich Quick: Outrageous Fortunes.

Forbes, crowned "America's LifeStyle Coach," is passionate about finding unique ways for people to get and stay healthy through food and exercise. She's known worldwide for starring in the feature film about raw food, Super Charge Me!

A regular presence on HSN, Forbes is known for selling her own line of branded lifestyle products including SpinGym and Love My Body fitness active wear as well as her Dual Trainer and Cool Towels. Her ebullient personality, charm and sincerity have contributed to her becoming known as "the Julia Roberts of infomercials."

On television, she is a familiar personality who has hosted series such as The X-Games on ESPN, Essentials on TLC (a daily talk show), and Zig & Zag Dog Game Show on Animal Planet. She spent five years as the original Fitness Host on Fit TV and the Cable Health Club as well as hosting series ABC Family, Pax-TV and MyNetwork TV.

With an eye and heart towards charity, Forbes, who has always been active with Big Brothers/Big Sisters, Clothes To Kids, Dress for Success, SPCA (hosting several telethons), the Dexter Fund, Revlon Run/Walk for the Cure, and many others, has now enrolled her business to give back.

SpinGym will launch Go Pink! SpinGym Empowerment, a fitness program for breast cancer survivors sponsored by proceeds of the new pinkSpinGym!

INTERVIEW 2

LisaAnderson

Personal Information

Full Name:
Lisa D. Anderson

Age:
55-1/2

Location:
Atlanta, Ga

Relationship Status:
Married for over 30 years!

Number of Children:
4 Fabulous Children (Melanie 26, Travis 23, Clay 19 and Paige 16)

Profession:
Wife, Mom, Personal Trainer, Group Fitness Instructor, Spin Instructor, Motivator, Fitness and Health Consultant for the Full Swing Magazine. http://www.livefullswing.com/contents.html

Educational Background:
Graduated from Southwest Miami High Class of '75, (Yes... 1975! ... LOL)

Certifications:
Keiser Spin Certification, ISSA Personal Trainer Certification, ISAA Sports Nutrition Certification
....

General Questions

What are you known for professionally?
Losing over 75lbs and changing my life at 49 years old and helping to motivate and inspire others to do the same.
......

Tell us about how you got into your line of work.
I was facing my 49th birthday and decided I did not want to be FAT and 50. It was then I began my Journey to a Healthier and Fit life. I had no idea just how much this Journey would change my Life!
......

How long have you been doing what you do?

I began my Personal Journey over 6 years ago. I have been in the 'training and fitness profession' now for over 5 years.
......

What do you enjoy most about what you do?
I ENJOY the whole aspect of what I get to do. I always say, "I am the luckiest girl I know". I love the impact that I have on other people's lives. Not to sound conceited in any way.. but while I am walking the walk, I love to talk the talk and share my own personal Journey with as people as I can. It's so fun when I run into somebody I haven't seen for awhile and they can't believe the person they are talking to is "ME". Change is POSSIBLE at any age.
......

What are you most passionate about professionally? What most excites you about your work & the contribution you can make?
I am most "passionate" about the PEOPLE I MEET and encounter. I am "passionate' about being able to help somebody accomplish things they never dreamed possible and they suddenly realize 'they can'. Can you imagine? I am so blessed and so lucky that I am given the opportunity and the ability to bring JOY and PRIDE back into a person's life.

Those "smiling from the inside" moments I call them. I wake up "EXCITED" every day about all of the different possibilities awaiting me, whether they be personal accomplishments or helping another person reach theirs. I am the walking "POSTER GIRL" for people over 50. My compassion and motivation and sincerity is infectious. I just can't help but be so excited!
......

What's the single most important reason for your success?
I would say the single most reason for my success professionally is my sincerity in helping others to live a Healthy and Fit life. The single most important reason for my

personal success is I finally decided if I did not change my life NOW and this time...WHEN would I. I am grateful for that 'bell' going off inside of my head telling me... "Lisa, this is YOUR TIME TO SHINE!"

What do you consider to be your greatest achievement?

I am proud of so many of my achievements. I would like to start off by saying my 4 Fabulous children are my greatest achievement. They all have a strong foundation and belief and such a great Love for each other and family and life.

Outside of my 'family' my greatest achievement...other than my initial weight loss of over 75lbs and having kept it off for over 6 years... is running a full marathon (26.2 miles) in October of 2012? Just 6 years ago I couldn't even walk on the treadmill at 3.2 MPH without holding on... Is it my SPRINT TRIATHLONS I train so hard for to accomplish (even though my darn bike still is my nemesis and tries to freak me out... LOL) or any of my other 'great feats' for the last few years?. No...in all honesty... I consider my greatest achievement other than the raising of my fabulous kids.. is my wonderful training partner, Carolyn Sanders and helping to encourage her to learn how to swim a few years ago before we did our first Iron Girl Sprint Triathlon together.

It's hard to explain..as it was Carolyn's achievement and not mine. In the end we both achieved overcoming our own fears by helping each other and cheering each other on. Carolyn couldn't even put her face in the water in January that year and by May she was swimming in an open lake, scared to death, swimming buoy to buoy and paddle boat to paddle boat until she reached the end of the swim portion.

My age group swam before hers so I did not know the whole race if she had made it through the water. As I was nearing the end of the final lap of my 5K run, I saw her running up the hill as I was running down... that was one of the greatest "moments' in my life. You take on a huge 'challenge' with another person and you are there the whole way for the ups and downs of training and you motivate each other and you lean on each other and you constantly remind each other that you can accomplish anything.

That day I learned that is true. I ran over and hugged her and told her I was so PROUD of her and that she did it! She hugged me back and reminded me as well, "Lisa, you did it, too". I certainly did. You have to realize that just over 6 years ago both Carolyn and myself had never done anything physical before. Carolyn and I had run some 5Ks and 10K races in our Journey to healthier and fit life, but this... THIS was a SPRINT TRIATHLON! I have to tell you, crossing that finish line, THAT MOMENT... words can not describe that feeling and it is "THAT FEELING" (that smiling from the inside moment) is what I try to share with as many people as I can.

We all deserve MOMENTS in LIFE like that as many times as we can get them. So to answer again my greatest achievement, I think it was during our IRON GIRL Training I definitely realized I have been given "GIFT"... a GIFT to help others believe in themselves. There were 5 girls in our Iron Girl Family that year. Carolyn and I went back the next year. I took over 50 women to their first Iron Girl Sprint Triathlon and from there husbands began doing them and participating along with some of my girl's children, they were so impressed by what the women had accomplished they wanted to do the same. You just never know when you open the door for 'one person'...just where it will lead.
......

How do you think women have changed over the years? Regarding business, sports and fitness.
I think there has been a HUGE change in business, sports and fitness for women over the years. Especially for somebody as old as I am... LOL. Back in my younger days growing up in Miami, Florida I was never exposed to 'sports' of any kind. I do not even remember any of my girlfriends 'playing sports'.

They took piano lessons and dance lessons but not like it is today with girls playing sports as much as the boys. Look at all of the Women TOP Athletes and also Sportscasters on TV now. You didn't see that a few years ago and what about women sports car drivers! We are no longer sitting on the sidelines or just being the 'cheerleaders'. Women are competing in sports just as the men.
......

Do you think women are competitive with each other? Why? Regarding business, sports and fitness.
Women are absolutely competitive with each other. Competition is a good thing. I think for the most part it is "friendly' competition and just like any sport it's anybody's race on any given day. The competition helps to fuel each ones' individual desire for greatness. Ultimately I always tell my peeps, It's just "YOU against YOU" in this Journey to a Healthier and Fit lifestyle. However, when it comes down to 'race day' I think deep down most people would like to be up on the Podium at some point. Crossing the finish line is always the most important part and then as you compete more and get stronger in your abilities that Podium and that 'win" sure does feel good!
......

What memorable competitions come to mind in your career?
I know personally just 'crossing that finish line" last October when I finished my Marathon. I felt like I was "KING OF THE WORLD" at that moment I didn't care who crossed before me, I just knew that I had crossed that "FINISH LINE".
......

What is the number one thing you like best about being into fitness?
The number one thing I like best about being into fitness is it is such a 'positive' experience. It helps me to keep on track in my own personal Journey. Like many other people, I had lost

weight before only to gain it back. Now that my life is all about "FITNESS"... I know there is no turning back! Some days are always harder than others, but ultimately, there is nothing better than feeling "in shape' and "strong in mind and body."
......

Is there anything wrong with wanting to portray women athletes, actors, etc as feminine and physically attractive?
Nothing at all wrong with wanting to portray women athletes, actors, etc and feminine and physically attractive. As always, Beauty is in the eye of the beholder. A healthy body is a beautiful body and very physically attractive.
......

How do you deal with cravings for junk foods, sweets and salty food?
We all have 'cheat days'. I remind my clients.. "This is a LIFESTYLE CHANGE" we are after...not a quick weight loss. Of course there are going to be splurges. The idea of NEVER eating another slice of pizza or having a bowl of ice cream or indulging in any of your favorite foods is 'crazy". We are "Living our life. I try to take the 'negative out' and replace it with 'positive reinforcement.' The point I try to promote is enjoy your 'cheat day' and do not feel guilty about it and beat yourself up over it.

No! Enjoy every bite. A splurge every now and then is just "Living your life" and enjoying it. That being said, just make sure you get 'back on your plan' the next day. What happens so often, even in my own personal experience, that one cheat day turns into another and another and another and before you know it, days and weeks and months and sometimes even years go by. Plan accordingly and then the following day go right back to healthy eating.

So how do I deal with 'cravings' for junk foods, sweets and salty food? Sometimes I deal with it...and sometimes...I just give in… Some days are good and some days need improving. Every day I just keep moving forward to this Healthy and Fit Life I am trying to lead and share with others. I always say…"if you bring it home…you will eat it". Don't bring it home! LOL. Hot air popcorn with a little parmesan cheese is my go to snack when I just need something. I also try to drink a big glass of water first and stay out of the kitchen. Bread is my temptation~ Oh my goodness…a nice crusty hot loaf of French bread? I keep telling myself…"step away from the bread'.

In the beginning of my Journey, however, I would always ask myself.. "How bad do you want it…and my answer was always the same… I want it bad!" I didn't even 'splurge on birthday cake the first year of my JOURNEY. Nope.. my mindset was so strong…it takes that commitment and determination. Some days it works and other days.. not so good… LOL. Keep focusing on 'your goal' and what you are trying to achieve.
……

Describe a typical day for you, starting from the moment you wake up in the morning.
I usually wake up at 7:00am. I drink a bottle of water that I keep on my night stand. This is another point I share with my PEEPS… you are dehydrated from the night before so drink a bottle of water before your feet even hit the floor! Water, water and more water throughout the day. I then make breakfast (usually a bowl of Steel Mill oatmeal with spinach and egg whites and a few berries) I am usually at the gym by 8:15 (after dropping my youngest daughter Paige at school).

I do my own workout prior to teaching my class at 9:45. Depending on the day of the week and what I am training for (during TRI season I will switch up swimming and running for 30 to 60 min) I teach my classes at the gym and I train my clients. I then will do my own weight training session for 30 minutes. I have a protein shake and/or an apple and almonds for a snack while at the gym and I will fix my lunch when I get home. I spend some time at the computer working on my Living Healthy Lisa Facebook and webpage and organizing myself and have another snack late afternoon (celery and peanut butter is a favorite in the afternoon).

Being conscious of drinking water throughout the day. I finish training my afternoon clients (3 days a week) and it's time to pick my daughter up from school. Soon it is time to fix dinner and I again sit at the computer checking emails, etc. I am sure you are familiar with the new 'old saying"..."Want to waste 5 hours...check your email for 5 minutes!" How true is that! On the days I do not have training clients my 'girls' and I try to meet at Stone Mountain Park to ride our bikes and run around the mountain. If you can 'conquer Stone Mountain" for your training, you can conquer your races! We also try to go up to the lake to practice our open water swimming as well. I am usually pretty exhausted early in the evening and I spend that time with my family. Again trying to avoid any late night snacking... and continue to drink water. Some nights my resistance is down and I find myself 'snacking' on popcorn with my husband while watching TV. LOL.
......

Health & Fitness Questions

What sports do you participated in for fun?
I was never a real 'sports participant' girl. I grew up in Miami, Florida and my sport of choice was "laying out in the sun". Literally. I could lay out in the sun from 8 to 5 and never be bored! I am lucky in that respect today (not so lucky regarding all the sun damage to my skin) that I have no 'sports injuries' like so many people have from playing sports, tennis elbow, bad knees, ankles, etc. I tease and say even at almost 56 years old...my body is brand new!
......

How long have you been playing those sports?
Now I am happy to say my 'sport of choice' are my Racing Events. Whether it's a 5K or 10K or Half Marathon or Full Marathon or Sprint Triathlon hopefully moving up to Olympic Distance soon and eventually a full Ironman. I have been doing this for about the last 5 years now.
......

What got you started in that sport?
I got started doing races for the fun of it and to see if I could actually do them. I will never forget when I ran my first mile! Oh my gosh...that was 4 times around the track without stopping and that was fabulous! I don't even remember why I entered my first 5K (3.1 miles) and then you just gradually increase to a 10K (6.2 miles) and then before you know it you are running a half marathon (13.1 miles) and you think you are crazy for running that far! Somehow... when you never believe you ever "could' let alone even want to... suddenly the idea of a FULL MARATHON (26.2 miles) suddenly seems like something you want to tackle... and I did! I love my sport of Triathlons as well. Everything just seems to lead into each other.... I love that! You just keep pushing a little bit harder .... And you cross that finish line!
......

What is your biggest accomplishment in your sports? Include fun sports and any athletic career.
I would have to say running my FULL MARATHON was a huge accomplishment. I loved every minute of the training and every mile. I started training May of last year and before I knew it..October was here. My training partner, Carolyn Sanders and I would meet at Stone Mountain part at 5:00am so we could get most of our training in for our long runs before it would get too hot! Loved that so much!

On another personal note... I did play 'DECK TENNIS" in Jr. High at Glades Jr. High... my only sport related 'claim to fame" is Deck Tennis which is a lot like Volleyball and Tennis

only you use a Rubber Ring. There are 2 people to a team. My partner was Sammi Siegal and we became Deck Tennis Champions in the 8th grade. I had a great end over end serve that the other team could not return. LOL.
......

What competitions have you entered? What were the outcomes?

As I previously stated I have entered RACE Competitions. I actually placed lst in my age division at one of my first 10K races I ran. That was pretty exciting. Last year at the Iron Girl Sprint Triathlon I placed 6th in my age group. I am proud to say that all Race EVENTS I have entered...I have crossed the Finish Line!
......

How do you motivate yourself and stay motivated?

I am so lucky... I just "AM MOTIVATED'. I just "AM". I am one of those lucky people at this stage in my life. As long as I stay "healthy" knock on wood. I know there is no turning back for me. I am so excited just to see what further transformation I can do with my body, my life and my Living Healthy Lisa Business. You have to have GOALS and PLAN. That is a huge part in keeping me motivated... besides I am having way too much FUN.
......

What are some of the main foods you would include in your shopping list to maintain a lean and muscular physique?

Chicken, Fish, Eggs, Fresh Veggies, Fruits, Nuts (Almonds and Walnuts) all Natural Peanut Butter or Almond butter, Steel Mill Oatmeal, Lean Meats (I love turkey sausage and bacon).
......

What is the most challenging thing you deal with about consistently staying in top shape?

NOT getting injured. Unfortunately, injury is bound to happen at some point in training. Other than that, I would have to say the motivation to continue challenging myself day after day...is something I look forward to.
......

Please describe your normal diet. What do you eat in a typical day to stay in shape?
I have steel mill oatmeal in the morning with spinach and chopped walnuts (or berries) with an egg. For the last 6 years I have been eating the whole egg...yes..yolk included. Just recently I have tried the liquid egg whites and I found I love them! Keep trying new foods...it is never ending. I have an apple and a few nuts as a snack.

Lunch is usually a salad with protein or a sandwich with Ezechial bread and avocado and fresh veggies galore. I top off with a little salsa or balsamic vinaigrette. I still "enjoy' my food. Snack is often some peanut butter and celery and dinner is usually chicken, lean meat of fish accompanied with brown rice or sweet potato and a veggie or side salad. I always put my 'dressing' on the side. Don't drown your salad with dressing! Those late night snack cravings...I try to control with occasional hot air popcorn.

I try to drink TONS of water throughout the day. Everyday is a work in progress. Some days run smoothly and according to plan..... other days... I try to keep those at a minimum and don't beat myself up over any indulges. I also try to remember one of my favorite sayings.. "Don't starve yourself FAT". The day can get away from you and before you realize it, it is dinner time and you haven't eaten anything since breakfast. PLAN and PREPARE. It is essential~ By planning and preparing your meals... your refrigerator can become your "GRAB and GO" Drive through if need be. LOL.
......

What type of exercises do you include in your routine to stay in shape?
I always try to mix it up. In other words, I strength train different body parts on different days. I mix up my cardio by swimming, biking and running on different days as well. Push ups and squats are a foundation for me. Throw in some burpees (Google if you are unfamiliar) and you pretty much have a solid foundation to work from.
......

A total beginner is about 35 pounds overweight. She doesn't really know where to start. What tips can you give her to follow the right track?
The most important beginning point.. Get focused. Believe in yourself. Believe in your JOURNEY. Acknowledge you are not going to drop 35 pounds overnight. Get excited about your transformation. Realize you truly can transform your body into anything you want to. You have to be patient. You have to ask yourself every day.. "How bad do I want this?" Drink water! If you drink diet sodas, begin weaning yourself off of them. Do NOT trick yourself into thinking drinking "zero" calorie drinks are OK. Think about 'portion' control. Realize that most of us really know what to do..it's making that commitment to ourselves that we are 'worthy' of this Journey to a Healthier and Fit life. That person screaming to come out... truly wants to.

If you Fall off the wagon one day... restart again the next day. Tomorrow is a new day. Do this for YOU and nobody else. Make a vision board and put it somewhere you can see it. Believe your "DREAMS" are possible! Bring those favorite tight pants from the back of the closet and put it in clear view where you can see them everyday. Look in the mirror. Really 'see' that reflection looking back at you.

Acknowledge that is YOU. LOVE yourself again. STOP making excused why you "CAN"T" and start reminding yourself why you "CAN". You must 'mentally' be prepared and

positive this time. Even though you have tried and stopped all of those other times in the past.. THIS time..is YOUR TIME". Contact me.. I am you biggest cheerleader and motivator. I understand the journey... I am there beside you every step of the way. We all 'need that person' along the way. Xoxo
......

What tips do you recommend for eating out at restaurants to make sure we don't gain too much weight/fat?

Don't even let them put that bread basket on the table... LOL. Seriously...why let it sit there and tempt you. It's like I stated previously..If you bring it home.. you will eat it! Just don't bring it home. If the waiter puts that bread on the table..you know you are going to eat it...OR you will get angry and frustrated at NOT wanting to. Broiled and baked.. NOT FRIED. Dressings on the side.

Eat half of your meal and take the other half home or 'share' a meal together. Don't 'overindulge' just because you are eating out. Same rules apply to your meal plan as if you were eating at home. There are so many 'healthy meal' options on the menus now...only be smart. Don't let them fool you! Just because a meal has only 450 calories... LOOK at where those calories are coming from. Those 100 calorie snack cookie treats...are still 100 calories..but look at the "sugar' content on the packages! Feel good about your food choices.
......

What exercises do you recommend for getting a bigger, rounder and fuller butt?

I love this quick 5 minute routine:

1 Minute Lunges + Lifts (left leg forward)
30 Seconds Lunge Pulses (left leg forward)

1 Minute Lunges + Lifts (right leg forward)
30 Seconds Lunge Pulses (right leg forward)

1 Minute Double Dip Squats (Pulse for 2 in the lower position and stand up. Immediately squat back down for 2 count)
30 Second Static Hold
30 Seconds Squat Pulses.
……

What are your top tips for developing toned and defined arms? Specific exercises, diet advice, etc.
Nutrition, nutrition, nutrition…is so important in every aspect. Keep it clean. Check the ingredients in the foods you are eating. Read the lable. If you cannot pronounce it, you really do not want to eat it!
I love this circuit: 10 exercises/10 reps each:
 Lateral raises, tricep extensions, bicep curls, close shoulder presses, tricep kickbacks, ventral raises, upright row, reverse curl, arm circles and tricep dips. This is great for women wanting to get nice toned arms and getting rid of that 'jiggle" (AKA: Bat wings…ugh!)

Eating a healthy and clean diet is beneficial for all over body toning and general fitness. Can you really 'spot" reduce? There is so much information going either way in this direction. I have been asked so many times…how many calories do you think I just burned taking your class? To be honest, my reply is always the same. I have NEVER focused on calorie burning or even calorie intake.. GASP~ Sorry…but I haven't. If I know I am eating healthy throughout the day and I am working out consistently and with intensity… the 'magic' will happen. I am walking proof of that.
……

What are your top tips for losing unwanted body fat? Specific exercises, diet advice, etc.
My top tips for losing unwanted body fat is again…eating a healthy diet. Drinking plenty of water. Focusing again on drinking half of your bodyweight in fluid ounces of water. I love this quote .. 'Get comfortable being uncomfortable".

Yes...you need to get out of your comfort zone at least 1 to 2 times a week. This means training with intensity is key. I love HIIT training myself. (High intensity interval training) You can do this on any piece of cardio equipment, the pool, outside on the track or simply on your street.

A great beginner HIIT session is simply jogging for 3 minutes at a comfortable pace then hard for 1 minute (your level 10 on a scale of 1 to 10...you want to NOT be able to go more than 1 minute at this intensity) and then a full 1 minute recovery. Repeat 5 times. Remember YOUR level "10" is YOUR level 10. Make sure you are working at a high intensity. You can have fun with HIIT. So many different variations. 30 seconds on 1 to 2 minute recovery. Repeat for a 20 to 30 minute workout. Remember... Keep it POSITIVE! Your goal is to live a Heathy and Fit Life. Get Excited. Challenge Yourself.
......

What are your top tips for gaining lean muscle mass? Specific exercises, diet advice, etc.
The old saying goes, more reps and lighter weights for lean muscle mass. Don't be afraid to push yourself. This is a great rule of thumb regarding pushing yourself:

While you don't want to workout too much, you want to make sure you cannot do one more repetition in a set because you are too exhausted. You want it to burn (this feeling is lactic acid stimulating muscle growth) and want to make the next set harder to do. Combine weight training along with your cardio. Mix it up. Don't become a slave to the Treadmill. Get outside and get some fresh air. Try other cardio machines as well. Hop on your bike.

 Three great strength training moves are the Deadlift, Squat and Bench Press. Master the basic movements first. Workout at least 3 times a week. Consume protein before and after your workout. Be sure to eat healthy carbs along with healthy fats. You want a well balanced meal plan. Another reminder you

should be drinking half of your bodyweight in fluid ounces of water every day. Don't fall slave to the scale. Take pictures frequently to monitor your transformation.
......

What are your top tips for improving breasts lift and shape? Specific exercises, diet advice, etc.
If you want to improve the tone and overall look of your breasts your best bet is to do muscle endurance style training using a regime of 3 sets 12-15 reps on a medium weight focusing on the pectoral muscles if you're looking for toning and definition. A great exercise for this is the Chest Fly. You can also use the Chest Machine at the gym. Push Ups. Chest to the ground push ups. Make sure you are getting your lats involved. Inhale down and exhale UP. Quality vs Quantity always.
......

What are your top tips for staying motivated on a fitness plan?
Stay excited. Take pictures. Pictures tell you the real story of what is truly happening to your body. So many times we rely on the 'scale' only to be disappointed. Take pictures and watch the 'magic' happen. Try new activities! Join a group. Find a training partner. Keep challenging yourself and see all the amazing things you can do that you never believed before. I am excited each day I wake up just to see what I can accomplish. I especially get excited when I see a client accomplish a "goal" they never believed they thought possible. Stay POSITIVE.
......

What is your training routine like? Please include a few details.
Depending on what my goals are..is how I train. I am currently in my Tri Training Season so I am focused on building up my endurance in my swimming, biking and running. I am also training for a half marathon in October hoping to complete it

under 2 hours. I am still focused on my strength training as well but building up my endurance and cardio training is my priority at this time. In the fall, I will be concentrating on building more lean muscle.

I am currently following a 3 day running training plan and building up mileage each week while at the same time building up my time in the pool. Each activity, swimming, biking and running are so different. They all are so 'different' in terms of the effect each event has on the body. I can run 3 miles at a certain pace of exertion and yet swim 100 yards in the pool is so much harder~ It's crazy but true.
……

What is the best way to get started in your industry?
I got started in this industry almost by 'accident'. I attended many of the local fitness classes offered by my gym and when one of the instructors was leaving, the supervisor offered me the opportunity to take over the class~ I was terrified at first. The thought of getting up in front of a room full of people and being 'in charge' was frightening. I was afraid nobody would want to come. She offered me the best advice… she said, "Lisa, those that like what you do will come, and those that don't …won't".

Wow. Ok I thought..I will give it a go. I am so glad I did. I found my passion in life. It might have taken me until I was 50 years old.. but I am truly blessed in every aspect of my life~ I went from being a group fitness instructor to a certified personal trainer when some of my participants asked me to personal train them. The rest is history… LOL.
……

What is the best way towards becoming a personal trainer?
Take a personal training certification course.
……

Have you suffered any injuries? What injuries?
Unfortunately I have "tweaked my back" a few times. You must train "smart' and 'listen to your body". I always remind my clients to "listen to your body" don't always listen to your trainer or instructor. If your body is sending you up warning signals about NOT doing something.. DON'T. Unfortunately I didn't always take this advice and being over 50 and never having trained before...there were probably a few 'moves" I have done that I really had no business doing or at least was not properly instructed.
......

What things do you currently do in your training that is key to your success?
Drink plenty of water. I try to get a good night's sleep. I stay focused on the foods I am eating. I make a plan and I stick with it. I have goals for myself. You have to have A GOAL and you have to have a PLAN. If you go to the gym, have a plan of what you are going to do before you get there. I incorporate different training principles on different days. I work different body parts on different days so there is a recovery phase in my Program. Rest and recovery is important as well.
......

Isn't it hard to stay fit? How do you manage that?!
Lucky for me I am at the gym everyday. I am surrounded by like minded people as well. I am the "motivator" for so many others. I never want to let myself down or anybody else down as well. I love this FIT and Healthy Lifestyle. I never want to go back to where I started. I know how easy that happens.
......

Business Questions

What is the most difficult part of starting your business?

The 'business' aspect of my business, Living Healthy Lisa,LLC has been all difficult. Thanks to some people who believed in me...I was able to set the wheels in motion. I would love to find a 'partner' who will help me on the business side of things very soon. LOL.
......

How have your entrepreneurial motivations changed since you first started?
I was very sceptical at first at even starting Living Healthy Lisa, but the more I was encouraged by family and friends, I was definitely motivated to start it up. Living Healthy Lisa began just a little over a year ago.
......

What's the biggest thing you struggle with as a business owner or entrepreneur?
There are so many parts I am struggling with. Not only the marketing end of it, but deciding on a brand and logo and all the aspects of moving my company in a forward direction to attract more followers and have more exposure.
......

How do you think running a business or being an entrepreneur has made you a better person?
I never ever dreamed of having my own company. My business has provided me an outlet in order to reach and encourage and motivate more people than I could on a daily basis going to and from the gym. I am so grateful and thankful for this opportunity.
......

How did you arrive at running this business? What path brought you here?
Living Healthy Lisa was actually envisioned by a friend of mine. I met him while swimming laps in the pool one day and I began talking to him in the lane next to me. We started talking about triathlons as he had just moved to Atlanta and

was looking for a group to get involved with. He started attending my classes at the gym and loved them. I found out he was a videographer and approached him about making a DVD for a fellow fitness instructor at the gym. He very calmly looked at me and said, I should make a DVD! Seriously? The thought never occurred to me.

We shot a few YouTube videos together. It was then he had a vision for Living Healthy Lisa...the original plan was for a web based type of TV Show. We have since gone separate ways but Living Healthy Lisa was born. I am so thankful to him for leading me to this path. He believed in me before I truly Believed in me. Sometimes...that really is all it takes... Believing in yourself to accomplish things you never dreamed possible.
......

What was the most difficult part of starting your business?
It still is difficult. I am at the very beginning stages but I keep moving forward.
......

What do you do on a daily basis to grow as a person/business person/entrepreneur?
I post on facebook daily anything from words of motivational quotes, to healthy recipe ideas. I post circuits and workouts that can be done at home. I try to reach my followers to help them in any way I can to live a healthy and fit life. Getting started is sometimes the hardest part. The whole journey can seem so overwhelming. I know. I had started and stopped myself in the past... Losing a few pounds only to gain a few more back. That is the worst thing we can do to our body. I am trying to make this Journey a Positive one. I want everybody to get excited about how GOOD they are going to Feel and Look.
......

What's unique about the service that you provide?
I am "UNIQUE" in myself…LOL. I say that honestly. I have that Type A energetic, get excited type of personality. I have been told I am like a 'firecracker'! I often get asked how much caffeine I consume and the answer is truly 'none".

I just feel when you are as passionate and committed as I am to help others live a Fit and Healthy Life… it is contagious. I pride myself on the fact that I truly am committed to putting the 'personal" in Training. You get "me".. every part of me that can help you in any way at all. My Iron Girl Triathlon Group call me "Mama Lisa"…I take care of everybody just like that.
……

Do you have any of your own branded products? If so, what are they?
I have put together an eBook Program called 10 Days to A New You. It's a complete 10 day workout program, meal plan, grocery list and exercise description Program. I take the guesswork out of it for you. I found that type of Program works best for me. Of course you can modify and change it to suit your own needs, but basically if you follow this Program for 10 days you will feel and see a difference. 10 Days… can absolutely get you started on your Journey.

I also put together an eBook called TABATA CITY. I love the Tabata method of training. It eliminates first of all any excuse of not having enough time or a gym membership! Each tabata is 8 rounds and lasts for only 4 minutes. You work each round for 20 seconds and rest for 10 seconds.

You can incorporate 8 rounds of the same exercise (i.e….push ups) or you can mix it up… alternating 2 exercises (Jumping Jacks and Squats) and repeat for a total of 8 rounds. You can do 4 exercises (Squats, Jumping Jacks, Push ups, High Knees) and repeat twice. TABATA CITY has 16 different Tabata groupings and from these 16 you can make a TON MORE.

So...if you are short on time..do a quick Tabata. We all have 4 minutes. If you have more time, add another Tabata~

I have YOUTUBES available demonstrating this method of training so you can have me in your living room~

Here is the YOUTUBE link to my Tabatas on YouTube:

http://www.youtube.com/user/livinghealthylisa?feature=watch

(Check out www.livinghealthylisa.com)

Exercise and staying fit and healthy CAN BE FUN. I promise!
......

Mixed Questions

What would be your ultimate achievement in any area of your life?
In my own personal fitness aspect... Completing an IRONMAN... WOW...that would be an ultimate achievement. Business wise- Living Healthy Lisa becoming a household name or even my own Talk Show! Lookout Ellen and Rachel Ray and Steve Harvey!
......

At present, what is your biggest challenge, and what are you doing to manage this challenge?
Challenges... One of my favorite quotes is:..."If you are not challenging yourself, you are not changing yourself." Amen to that one! An immediate challenge is figuring out how to get Living Healthy Lisa into a profitable business and help to motivate others to live a Fit and Healthy Life. I make little strides every day. I am been so fortunate to have had my story

told twice on 2 of my Local TV stations. That alone helps get my 'name' out there locally.

You can see my FOX 5 TV appearance at this link…this was broadcast prior to the completion of my Marathon in October of 2012 and used as a lead in to their Heart Trek 5K Race. It was such an honor indeed. …. Here is the link to the FOX 5 clip that was on TV:

http://www.myfoxatlanta.com/story/19607690/woman-learns-its-never-to-late-to-change

I was also featured in SHAPE MAGAZINE recently as 1 of 16 trainers who transformed their life. Here is the article on page 8:

http://www.shape.com/weight-loss/success-stories/16-fitness-experts-who-used-be-fat?page=8

In March this year I was again featured and LIVE in the STUDIO for CBS Channel 46 Better Mornings Atlanta. They again shared my story to help encourage others as I was not only running the Publix Half Marathon but training a group of people for their very first race. What an amazing experience. "LIVE" in a TV studio on the air.

Really? Yes, really. I also have the link of the replay. I even somehow managed to do the weather with our local weatherman, Paul Ossmann. It was so fun. I remember Brandon, the host asking me this basic question, "Lisa, Did you imagine 6 years ago when you began your Journey that you would ever run a Marathon or Half Marathon?" I answered honestly, 'Are you kidding me…I never even dreamed 6 years ago I would be on TV." I have now been on TV twice!
It continues to amaze me that by making the decision to Live a Fit and Healthy Life has changed my life in so many incredible ways.

······

What things do you believe differentiates you from your contemporaries?

I just am so committed and so passionate about helping others to live a Fit and Healthy Life. It takes time. I always strive that. This is a JOURNEY. This is a Lifestyle Change. This is NOT about losing 10 lbs fast or dropping a dress size. So many others focus on just the rapid weight loss. I want to change your whole LIFE. I don't want you to lose the weight only to gain it back again.
······

Have you ever experienced a breakthrough, and if so, what led to it?

The day I ran on a level 10 MPH on the Treadmill just to see if I could, was a huge Day for me. I can so easily remember when I started my Journey and I was walking 3.2MPH on the Treadmill holding on for dear life wondering if I would ever be able to 'let go'. Running that fast that day just again proved to myself that I really could do things I never dreamed possible before. From that day on I continue to challenge myself to see how far or how fast I can really go!

We all put limitations on our own abilities... instead of challenging ourselves and seeing what 'magic' is really inside. I love when I take a client out of their 'comfort zone' and they get that look in their eye after they have accomplished something they never knew they could do!~ It is so rewarding for the both of us. I call it the 'smiling for the inside' moments that I so love to share with everybody. It is so wonderful when other people are proud of us...Even better when we ourselves our Proud of us.
······

Who has been the biggest influence on your life? What lessons did that person teach you?

I have an old friend who has always believed in me and constantly supported me in everything I ever attempted to do. Unfortunately, I never believed in myself and therefore, until 6 years ago...I never even tried to do anything. Not really. Can simply 'believing' in yourself make a huge difference? Absolutely. I constantly tell my clients.. "I believe in YOU... now YOU need to Believe in YOU."
......

Do you have a saying or motto that you live your life by?
I have so many. One of my favorites is.."It's Never too Late to be Great". I am a prime example of this. Just because I never did anything physically active before my 50th birthday..I am certainly living an active and "great life" now. Don't use the excuse...well..I've always been overweight and out of shape..I'm too old to change. WRONG!
......

Where do you draw your inspiration from?
My family, my friends, my clients...myself. I ask myself every day as I always have.. "How bad do you want this..." and I answer the same.."I want it bad". I have a great core of people surrounding me with love and passion and motivation as well. This is not a Journey you have to take alone. I always say... "sometimes it just takes somebody else to open the door for you...Let me be that person for YOU".
......

What were your biggest personal battles and how did you confront them?
Currently, my own personal fitness/training battle is myself vs my bike. Sounds crazy I know. I put these really great peddles on my bike and now I am fearful of clipping in and clipping out. It's just silly. I know that. First of all, I don't even have to keep the pedals on my bike (for all the bikers out there I now have speed play zeros on my road bike), but I am too stubborn to switch them out. I WILL Conquer this battle.

Again, it's just me against me. I go around encouraging and motivating others they can do anything they wan to.. I WILL DO THE SAME. I can't just talk the talk...I must walk the walk..and I will continue to be a better person (and biker) for it.. LOL. I am currently making myself clip and clip out in my neighborhood before I go back and tackle Stone Mountain. My next Sprint Triathlon is in August. Come on Lisa ... I can do this. (Shout out to my 'girls' who continue to inspire me and encourage me, too).
......

If you could paint a picture of any scenery you've seen before, what would you paint?
The sunset at the beach or the sunrise. I am not picky.
......

What are some goals you are still trying to accomplish?
My goals currently are getting back on that bike. Getting my business up and running and reaching as many people as I can to encourage them that they too, can lead a Fit and Healthy Life. We must be the role models for our children, too. I am about to start a new "PROGRAM"...to see just how shredded and lean I can transform my body into. I am very excited. For the first time in my JOURNEY I will actually have a "COACH" to help me. You know the old saying.."Even a trainer needs a trainer". Part 2 of my own Transformation Journey is about to begin.
......

What are the most important lessons you've learned in life?
Believe in yourself. Love yourself. Be PROUD of who you are. SO many times we focus on the negative when there are so many positive aspects we tend to ignore. Don't put off tomorrow what you can do today. Those 'tomorrows' turn into years before we know it.

What are you proudest of in your life?
My 4 FABULOUS KIDS. A husband who loves me unconditionally for over 30 years and puts up with me...those are lots of moments for sure! My childrens' achievements. I have 2 college graduates from the University of Georgia (Melanie and Travis) My son Clay is about to start his sophomore year at the University of Georgia and my youngest daughter Paige is about to be a junior at Lakeside High School. Crossing every finish line of every race. Watching my friends/clients cross their own finish lines no matter what that 'line' is. Having somebody randomly come up to me to tell me 'thank you' for inspiring them.

How do you set your goals?
I set my goals according to the time of the year.. LOL. In the spring through Fall I am concentrating on my Triathlon and Race Goals. The other times of the year I am focusing on my personal body transformation goals. Both require a lot of thought and hard work and patience.

What else would you do if you weren't in your current line of work?
I have no idea. It took me until I was 50 years old to find my passion... I know this is my MISSION.

Do you believe in the Law of Attraction?
I do believe what goes around comes around and if you put "GOOD OUT" ...GOOD will come back.

What is your diet like?
I have to say most days my diet is pretty good. I have to admit like most of us I find the nutrition portion to this plan of living

a Fit and Healthy Life the most difficult. I worry I don't eat enough and I find that common in most people.

We all think 'depleting' calories is the answer to dropping quick weight. I remind people all of the time to think of our body like a car. It takes fuel (food) for it to run properly. I try to incorporate protein and carbs and healthy fats with each meal. I use protein shakes on occasion when I haven't take the time to prepare my meal and I am constantly 'on the go'.

I do have my days when I enjoy a great slice of pizza or a piece of cheesecake. I try to do moderation. I also feel that if there is something you absolutely are craving and feel like you have to eat it... Go ahead and eat it and get it over with and enjoy it guilt free. I find too many times you will eat a lot of other 'food' that you really don't want to keep yourself from eating that 'splurge'. Eat it and enjoy it and get back on your plan the next day!
......

What's your favorite food?
I love a hot loaf of French crusty bread right out of the oven. I don't even have to have butter on it... LOL.
......

What would we find in your refrigerator right now?
Spinach, eggs, milk, natural peanut butter, celery, carrots, hummus. Baked chicken, sweet potatoes (already cooked). Ezechial bread. Steel mill oatmeal (a container already cooked). Salsa, mustard, balsamic vinegar. Uh Oh...I have lemon sorbet in the freezer..LOL.. my husband brought that home. Yes I will indulge in a few bites from time to time since it is sitting in there. Like I say... "If you don't bring it home, you won't eat it". Plan and prepare your meals. Keep Tupperware type containers on hand and fix your meals in bulk so you are not constantly having to cook your meals, but they are already ready for you to eat!
......

If you had the opportunity to get a message across to a large group of people what would your message be?
Living a Fit and Healthy LIFE is the best gift you can give yourself. Seriously my friends, without good health... we have nothing. Why do we have to wait until the doctor finds something wrong with us. So many times that is the only time people begin their Journey...out of a health crisis. Take a few steps every day and be amazed how much better you will feel in a short amount of time.

It truly is never too late to be great! Look in the mirror...Really look in the mirror... do you like the reflection looking back at you? Do you get up every day feeling good and anxious to face a new day? We should not focus on just losing weight, but focus on living a Fit and Healthy Life. There are so many rewards along the way. I love sharing my before pictures... or my blue sweatpants that were too small when I bought them and I refused to take them back. You can tell people you have changed your life but until they see the pictures, actually see the pants... then it becomes a REALITY to them. If I can do it.. YOU can do it. Let me help you.
......

Where do you see yourself in 5 years?
Hopefully continuing to have an impact on changing people's lives. I still love the original concept of Living Healthy Lisa being an internet based Talk SHOW. That would be so incredible! I want to 'share' stories. WE ALL have a story. You never know when YOUR story will influence somebody else.
......

What are you best at?
Truly caring about others!
......

What books do you like to read?

Fitness... all kinds. How to run races..how to strength train... how to get better at triathlons..it's nonstop. However, I do have Think and Grow Rich on my desk to begin shortly.
......

What is your favorite type of music?
I love all kinds of music. I am a rock and roll girl from the 70's...but there is plenty of good music today, too. My 4 kids help keep me in the loop..
......

Tell us a time in your life that was a time you'll never forget?
Crossing that finish line for my marathon... Oh my goodness... What a moment...and I got to share the whole experience with my wonderful training partner and awesome friend, Carolyn Sanders!
......

What things do you find yourself doing that you said you'd never do?
Living this life actively. Lifting weights? Running? Biking? Doing races? Teaching fitness classes? Talking in front of people? I never believed I would ever do anything like this and I am so glad I was WRONG!
......

What are some qualities that you value in a person?
Honesty. Compassion. Humor. Laughter. Positivity.
......

Where did you grow up and what was it like?
I grew up in Miami, Florida. Need I say more? It was fabulous! Senior year of high school we started at 7am and done at 12:00pm. My kids are so jealous. Shout out to Southwest Miami High School Class of 1975!
......

Name 5 of your favorite movies.

The Original Willy Wonka and the Chocolate Factory (The girl who plays Violet, the bubblegum girl is Denise Nickerson and she sat in front of me in the first grade. My kids thought this was so cool when they were little. My celebrity 'claim to fame'). Warrior. Remember the Titans. The Notebook. PS I love YOU.
......

What TV shows do you like?
Grey's Anatomy. How I Met Your Mother. Scandal. Extreme Weight Loss. Prison Break (they took it off the air but I loved watching that with my son, Travis). I loved the boxing show The Contender. We don't have cable.. LOL.. so my choices are limited.
......

What do you enjoy doing on a Sunday afternoon?
I love getting up for an early morning run and then spending time with my family. It's so nice now when all 4 of my kids are home at the same time. Those little things we take for granted.
......

Is there anything in particular that you wish you could do over? What is it?
No regrets. That was my "motto" this year. I am sticking to it.
......

What personality traits in your mind are best suited for your job, career, etc?
Compassion. Friendliness. Cheerful. Positive attitude. Patience.
......

What is your favorite drink?
A cold dark Guinness. Yep...It certainly is.
......

What is your favorite color?

Today it is neon Green.
......

Name a movie that touched you in some way.
I just saw the Spirit Of Marathon II. I am so inspired to run another marathon now~ I loved every aspect of it the first time.
......

When in life have you felt most alone? Why?
The year my mom passed away. That was a hard Journey all in itself and at the same time I was facing turning 50. My children were growing up way too fast. I had no idea what I was going to do with my life. I was a big black hole. I didn't like the reflection staring back at me in the mirror. Thankfully, I was able to fight my way back and changed my body and I changed my life.
......

What would be impossible for you to give up?
My feeling of a 'close family' unit. We are all so blessed in that way. My family is #1 in my life and we all feel that way about each other.
......

Why would someone not want to work with you?
I get a little 'over the top' with my excitement and passion... is that a bad thing?
What activities did you enjoy in school?
I had a great time in school. I wasn't involved so much as 'school activities' but had a great group of friends and a very active 'social life'.
......

What kind of child were you?
Quiet and shy actually. Most people find that unbelievable.
......

How do you want to be remembered?
A woman who truly cares about trying to help improve people's lives by helping them to get Fit and Healthy from the inside out.
......

We all have vices, what are yours?
Talking too fast. I have to remind myself to slow down and breathe. One of my clients told me, "Lisa, I believe everybody has a certain number of words they must get out everyday and YOU have a lot of words" LOL. Talking to everybody about living a fit and healthy life... I'm sure there are some people that just don't want to hear about it..but I still try. I also know I spend way toooo much time at the computer.... Always trying to work on my business. Sometimes I know I should just 'walk away'...tomorrow is another day! I also 'crack' my gum...it annoys me when other people do it... LOL.
......

What is one of your favorite quotes?
We do this today because We Can, we don't known what tomorrow brings. So true.. think about it.
......

What chore do you absolutely hate doing?
ALL of them. LOL.
......

What is your best feature?
Being friendly.
......

What was the last experience that made you a stronger person?
Falling off my bike at the end of the Iron Girl bike portion and realizing it's ok to fall....Just get back up and finish the race. I still finished in 6th place, too. LOL.
......

If you could change something physical about yourself, what would it be and why?
I guess one of the best things about getting 'older' is that we learn to accept ourselves as we are. However, that being said, I still would love to have more defined muscles and ..that 6-pack AB look, although after 4 C-Sections, I'm pretty happy.
......

Besides money, what are your favorite ways to compensate people?
HUGS and high fives. A genuine HUG. One that comes from the inside out. I also will sometimes trade out personal training sessions.
......

When was the last time you tried something new?
Yesterday. Every day I get on my bike with those speed play peddles..it feels 'brand new' again. I can't wait until I feel comfortable with them and realize I really do love to ride my bike!
......

How would you describe yourself in three words?
Passionate, compassionate, friendly.
......

What is one thing you are not?
Shy.
......

Do you think crying is a sign of weakness or strength?
Crying is such an incredible emotion. I cry for so many different reasons...crossing a finish line, watching a Hallmark commercial, seeing a friend accomplish a goal they never believed they could.
......

What makes you angry?

Standing in a long line and it's not moving. I'm not a very patient person.. sorry.
......

What makes you laugh?
Me. My kids constantly shake their heads at me...I really can crack myself up... and I find myself laughing all by myself.
......

What are you afraid of?
Being a disappointment to those I love.
......

What would be the first thing you would do if today was your last day?
Way too sad to even think about!
......

What's your vision of a perfect society?
Everybody just getting along and helping each other. Sound corny? Maybe... but that would be wonderful if it could happen.
......

Is it possible to lie without saying a word? How?
Yes. Just by somebody's body language.
......

What's something you check daily?
I check my email and facebook daily. Doesn't everyone?
......

Are you an emotional person?
A very emotional personal.
......

What's your own definition of happiness?
Living my life...having those I love around me and staying healthy.

......

Which famous person would you like to interview and which questions would you ask him/her?
I actually would love to interview Tony Horton from P90x..and I would love to ask him to partner with me...WE would be a dynamic TEAM! LOL. I actually did meet Tony a few years ago at a book signing he did here in Atlanta and he took pictures with each and everyone of us, too.
......

If you could choose to be born with a particular natural skill what skill would it be?
A natural 'athletic' skill. I do believe some people are just 'born' that way.
......

What advice would you give someone who wanted to do what you do?
Be patient with people. Be positive. Realize that just because people want say they want to do this Journey, many really do not. It's not an easy business to build up a clientele with, but those that follow you are loyal.
......

Do you have any secrets you want to share with the few of us reading this? We won't say anything....promise!
You really can do anything YOU want to..YOU just have to want to. If you need some help..or some guidance... feel free to contact me...that is why I'm here. Lisa.anderson1957@gmail.com or Facebook me at Living Healthy Lisa.
......

Are there any words of wisdom you'd like to pass along to us?

Believe in YOURSELF. This Journey to a Fit and Healthy Lifestyle is just that. It is a way of life. Rejoice in the choices you make every day. Don't give up...the "magic' is just about to happen and it is so worth it. I always say...if everybody knew what it felt like to feel good, they wouldn't want to feel any other way~ Most people have forgotten or maybe they have actually never known.
......

Did you enjoy answering these questions? On a scale from 1 – 10. 1= I hated it. 10= I really enjoyed it.
    5.   Thank YOU Andy though for this great opportunity!

....

About Lisa

I truly do just want to help and reach as many people as I can to lead a Healthy and Fit Life. I know from experience what it feels like 'on the other side' and I want others to realize, they, too can just feel good again along with looking good, too.

I have been featured in Shape Magazine and my role as Coach for the Live Full Swing Digital Magazine..the editor, Sherry, shared her First Iron Girl Sprint Triathlon Story and I was her "coach". I am also the Fitness and Healthy Correspondent for this magazine now.

As a FUN fact..I was recently shown on the Katie Couric show as one of many people who have trouble "sleeping through the nite"... LOL. I appear in the first 3 seconds. My uploaded YOUTUBE video was NOT shown in full, but still FUN to appear at all on the show.

I am about to be featured in a local showing in Atlanta of "WHAT NOT TO WEAR".. being aired in August, Comcast channel 5. This should really be FUN! After losing 75lbs and wearing nothing but workout clothes..they are going to help me in my "IMAGE" now that I am a business owner and the over "50" phase in life, too. As my daughter tells me.."Mom, just because you can wear something, doesn't mean you should.."

I offer PERSONAL TRAINING, ONLINE TRAINING (yes it works) and Coaching for Races.. if anybody needs help just getting started, too.

My 2 eBOOKs are 10 Days to a NEW You and TABATA CITY.

I may be contacted at:
lisa.anderson1957@gmail.com or lisa@livinghealthylisa.com

Visit my webpage at: www.livinghealthylisa.com and also please LIKE my Facebook page as Living Healthy Lisa. Both sites have some great information as well as pictures and motivation.

Here is the link to the FOX 5 clip that was on TV:
http://www.myfoxatlanta.com/story/19607690/woman-learns-its-never-to-late-to-change

Check out Live Full Swing Digital Magazine Article:
http://www.livefullswing.com/

Click on Pure 50 the first triathlon article.

I was recently posted in Dax Moy's Personal Trainer Article: (My posting is towards the end).
http://www.daxmoy.com/london-personal-trainer-top-fatloss-tips-from-top-fatloss-trainers/
http://www.youtube.com/user/livinghealthylisa?feature=watch
http://www.shape.com/weight-loss/success-stories/16-fitness-experts-who-used-be-fat?page=8

INTERVIEW 3
Michelle Brown

Personal Information

Full Name:
Michelle C Brown

Age:
42

Location:
Los Gatos

Relationship Status:
Single

Number of Children:
0

Profession:
Personal Trainer, Fitness Nutrition Specialist, Wellness Coordinator

Educational Background:
AA Liberal Arts

Certifications:
NASM CPT and FNS, CPR/AED Rock Doc Cert
....

General Questions

What are you known for professionally?
Transformations – body transformations through diet and exercise. I am a National Level Figure Competitor, which keeps me looking in touch with what I do. I'm known for having fun in my programs. One of the things I tell clients is if we are not laughing at least a couple times during our workout, it is not a good workout. I'm also known for helping clients build muscle.
......

Tell us about how you got into your line of work.
I have always enjoyed working with people in a way that is beneficial to them. I have worked in Physical Therapy, been a medical assistant, and worked in sales in Real Estate. I enjoy being helpful to another person's success. I realized that my

work had taken over priority and that my health and fitness level were not what they use to be. I then researched personal training and found a trainer for myself. I started hitting all of my goals quickly and after cleaning up my horrifying diet and dropping 17lbs I needed a new goal.

I found that goal in competing in a Bodybuilding competition. I got a coach. I trained and did the diet. I then went on stage and took a 2nd place. After this great accomplishment I went onto a second show where I won the Open Division (meaning all ages) I was 37 at the time. I had developed a passion for training and nutrition. I decided to become a Certified Trainer. I have continued to compete and now am at a National Level working toward getting my Pro Card. I opened my business Active Life Fitness and continue to be a Personal Trainer and a Fitness Nutrition Specialist as well as a Competition Coach.
......

How long have you been doing what you do?
5 years
......

What do you enjoy most about what you do?
Working with my clients. They are fascinating people who come from all different walks of life.
......

What are you most passionate about professionally? What most excites you about your work & the contribution you can make?
Results! I couldn't be more excited to see someone come to me with a vision of how they want to see themselves and be able to create a plan for them to get there. Then when they get there it is so amazing to see the satisfaction the client gets from their newly developed healthy lifestyle. Being the person to guide them through this tough process excites me and gives

me energy and the feeling of accomplishment that is beyond amazing.
……

What's the single most important reason for your success?
My ability to care about my clients and have the personality to motivate them during the tough times.
……

What do you consider to be your greatest achievement?
Turning my clients health around…from seeing diabetes go away, disabilities eased, pain removed, and blood work improved these are the greatest achievements anyone can ask for in my industry.
……

How do you think women have changed over the years? Regarding business, sports and fitness.
Many things have changed over the years. Women have come into their own and taken the business and fitness worlds to a whole new level. With the Rights for women changing over the years allowing us to be on a more level field with men has exploded women in business and in the sports and fitness arenas. Women have really taken old concepts and put a completely different flare on them. We are now much bolder, stronger, and are much more driven than ever in every industry especially sports and fitness.
……

Do you think women are competitive with each other? Why? Regarding business, sports and fitness.
I do believe women are competitive with each other, but in a different way than men. I think that women are competitive but with a more appreciative spin. I believe that intuition and appreciation play a role in our competitiveness. We have the drive and moral to compete but also the ability to truly

appreciate others on the same or higher level. Thus giving us an advantage over the competitive male who tends to be more judgemental and angry with their competition.
......

What memorable competitions come to mind in your career?
My first Figure competition in 2008. The Contra Costa Bodybuilding Show. Walking into this new adventure I did not know what to expect. The journey to these types of competitions are really what it is about. The competition itself is relatively quick compared to the many months of preparation. Walking into registration for the show I recall looking at the other females and thinking, why am I even here? These women look amazing. I don't have a chance. Then going through and earning a 2nd place in the Open Division, as well as a 3rd in the Masters (35+ age group). This was a mind blowing, life changing experience I will never forget.
......

What is the number one thing you like best about being into fitness?
It's good for you. It's healthy, extending your life and fitness brings you happiness, through endorphins as well as just feeling good about how you look.
......

Is there anything wrong with wanting to portray women athletes, actors, etc as feminine and physically attractive?
That's a tough one. Yes and No! Some women are just naturally attractive and very feminine while others aren't at that same eye appealing level. I think people should be shown as they are. Meaning as their personalities are. Not just their look. As an example I tend to be more of a tomboy type although I am told I am very attractive. I would prefer to be portrayed more rugged and strong vs pretty and elegant.

......

How do you deal with cravings for junk foods, sweets and salty food?
I deal with this frequently as dieting is extremely strict with Bodybuiding competitions. I mainly will make healthy versions of things I crave or find a healthy replacement to solve the craving. Honestly with cravings while I'm competing...I have no choice to just get over it and call it a day.
......

Describe a typical day for you, starting from the moment you wake up in the morning.
Currently I wake up at 4am and do fasted cardio for 45 min and either a quick shoulder or leg/glute weight set. I then shower, load my cooler with food for the day, cook my breakfast, take my stack of supplements then head out the door for my first clients starting at 6am.

I usually have clients till 10 or 11 (which I have to squeeze in a meal in between them) I will either run errands or get in a weight workout. Then check emails and return calls. Grab my lunches (I eat every 2.5 hours to keep on track form comp) Head back to the studio and train more clients from 2pm till 6 or 7pm. Then I'm off to do evening cardio and posing.

Once I'm done with that I need to go home and prep food for the day after eating my last meal. I prep/cook the bulk of my food on the weekends so that I can just pull it out of the fridge, measure it, and put it in containers the night before. Grab my evening supplements and take them. Once I'm done with that I head to my computer to prepare client nutrition agendas, programs, marketing, etc for the next day. I try to get to bed by 11pm so I can get some much needed sleep. Then the alarm goes off and I start all over again.
......

Health & Fitness Questions

What sports do you participated in for fun?
Softball, tennis, running races, Motocross, gymnastics, cheerleading.
......

How long have you been playing those sports?
Softball I've played since I was 4 – my favorite sport! Tennis I played for 20 years off and on. Running I've always loved and continue to race and have run for 30 years. Motocross is new to me and am learning more and more...I just started this last year. I competed in gymnastics when I was young and did that for 4 years. Cheerleading I did for 8 years.
......

What got you started in that sport?
My dad got me started actually in baseball. Tennis was my ex husband who was a tennis pro. Running was a friend in High School and Motocross was a significant other. My parents put me in gymnastics to keep me busy. After that I saw cheerleading and joined that on my own so I could do more tumbling.
......

What is your biggest accomplishment in your sports? Include fun sports and any athletic career.
I've been fortunate to have many although I believe competing on the National Stage in Bodybuilding is a huge accomplishment due to the nature and time consumption of the sport. It takes months even years to get to be on that stage and make it happen.
......

What competitions have you entered? What were the outcomes?
2008 Contra Costa Bodybuilding – 2nd Place Masters Figure B, 3rd Place Open Figure C.

2008 San Jose Bodybuilding Championships – 1st place Open Figure C, 2nd place Masters Figure B.
2012 San Francisco Bodybuilding – 1st Place Masters 35 + Figure B, and 2nd Place Open Figure C.
2012 Nationals Atlanta Georgia – 16th place.
2013 Contra Costa Bodybuilding – 1st Place Open Figure C and 1st place Masters Figure B.
2012 Jr USA's National Bodybuilding – 7th Place.

How do you motivate yourself and stay motivated?
I use motivational images, videos, Vision Boards, Pro Card winners.
……

What are some of the main foods you would include in your shopping list to maintain a lean and muscular physique?
Egg whites, talapia, chicken, broccoli, asparagus, sweet potatoes, oatmeal, brown rice.
……

What is the most challenging thing you deal with about consistently staying in top shape?
The diet and workout schedule is gruelling especially when having your own business.
……

Please describe your normal diet. What do you eat in a typical day to stay in shape?
I do carb cycling with 6 meals a day with 5-6 oz protein, 1 cup veggies, and 5 oz carbs when allowed....foods are Egg whites, talapia, chicken, broccoli, asparagus, sweet potatoes, oatmeal, and brown rice.
……

What type of exercises do you include in your routine to stay in shape?

Lots of cardio mainly on the Step Mill – I call it the Gauntlet and then a full boar weight lifting routine hitting different body parts each day.
......

A total beginner is about 35 pounds overweight. She doesn't really know where to start. What tips can you give her to follow the right track?
Number one tip is diet is about 70% of weight loss 20% cardio, and the rest is strength training. I would first adjust to having no starchy carbs after 4pm. This will help you cut out energy going in and turning to fat stores when you are more likely to be moving less. Then increase your protein to keep muscle on as we lose fat.
......

What tips do you recommend for eating out at restaurants to make sure we don't gain too much weight/fat?
Easy choice pick fish – simply grilled fish, eliminate the carb and ask for extra veggies. Have all sauces on the side and drink at least 3 glasses of water while you are there.
......

What exercises do you recommend for getting a bigger, rounder and fuller butt?
If you want it you will SQUAT for it! Weighted squats and lunges...key to a firm booty.
......

What are your top tips for developing toned and defined arms? Specific exercises, diet advice, etc.
If you want definition you must make sure you are trimming the fat off your body....cardio is key to get the extra burn. Of course there is no way to spot train fat away. Diet is the most important in fat loss. Keeping a lower fat diet that has low sugar will help to increase you efforts.
......

What are your top tips for losing unwanted body fat? Specific exercises, diet advice, etc.
Get the most burn you can using plyometrics and HIIT types of training. Plyometrics is really the art of jumping. Power moves…squat to jump up and repeat or Split lunge jumps. Get into a lunge position jump up and switch legs to land in the opposite lunge. This is intense to say the least. As for HIIT…it is high intensity interval training. You see it everywhere these days. That's because it actually works.

Let's use running as an example: Run at your normal steady pace for 1 min then for 30 seconds go as fast as you can, and repeat this interval. If you are doing it right you won't be able to do this for a long period of time. 20-30 minutes is considered a really good workout time for this kind of training. Interval training is truly the best for burning fat.
……

What are your top tips for gaining lean muscle mass? Specific exercises, diet advice, etc.
First and foremost diet here again is extremely important. You can lift all you want but without the proper intake you will be left without gaining the muscle you are looking for. For gaining lean muscle you need to eat a high protein higher carbohydrate diet. For protein intake you want at least 1gram of protein per pound of body weight. You can even go to 1.5g/pound.

So if you are 120lb female you need to take in a minimum of 120 grams of protein. Protein alone will not create growth. You need to add weight by increasing your carb intake. When trying to gain lean muscle you want to eat good complex carbs such as; oatmeal, brown rice, sweet potatoes, yams, etc. Each meal should contain protein, carbs, vegetables, and some fat. Usually this is in the protein, but you want to get in some good fats as well. Omegas are important to build. Avocado,

almonds, ground flax, olive oil, EFA's are essential to ones diet.
......

What are your top tips for improving breasts lift and shape? Specific exercises, diet advice, etc.

To lift the chest there are a variety of exercises to do. My favorite is chest fly's. I like to do these on the cable machine. Place cables at chest height and at a weight that is challenging for you. Start with arms extended back and pull with straight arms forward until your hands are facing each other. Make sure to squeeze at the chest and not to use pure arm strength.
......

What are your top tips for staying motivated on a fitness plan?

Staying motivated can be tough. If you are a visual person create a vision board with images of your goals and inspirations. Place it in an area you see frequently...I like it by my closet so as I am getting dressed I can envision myself reaching my goal. Also document all your measurements and weights from the beginning. Don't wait till you lose some first. Start off with measurements and then you can really see your full journey.
......

What is your training routine like? Please include a few details.

My day starts off with morning fasted cardio of about 30-45 min and some plyo for about 20 min. Then I take my supplements eat meal #1 and off to work. I eat every 2-3 hours. Later in the day in the afternoon I get my weight workout in. This is a plan that I do different muscle groups on different days. I do weights 6 days a week hitting legs 3 times since that is my trouble area. I always get in my meal post workout within 30 minutes to ensure good recovery for my muscles. After my weight training I get in my second round of cardio that ranges from 30minutes to 1 hour.
......

What is the best way to get started in your industry?
First make sure you are in shape. No one wants to workout with trainers that are not in shape themselves. Get your certification and get to one of the big box gyms. Here is a great place to learn and have the opportunity to pick up clients that you can always take with you when you move to another location.
......

What is the best way towards becoming a personal trainer?
I believe you should get certified through NASM. It is one of the best programs out there.

Have you suffered any injuries? What injuries?
Yes. Nothing major but many muscle strains. It is important to take care of your body. I have a whole team of professionals to assist me with this. Chiropractic care, acupuncture, massage, supplement expert, and a coach.
......

What things do you currently do in your training that is key to your success?
Push hard. Stick to the plan. Every successful athlete has a plan and a coach. Stick to it.
......

Isn't it hard to stay fit? How do you manage that?!
Yes, it is not always easy. I enjoy looking ultra fit and the price to pay for that is discipline. I plan for it every day. That is the only way to get through it.
......

Business Questions

Tell us about your first entrepreneurial experience as a kid or older.
I had my first baby sitting job and I had to negotiate getting off work by my bedtime.
......

What is the most difficult part of starting your business?
Fear of the unknown. Having to build business from scratch.
......

How have your entrepreneurial motivations changed since you first started?
I am now more focused on quality of clients than quantity.
......

What do you consider to be success as a business owner or entrepreneur?
Referrals!
......

What's your least favorite part about being a business owner or entrepreneur?
Book keeping/paperwork.
......

What's the biggest thing you struggle with as a business owner or entrepreneur?
Spending too much time on little insignificant issues when time could be better spent bringing in new business.
......

How do you think running a business or being an entrepreneur has made you a better person?
It makes me appreciate attributes in others much more.
......

How did you arrive at running this business? What path brought you here?

I started working out with a trainer. I progressed and hit all my goals. Creating more and more goals as I went along. I then hit a huge goal when I won my second Figure Competition and said I want to help others get this type of feeling. The feeling of true accomplishment.
……

What was the most difficult part of starting your business?
Letting go of my stable weekly pay check at my day job.
……

What do you do on a daily basis to grow as a person/business person/entrepreneur?
Meet with other small business people, learn from my successes as well as my failures, and keep pushing.

What's unique about the service that you provide?
Customized transformation. Each program is customized to the client and that client gets a coordinator who truly cares about their path.
……

What entrepreneurial hacks have you developed to stay focused and productive in your day-to-day?
Making sure there is a plan. Food plan, workout plan, errand plan, schedule stacked. Organization!
……

Do you have any of your own branded products? If so, what are they?
Not yet!
……

Mixed Questions

What would be your ultimate achievement in any area of your life?
Get my IFBB Pro Card.
……

If you could be any character in fiction, who would you be?
Tinker Bell.
……

At present, what is your biggest challenge, and what are you doing to manage this challenge?
Location. Currently I am running to a variety of studios to fit in my clients at places I can sublease. I am working toward getting my own location.
……

What things do you believe differentiates you from your contemporaries?
Energy, personality, and creativity.
……

Who has been the biggest influence on your life? What lessons did that person teach you?
Geno Johnson – he was my coach/trainer for my first bodybuilding show. He taught me to stay the course. Slow and steady it will happen. Just don't stop. No matter what comes your way keep carrying on. In the end you will be successful. He also taught me that actions speak louder than words. Amazing man.
……

Do you have a saying or motto that you live your life by?
Yes, When in Doubt...Workout!
……

Where do you draw your inspiration from?

Everywhere! I see it in others. Someone working out for the first time, an experienced fitness person pushing limits, my clients inspire me to be better.
......

What were your biggest personal battles and how did you confront them?
Believing that I could do it. It was really hard but I just threw myself in and said you will sink or swim...but something is going to happen.
......

What were the most difficult decisions you had to make during your lifetime? Why?
Just had to make one of my most difficult decisions. I was scheduled to do my next National show in just 6 weeks. An injury has been holding me back and not being able to do my full workouts. Meaning my result was not going to be 100%. So weighing it out the cost of $2000 for a show I can't give my all for and possible seriously injuring my arm. I had to pull out of the show and take care of my body. Very difficult as I have come so far and ready to get out there and get my Pro Card.
......

If you could paint a picture of any scenery you've seen before, what would you paint?
Tuscany hills, with rolling hills, vineyards, and beautiful landscape.
......

What are some goals you are still trying to accomplish?
Convert studio clients into private clients.
......

What are the most important lessons you've learned in life?

Be kind, always smile, helping others always makes you feel better, and although most of us want a partner in life you can only get through it on your own.
......

What are you proudest of in your life?
I have completely changed to a healthy lifestyle.
......

How do you set your goals?
Strive for the best, but always make achievable goals.
......

What else would you do if you weren't in your current line of work?
Physical Therapy.
......

What are your religious beliefs/spiritual beliefs?
I believe in a higher power and that we are destined to do certain things.
......

Do you believe in the Law of Attraction?
Yes.
......

What is your diet like?
Healthy. Lots of protein, veggies, and good complex carbs.
......

What's your favorite food?
Apples.
......

What would we find in your refrigerator right now?
Chicken, talipia, avocado, asparagus, broccoli, water, egg whites.

......

If you had the opportunity to get a message across to a large group of people what would your message be?
If you want to feel good and look even better upgrade your life with a healthy lifestyle.
......

Where do you see yourself in 5 years?
Own my own studio and have other trainers under me.
......

What are you best at?
Customer Service.
......

What books do you like to read?
Not much of a reader. I do read educational materials and of course all the fitness mags!
......

What is your favorite type of music?
Top 40.
......

Describe your parents, what are they like?
Very different from me. They have not turned a new leaf as of yet. They are overweight and do not live a healthy lifestyle. They will change one day.
......

What were your dreams as a child and did you achieve any of them?
I wanted to get married and have children. I got married.
......

Tell us a time in your life that was a time you'll never forget?

I was diagnosed with cancer in 1997. I went to my regular yearly appointment and when the results came back I was told I had stage 3 cervical cancer. That day changed my life forever.
……

What things do you find yourself doing that you said you'd never do?
Eating broccoli…I use to hate that stuff!
……

What are some qualities that you value in a person?
Integrity, humor, empathy, professionalism, spunk, and quick wit.
……

Where did you grow up and what was it like?
Fremont California, it was good. My parents didn't have much but I never knew that.
……

Name 5 of your favorite movies.
Father of the Bride, Lord of the Rings, Hangover, Fried Green Tomatoes,
……

What TV shows do you like?
Grey's Anatomy, So you think you can dance.
……

What do you enjoy doing on a Sunday afternoon?
Hiking, being outdoors. Time to relax…
……

You are stranded in the Amazon rain forest. What 3 items would you want to have with you and why?
Knife, water, and waterproofs. Knife to protect and kill for food, water to stay hydrated and waterproofs to stay dry.

……

Is there anything in particular that you wish you could do over? What is it?
My second marriage. I wish we would have waited longer to get married. It might have worked out then.
……

What personality traits in your mind are best suited for your job, career, etc?
Perky, intuitive, communicative, patient, caring, determined, goal oriented, and organized.
……

What is your favorite drink?
Vitamin Zero Water.
……

What is your favorite color?
Turquoise.
……

Name a movie that touched you in some way.
Rudy.
……

When in life have you felt most alone? Why?
In the midst of my marriage. We were having hard times to say the least and I just felt more along than ever. I never experienced that especially when I had a partner that was supposed to be there for me.
……

What would be impossible for you to give up?
My spirit.
……

Why would someone not want to work with you?

Someone may not want to work with me if they are not serious about achieving results.
......

What activities did you enjoy in school?
Many...gymnastics, softball, cheerleading, dance, track, cross country.
......

What kind of child were you?
Talkative, athletic, attention getter!
......

If you could be a superhero, what would you want your superpowers to be?
Heal pain, enable others to see a different outlook, give positivity.
......

How do you want to be remembered?
Kind, giving, inspiring, and a hard worker.
......

We all have vices, what are yours?
Truvia (sweetner) , Red Wine.
......

What is one of your favorite quotes?
Just do it.
......

What chore do you absolutely hate doing?
Cleaning the bathroom.
......

What is your best feature?
My smile.
......

What was the last experience that made you a stronger person?
Getting a divorce.
......

What makes you uncomfortable, besides these questions?
Confrontation.
......

If you could change something physical about yourself, what would it be and why?
I would have leaner legs. It's always been a tough spot for me. Even getting as lean as I do for competition. It's always so hard to get them to do what I need them to do.
......

Besides money, what are your favorite ways to compensate people?
I like to make things for people. Personalized gifts.
......

When was the last time you tried something new?
Last week. I like trying new things. I also have a bucket list that I am crossing off things from often.
......

How would you describe yourself in three words?
Energetic, happy, giving.
......

What is one thing you are not?
Dishonest.
......

Do you think crying is a sign of weakness or strength?
Strength.

......

What makes you angry?
Being underestimated.

......

What makes you laugh?
Most everything.

......

What are you afraid of?
Being alone.

......

What would be the first thing you would do if today was your last day?
Get to my family!

......

What's your vision of a perfect society?
One that everyone is positive and kind to one another.

......

Is it possible to lie without saying a word? How?
Yes...body language, facial expressions.

What's something you check daily?
Facebook and Instagram.

......

Are you an emotional person?
Very much so.

......

What's your own definition of happiness?
Feeling good about who you are and being able to be that person around everyone.

......

If you could choose to be born with a particular natural skill what skill would it be?
To sing.
......

What advice would you give someone who wanted to do what you do?
Learn as much as you can from every source possible. It's the best career out there.
......

While you are watching TV in your home a penguin walks through the door wearing a sheriff's hat and badge. What does he say?
You are under arrest for shear laziness...get off the couch and workout!
......

Do you have any secrets you want to share with the few of us reading this? We won't say anything....promise!
I use to be overweight and ate fast food daily, even more than once a day.
......

Are there any words of wisdom you'd like to pass along to us?
Eat healthy and exercise to feel good. Not just to look good.
......

Did you enjoy answering these questions? On a scale from 1 – 10. 1= I hated it. 10= I really enjoyed it.
Yes. 9!

About Michelle

Michelle Brown:

Active Live Fitness
michelle@myactivelifefitness.com
http://www.myactivelifefitness.com
http://www.facebook.com/myactivelifefitness

INTERVIEW 4
Dr. JaNee' G. Mobley

Personal Information

Full Name:
Dr. JaNee' G. Mobley

Age:
30

Location:
Albany, Georgia

Relationship Status:
Married

Number of Children:

o
Profession:
Life & Business

Educational Background:
Pharm D.

Certifications:
Life Coach Certification
....

General Questions

What are you known for professionally?
Coach, Consultant, Motivational Speaker, Registered Pharmacist.
......

Tell us about how you got into your line of work.
I've always loved inspiring people to live their best lives. I love showing people the best that is already within them. When I first discovered coaching after hiring a coach, I knew that this is what I was created and called to do.
......

How long have you been doing what you do?
Speaking and coaching: 2.5 years.
Pharmacist: 4 years.
......

What do you enjoy most about what you do?
I enjoy proving the best in people. I love seeing people see their true potential, discover their purpose and building thriving businesses.
......

What are you most passionate about professionally? What most excites you about your work & the contribution you can make?
I am most passionate about serving others. To help people through believing they can reach their full potential, build confidence and creating business that soar, it adds greater to this world.
......

What's the single most important reason for your success?
The reason for my success is my relationship with God. It keeps me grounded, focused and humbled.
......

What do you consider to be your greatest achievement?
My greatest achievement so far is my perseverance to continue my journey of purpose.
......

How do you think women have changed over the years? Regarding business, sports and fitness.
Women have really taken hold of their contribution to this earth. I believe that now women realize the power, poise and purpose that they have. Women are now leading entrepreneurship and business.
......

Do you think women are competitive with each other? Why? Regarding business, sports and fitness.
I believe that there is some competition, but not enough to really take notice.
......

What is the number one thing you like best about being into fitness?

Being into fitness for me allows me to be healthy to better walk in my purpose. It also allows me to be a living example of how you can better serve the world when you are healthy.
......

Is there anything wrong with wanting to portray women athletes, actors, etc as feminine and physically attractive?
In my opinion, no.
......

How do you deal with cravings for junk foods, sweets and salty food?
I indulge, but plan ahead to indulge. I will reduce my carbohydrate intake or increase my workout for the day.
......

Describe a typical day for you, starting from the moment you wake up in the morning.
I pray, read the Verse of the Day, visualize, and state my affirmations.
......

Health & Fitness Questions

What sports do you participated in for fun?
None.
......

How do you motivate yourself and stay motivated?
I journal, personally develop through reading and masterminding. I also stay motivated by my team of supporters (friends and family).
......

What are some of the main foods you would include in your shopping list to maintain a lean and muscular physique?
Chicken, turkey, veggies, almonds, oatmeal, fruit, whole wheat products, brown rice, olive oil.
......

What is the most challenging thing you deal with about consistently staying in top shape?
Cravings.
......

Please describe your normal diet. What do you eat in a typical day to stay in shape?
My meals vary typically depending upon my day.
I eat egg whites, turkey bacon, fruit, a fish, salad, a sweet potato, brown rice, and most baked chicken.
......

What type of exercises do you include in your routine to stay in shape?
Cardio (walking, Zumba) 3-5 days a week
Strength training (twice per week).
......

A total beginner is about 35 pounds overweight. She doesn't really know where to start. What tips can you give her to follow the right track?
Believe that you can do it. Whatever the mind believes, it can surely achieve. Take one step at a time. Commit to one thing initially. Maybe it is walking for 30 minutes a day. Do what you know that you can and will commit to.
......

What tips do you recommend for eating out at restaurants to make sure we don't gain too much weight/fat?

Plan ahead. If you know that you want to indulge, plan your meals ahead of time. Cut back on having a large lunch if you know that you want to go all the way for dinner. Make sure that you get in a great workout as well.
If you don't want to indulge, stay away from the appetizers if you know that you are going to have a full meal as well. Ask for a take-out box and put ½ of your food in that container so that you won't eat all of it.
......

What exercises do you recommend for getting a bigger, rounder and fuller butt?
Squats, hip extensions and lunges.
......

What are your top tips for developing toned and defined arms? Specific exercises, diet advice, etc.
Arm lifts, triceps dips, bicep curls, arm rotations, push ups.
......

What are your top tips for losing unwanted body fat? Specific exercises, diet advice, etc.
Stay away from sugar. Cardio, cardio, cardio.
......

What are your top tips for gaining lean muscle mass? Specific exercises, diet advice, etc.
Make sure that get protein with each meal. You can also consume protein shakes (be careful of the sugar content and the amount of protein that you are getting daily). Strength train 2-3 times weekly.
......

What are your top tips for improving breasts lift and shape? Specific exercises, diet advice, etc.
Push ups and chest press exercises.
......

What are your top tips for staying motivated on a fitness plan?
Support, support, support.
Remember the reason why you started initially.
Reward yourself for each accomplishment.
......

Have you suffered any injuries? What injuries?
No.
......

What things do you currently do in your training that is key to your success?
I do a lot of mind work. I motivate myself which really keeps me on task. I also make an effort to plan ahead of time for my meals and workout.
......

Isn't it hard to stay fit? How do you manage that?!
YES. It is hard to stay fit. It is something that I have to consciously focus on because it is so easy to get back into old habits. The way that I deal with this is I constantly remind myself why I started this in the first place. I look at my family and it really gets me motivated because I want them to be healthy, but I must first be the example.
......

Business Questions

Tell us about your first entrepreneurial experience as a kid or older.
My first entrepreneurial experience was in a network marketing company. I loved that experience because it really helped me overcome fear of rejection. It also showed me the importance of personal development, mentorship, the power of associate, and attitude in your business.

What is the most difficult part of starting your business?
I really can't answer that question because I didn't have any difficulty starting my business.

How have your entrepreneurial motivations changed since you first started?
My motivation now is focused more so on serving and inspiring change in other people's lives. My motivation is more service oriented.

What do you consider to be success as a business owner or entrepreneur?
I believe success is a state of mind. A person determines what success is for them. By knowing that, they will know when they have attained it.

What's your least favorite part about being a business owner or entrepreneur?
Coming across negative people.

What's the biggest thing you struggle with as a business owner or entrepreneur?
Staying focused. Remaining focus is something that I have to consciously and continuously work on.

How do you think running a business or being an entrepreneur has made you a better person?
It has taught resilience, perseverance, patience, endurance, work ethic, organization, and so much more. It has indeed made me into a better person.

......

How did you arrive at running this business? What path brought you here?
When I graduated from pharmacy school, I realized 5 months into my career that I didn't like it. It wasn't me. So, I hired a coach, and it was through working with a coach that I discovered what my purpose was and I am so glad that I made that investment because it really changed my entire life.
......

What was the most difficult part of starting your business?
I didn't have any difficulties because I started with an expert.
......

What do you do on a daily basis to grow as a person/business person/entrepreneur?
Read.
Pray.
Surround myself with positive and supportive people.
Attend live personal development events.
Have a coach.
Be apart of a mastermind group.
......

What's unique about the service that you provide?
My service is focused on the individual, not their business nor their circumstance. I believe that when you improve the individual, you change everything and everyone around them no matter how their situation maybe.
......

What entrepreneurial hacks have you developed to stay focused and productive in your day-to-day?
A calendar.
An accountability partner.
......

Do you have any of your own branded products? If so, what are they?
I am currently working on my home study system.
......

Mixed Questions

What would be your ultimate achievement in any area of your life?
My ultimate achievement in life is to help my family, clients and students live a whole and purposeful life.
......

At present, what is your biggest challenge, and what are you doing to manage this challenge?
Staying focused. I am handling this by creating a list of reminders and a calendar that helps me to organize it all.
......

What things do you believe differentiates you from your contemporaries?
What makes me different is my individuality. I am not conformed to a certain ritual, but I allow myself to really connect with my clients and focus on their challenges in order to get them the breakthroughs that they need.
......

Have you ever experienced a breakthrough, and if so, what led to it?
Yes. I was lead to this breakthrough by my life coach. She asked me a series of questions which assisted me in getting the answers that I needed in order to move forward.
......

Do you have a saying or motto that you live your life by?
GO FOR IT! NOW IS YOUR TIME!
......

Where do you draw your inspiration from?
From others who are successful or are working towards their goals.
......

Made any mistakes that helped or hurt you in a way that you would like to share?
One of my lessons in life that I'd like to share is for so long I got so much information. I've had a coach, mentors, gone to events, read books and magazines, but did nothing with the information that I received. Once I realized this, I made a conscious decision to implement the information that I receive.
......

What were your biggest personal battles and how did you confront them?
One of battles that I encounter is the battle of my mind. It tries to plague me with fear when it is time to play a bigger game, but I have learned to tell myself a better story. When fear tells me that I can't, I tell it that I can do all things through Christ who strengthens me. I also have other affirmations that I state to get me back on track.
......

What were the most difficult decisions you had to make during your lifetime? Why?
Learning to say no to people. This was hard for me because I used to struggle with making everyone happy because I didn't like for people to be upset with me.
......

If you could paint a picture of any scenery you've seen before, what would you paint?
The beautiful clear blue water in Nassau, Bahamas. I would paint how the waves rippled. Um! I get excited visualizing it.
......

What are some goals you are still trying to accomplish?
Writing my first book.
Completing my home study system.
Being featured on my local news station for my business.
......

What are the most important lessons you've learned in life?
Always have a financial cushion.
The key to great wealth is entrepreneurship.
Having support is key to success.
Stay positive.
Learn how to say no.
Make sure that your business endeavours align with your brand.
Keep a mentor and coach.
......

What are you proudest of in your life?
Graduating from pharmacy school.
Walking in my purpose.
Developing a healthy lifestyle.
......

How do you set your goals?
I right them all down and number the most important and out of that, complete the simplest one first to motivate me.
......

What else would you do if you weren't in your current line of work?
Bake.
......

What are your religious beliefs/spiritual beliefs?
I believe God sent Jesus Christ, his son, to die for my sins. He is the creator of heaven and earth.

......

Do you believe in the Law of Attraction?
Absolutely!
......

What is your diet like?
Honestly, it varies, depending upon my schedule and craving. I make sure that I get my veggies in for the day though.
......

What's your favorite food?
Spaghetti.
......

What would we find in your refrigerator right now?
Almond milk.
Shredded Cheese.
Chicken.
Water.
Leftovers (lol).
......

If you had the opportunity to get a message across to a large group of people what would your message be?
Love the skin that you're in. When God created you, He broke the mold. Never try to be anyone else but yourself!
......

Where do you see yourself in 5 years?
Still married with 3 children (2 sons and one daughter or just 3 sons).
At millionaire status in my business.
Featured on talk shows and Essence, Oprah and Forbes magazines.
Hosting my own women's conference.
Best selling author.
......

What are you best at?
Speaking.
Coaching.
Inspiring.
Motivating.
Marketing.
......

What books do you like to read?
Personal development, self help books.
......

What is your favorite type of music?
Gospel.
Jazz.
R & B.
......

Describe your parents, what are they like?
My father was a very vocal, caring, hard-working man who prided himself in his family. He loved to cook and make people laugh.
My mother is reserved, kind-hearted, sensitive, comforting, supportive and so loving. She prides herself in being a wonderful mother.
......

What were your dreams as a child and did you achieve any of them?
My dreams as a child was become a teacher and an airplane pilot. I am achieving my dreams being a teacher through my business.
......

Tell us a time in your life that was a time you'll never forget?

When my mother told me that my father passed away. I was devastated. I was broken. It was a horrible moment for me at that time.
……

What things do you find yourself doing that you said you'd never do?
Speaking.
Reading.
Writing.
……

What are some qualities that you value in a person?
Integrity.
Honesty.
Perseverance.
Good work ethic.
Team player.
Optimism.
……

Where did you grow up and what was it like?
Miami Gardens Florida.
It was a friendly neighbourhood where we knew our neighbours and looked out for one another. All of the kids would play together. Parents would carpool for school pick up. It was a pretty good neighbourhood.
……

Name 5 of your favorite movies.
The Ultimate Gift.
Last Holiday.
Just Wright.
Facing the Giants.
Fast and the Furious.
……

What TV shows do you like?
Oprah's Next Chapter.

Iyanla Fix My Life.
Scandal.
Criminal Minds.
19 Kids and Counting.
......

What do you enjoy doing on a Sunday afternoon?
Relaxing and enjoying my family.
......

You are stranded in the Amazon rain forest. What 3 items would you want to have with you and why?
A map or compass for direction. Water to stay hydrated.
......

Is there anything in particular that you wish you could do over? What is it?
No because each experience has made me into a better individual.
......

What personality traits in your mind are best suited for your job, career, etc?
My spirit of optimism, perseverance.
......

What is your favorite drink?
Water.
......

What is your favorite color?
Purple.
......

Name a movie that touched you in some way.
The Ultimate Gift.
......

When in life have you felt most alone? Why?
When I lacked confidence, because I felt like I was the only one who was going through it at the time.
......

What would be impossible for you to give up?
My God-given purpose because I am so focused on achieving and making it happen.
......

Why would someone not want to work with you?
If they are not truly ready to change the course of their lives. If they are serious, nor want accountability.

What activities did you enjoy in school?
Art.
......

What kind of child were you?
I was a child who didn't need much entertainment. I didn't mind being by myself or playing dolls and teacher by myself. It was very easy to entertain me.
......

If you could be a superhero, what would you want your superpowers to be?
Wonder woman.
......

How do you want to be remembered?
As a loving and devoted woman of God, wife, mother, servant. A woman who gave life her all and accomplished her purpose and shared it with the world.
......

We all have vices, what are yours?
I can be judgemental.
......

What is one of your favorite quotes?
Be the change that you want to see in the world. –Mahatma Gandhi.
......

What chore do you absolutely hate doing?
Mopping.
......

What is your best feature?
My personality.
......

What was the last experience that made you a stronger person?
Being fired from my job.
......

What makes you uncomfortable, besides these questions?
Negative people.
......

If you could change something physical about yourself, what would it be and why?
I have come to a place in my life where I love me so me just as I am.
......

Besides money, what are your favorite ways to compensate people?
Through service and advice.
......

When was the last time you tried something new?
I can't remember.
......

How would you describe yourself in three words?
Optimistic, Positive and Encouraging.
......

What is one thing you are not?
Pessimistic.
......

Do you think crying is a sign of weakness or strength?
No.
......

What makes you angry?
Negativity and foolishness.
What makes you laugh?
Babies and people.
......

What are you afraid of?
God.
......

What would be the first thing you would do if today was your last day?
Give more, live more and be even more than I am now.
......

What's your vision of a perfect society?
Where we all can live in peace, love and unity.
......

Is it possible to lie without saying a word? How?
Yes, if you consider body language.
......

What's something you check daily?
My bank account.
......

Are you an emotional person?
Yes.
......

What's your own definition of happiness?
Happiness is a feeling of emotion that is based on a conscious choice. Regardless of your environment or situations no-thing will steal your beautiful moment.
......

Which famous person would you like to interview and which questions would you ask him/her?
Oprah.
......

If you could choose to be born with a particular natural skill what skill would it be?
I really can't think of anything.
......

What advice would you give someone who wanted to do what you do?
I would say to make sure that this is what you want to do and what you're supposed to do because if you are not sure, the road can be very difficult and discouraging. Get a coach and mentor. This is so vital if you really want to succeed. It is so much easier going on a journey when you have someone who has been there and can help you avoid a lot of the pitfalls and difficulties. Stay focused and always work harder on yourself than you do anything else.
......

Are there any words of wisdom you'd like to pass along to us?
In order to truly be a gift to the world and those that you love is first love yourself and take care of yourself. You can't possibly be as good for others if you are not at your best.
......

Did you enjoy answering these questions? On a scale from 1 – 10. 1= I hated it. 10= I really enjoyed it.
7.

....

About JaNee'

Dr. JaNee' Mobley

Unveiling Your Next Level Strategist, Mentor & Coach

Unveiling You Enterprises

http://www.unveilingyouenterprises.com

https://www.facebook.com/unveilingyouenterprises

www.twitter.com/drjaneemobley

www.linkedin.com/in/janeemobley

www.youtube.com/nowisyourtime

INTERVIEW 5

Iva Franks-Singer

Personal Information

Full Name:
Iva Franks-Singer

Age:
Age range 45 to 50

Location:
All of California

Number of Children:
1.

Profession:
Actress

Educational Background:
Some College

....

General Questions

What are you known for professionally?
Acting.
......

Tell us about how you got into your line of work.
I've been an artist since I can remember so it was inevitable.
......

How long have you been doing what you do?
Professionally... 26 years.
......

What do you enjoy most about what you do?
I love being creative!
......

What are you most passionate about professionally? What most excites you about your work & the contribution you can make?
You know that feeling you get when you fall in love? That's how I feel when I'm working as an actress... The contribution is vast. I have the opportunity to do a lot of charity work, PSA's and I have more exposure as a victims rights advocate due to my profession.
......

What's the single most important reason for your success?
Perseverance, I never gave myself an expiration date and I don't know how to quit.
……

What do you consider to be your greatest achievement?
I haven't reached it yet.
……

How do you think women have changed over the years? Regarding business, sports and fitness.
They way we're viewed and respected. As well we have more liberties then ever before. Not only in the U.S. but in other countries.
……

Do you think women are competitive with each other? Why? Regarding business, sports and fitness.
I think people in general are competitive. If you're not, good luck.
……

What memorable competitions come to mind in your career?
Every time I audition I'm competing.
……

What is the number one thing you like best about being into fitness?
I like feeling good when I wake up in the morning. I like fitting into my clothes without angst. I want to be an very healthy and agile older person, when that time comes.
……

Is there anything wrong with wanting to portray women athletes, actors, etc as feminine and physically attractive?
Absolutely not. Women are beautiful creatures and we should be proud of that.
......

How do you deal with cravings for junk foods, sweets and salty food?
I usually don't have cravings. However, frosting is my kryptonite. It's not a craving but if it's in my view I may eat it!
......

Describe a typical day for you, starting from the moment you wake up in the morning.
I get up and make the bed, feed the cats and dog. Then I get my green tea and some almonds and go to my computer to check my emails. My days are usually not the same. Depending on my schedule they can go anywhere. I try to work out before 3PM. I try to be in bed by 11:30.
......

Health & Fitness Questions

What sports do you participated in for fun?
Golf, hiking, swimming. Trying to learn tennis.
......

How long have you been playing those sports?
Golf, almost 30 years. All other sports, since I was a kid.
......

What got you started in that sport?
All my friends.
......

What is your biggest accomplishment in your sports? Include fun sports and any athletic career.
I have trophies for golfing! Yea! I used to race BMX and run track. I won awards, but that is when I was a youngster.
......

What competitions have you entered? What were the outcomes?
Golf tournaments, you win some you lose some. It's all fun.
......

How do you motivate yourself and stay motivated?
Stay focused. Stay positive.
......

What are some of the main foods you would include in your shopping list to maintain a lean and muscular physique?
Chicken breast, fish, love salmon. Lots of greens. Love tomatoes. High proteins. Energy foods.
......

What is the most challenging thing you deal with about consistently staying in top shape?
Hormonal issues.
......

Please describe your normal diet. What do you eat in a typical day to stay in shape?
Almonds or pure protein for breakfast. A salad with some protein and lots of veggies for lunch and a light dinner, fish or chicken.
......

What type of exercises do you include in your routine to stay in shape?

Cardio and body sculpting. I have a tendency to bulk up so I have to sculpt. Pilates, Turbo Jam, P90X and my trusty treadmill.
......

A total beginner is about 35 pounds overweight. She doesn't really know where to start. What tips can you give her to follow the right track?
Try not to get discouraged. Stay focused and surround yourself around like-minded people. Create a routine and stick with it. It's a life style change not a diet.
......

What tips do you recommend for eating out at restaurants to make sure we don't gain too much weight/fat?
No bread. Get in the habit of ordering fish and chicken. There are a lot of really great menu items that are not fat filled. Light on the dressing if you're having a salad.
......

What exercises do you recommend for getting a bigger, rounder and fuller butt?
I don't.
......

What are your top tips for developing toned and defined arms? Specific exercises, diet advice, etc.
Isometric exercises. Light weights and a lot of reps. Don't worry you wont bulk up.
......

What are your top tips for losing unwanted body fat? Specific exercises, diet advice, etc.
Build muscle and do cardio. Having more muscle helps burn more fat. Everything I wrote about above pertains to this question.
......

What are your top tips for gaining lean muscle mass? Specific exercises, diet advice, etc.
Light weights and lots of reps for all exercises.
......

What are your top tips for improving breasts lift and shape? Specific exercises, diet advice, etc.
My favourite is the butterfly. Either on a bench or the machine.
......

What are your top tips for staying motivated on a fitness plan?
Love yourself more than you love food. Love being in shape more than you love cookies. Whenever you start to eat something fattening, think of how horrible you feel trying on pants that are too tight.
......

What is your training routine like? Please include a few details.
6 days on 1 day off. An hour of cardio everyday and arms, legs, abs I switch off during the week.
......

What is the best way towards becoming a personal trainer?
Go to a gym and train with a trainer. Then take classes and become certified in whatever style you want to teach.
......

Have you suffered any injuries? What injuries?
Yes, nothing to do with training.
......

What things do you currently do in your training that is key to your success?

See above.
......

Isn't it hard to stay fit? How do you manage that?!
At this age, yes. I get mad and work harder.
......

Business Questions

Tell us about your first entrepreneurial experience as a kid or older.
I was very competitive as a Girl Scout selling cookies.
......

What is the most difficult part of starting your business?
Licensing, insurance all the red tape.
......

How have your entrepreneurial motivations changed since you first started?
The economy changes so you have to adjust accordingly.
......

Mixed Questions

What would be your ultimate achievement in any area of your life?
To keep acting until I'm in to my golden years.
......

If you could be any character in fiction, who would you be?

Cynthia Ann Parker.
……

At present, what is your biggest challenge, and what are you doing to manage this challenge?
To keep working. My business is hot and cold. Very unpredictable.

What things do you believe differentiates you from your contemporaries?
My drive to keep moving forward.
……

Have you ever experienced a breakthrough, and if so, what led to it?
Yes, never listening to others saying I can't.
……

Who has been the biggest influence on your life? What lessons did that person teach you?
Sal Dano, my past acting coach.
……

Do you have a saying or motto that you live your life by?
Yes, there are no rules.
……

Made any mistakes that helped or hurt you in a way that you would like to share?
Yes, I let others in my life advise me. (relationships, they don't always have your best interest at heart).
……

What were your biggest personal battles and how did you confront them?
My stalker. I'm a victim's rights advocate now.
……

What were the most difficult decisions you had to make during your lifetime? Why?
Can't think of any, there were a lot.
......

If you could paint a picture of any scenery you've seen before, what would you paint?
I love painting flowers, trees and hill sides.

What are some goals you are still trying to accomplish?
Emmy, Oscar, a really great series.
......

What are you proudest of in your life?
My daughter.
......

How do you set your goals?
Post-its.
......

What else would you do if you weren't in your current line of work?
Search and Rescue Paramedic or ER Doctor.
......

What are your religious beliefs/spiritual beliefs?
I'm not religious, I'm spiritual. Messianic Jew.
......

What's your favorite food?
Italian.
......

If you had the opportunity to get a message across to a large group of people what would your message be?
You are beautiful. It's not how others see you; it's how you see yourself.

......

Where do you see yourself in 5 years?
Not a clue. Hopefully happy!
......

What are you best at?
Whatever I put my mind to.
......

What books do you like to read?
Inspirational books.
......

What is your favorite type of music?
All.
......

Describe your parents, what are they like?
My mom is strong.
......

What were your dreams as a child and did you achieve any of them?
I'm living them.
......

Tell us a time in your life that was a time you'll never forget?
Getting cast on Las Vegas.
......

What are some qualities that you value in a person?
Honesty and self respect.
......

Where did you grow up and what was it like?
Clovis CA. My life was like pretty much like St Elmos Fire. I was lucky.

......

Name 5 of your favorite movies.
Citizen Kane, Casino, Mommy Dearest, Moonstruck, When Harry Met Sally.
......

What TV shows do you like?
Downton Abby, Magic City, Friends.
......

What do you enjoy doing on a Sunday afternoon?
Different things. Antique shop, swim, BBQ.
......

You are stranded in the Amazon rain forest. What 3 items would you want to have with you and why?
Swiss Army knife. Survival book on plants I can eat, Plastic tarp.
......

Is there anything in particular that you wish you could do over? What is it?
Be happy on all levels.
......

What personality traits in your mind are best suited for your job, career, etc?
Determination.
......

What is your favorite drink?
Green tea.
......

What is your favorite color?
Red.
......

Name a movie that touched you in some way.
So many.
......

When in life have you felt most alone? Why?
I have a large family and God is always with me.
......

What would be impossible for you to give up?
My family.
......

Why would someone not want to work with you?
Competition.
......

What activities did you enjoy in school?
Gym.
......

What kind of child were you?
Total tomboy.
......

If you could be a superhero, what would you want your superpowers to be?
Kwai Chang Caine.
......

How do you want to be remembered?
I don't really know.
......

We all have vices, what are yours?
Gum, I have to have gum.
......

What chore do you absolutely hate doing?
Taking out the trash.

......

What is your best feature?
Confidence.
......

What was the last experience that made you a stronger person?
Having to defend myself against my stalker.
......

What makes you uncomfortable, besides these questions?
I don't answer question about my relationships or sex.
......

If you could change something physical about yourself, what would it be and why?
My feet are too fat! LOL.
......

Besides money, what are your favorite ways to compensate people?
Support as a friend.
......

When was the last time you tried something new?
I'm always trying new things. I can't really think... hmmm.
......

How would you describe yourself in three words?
Honest, confident and determined.
......

What is one thing you are not?
A pacifist.
......

Do you think crying is a sign of weakness or strength?
No, it's a great release.
……

What makes you angry?
People who lie and have no respect for others.
……

What makes you laugh?
So many things.
……

What are you afraid of?
I don't really know.
……

What would be the first thing you would do if today was your last day?
I'd take my pets and go to be with my family.
……

What's your vision of a perfect society?
Less Government, happier, healthier.
……

Is it possible to lie without saying a word? How?
Yes, lying by omission.
……

What's something you check daily?
Email, Ebay, Casting.
……

Are you an emotional person?
Yes.
……

What's your own definition of happiness?

Everything good in harmony.
……

Which famous person would you like to interview and which questions would you ask him/her?
Judas Iscariot, I'd like to ask him if it was really worth it? ☺
……

If you could choose to be born with a particular natural skill what skill would it be?
To play the piano and sing.
……

What advice would you give someone who wanted to do what you do?
You have to be willing to sacrifice a lot, eat Top Ramin and willing to be broke at times. Pretty much you have to love being an artist more than you love having tons of money.
……

While you are watching TV in your home a penguin walks through the door wearing a sheriff's hat and badge. What does he say?
I know you're hiding the ice, point me to the fridge!
……

Do you have any secrets you want to share with the few of us reading this? We won't say anything….promise!
No. ☺
……

Did you enjoy answering these questions? On a scale from 1 – 10. 1= I hated it. 10= I really enjoyed it.
5. Some of them were repetitive. I don't have answers for others. ☺

……

About Iva

http://www.ivafranks.com (personal website)

http://www.imdb.com/name/nm0291655/ (IMDB)

www.jodisvoice.org (I'm on the Board of Directors) Victims Rights against stalking

www.reelfestivalforwomen.org (I sit on the Board of Directors & oversee all documentaries)

INTERVIEW 6

Jessica Li

Personal Information

Full Name:
Jessica Li

Age:
31

Location:
Toronto, Canada

Relationship Status:
Separated

Number of Children:
3

Profession:
Raw Chef, Certified Personal Trainer, Business Owner

Educational Background:
B.A. (Psychology, Criminology)

Certifications:
Personal Trainer, Raw Chef Intensive, Dental Hygiene, Psychiatric Aide, Long Term Care Worker
....

General Questions

What are you known for professionally?
Being a raw chef and fitness expert who inspires, motivates, and transforms clients to a higher place in their health.
......

Tell us about how you got into your line of work.
I've been passionate about health and fitness since first stepping into a gym in 2001. I saw first hand how taking care of myself transformed me into a body and state of mind that I never thought possible.
......

How long have you been doing what you do?
I have been in health care since 2000 and became a raw chef in 2012 and a personal trainer in 2013.
......

What do you enjoy most about what you do?

I love seeing a client's "aha" moment go off for them because once they get to that point a whole new mind set comes into play and they have even more motivation and drive to maintain their newfound health. And they spread the word of health to others around them, whether verbally or by simply being walking proof".
......

What are you most passionate about professionally? What most excites you about your work & the contribution you can make?
I am dedicated to spreading knowledge of health to others. I love when clients achieve their goals or learn something new and share it with the people around them because it inspires even more people to look at their own health and figure out how they too can improve.
......

What's the single most important reason for your success?
A strong work ethic.
......

What do you consider to be your greatest achievement?
Taking the worst thing that happened to me, being almost killed by my husband in a domestic violence attack and using that incident as a catalyst for leaving the relationship, starting my own business and finally living out my dreams.
......

How do you think women have changed over the years? Regarding business, sports and fitness.
More women are doing things that traditionally men would mostly do, whether it be business, sports and fitness, or any other field. Women have become more independent and now have a wealth of resources thanks to the Internet There's a

reliable platform for them to find out how to workout, who the top coaches are to see, and to see what other women are doing.
......

Do you think women are competitive with each other? Why? Regarding business, sports and fitness.
Definitely can be competitive, some more than others. But I see more women supporting each other than anything. We relate to female issues but at the same time we want to be the best in our field.
......

What is the number one thing you like best about being into fitness?
Seeing how it can dramatically transform a person.
......

How do you deal with cravings for junk foods, sweets and salty food?
After being on a high raw food diet for awhile now, I rarely get cravings for that kind of stuff. And if I do, I just throw some hazelnuts, raw cacao, and yacon syrup in a processor and BAM! I have enough to quickly satisfy my sweet tooth. It takes me about two minutes to make. I make other versions as well. If I'm on the road and feel the need for sweet, I'll aim for a health store and check out their selection but I'm anal about labels so if nothing in the store is really healthy in my books, then I'll grin and bare it and move on. I don't sacrifice my health for any preservatives or other harmful chemicals in foods.
......

Describe a typical day for you, starting from the moment you wake up in the morning.
<u>Typical day:</u>

6am= alarm goes off

6:15= still in bed but may be reflecting on life's blessings, what's on the agenda for the day, and what new goals I want to accomplish. This is my dose of motivation and then I roll out of bed ready to rock

6:20am= brush teeth, put contacts in, have a capsule of EGCg

6:25am= plank for as along as I can (I challenge myself to beat the previous day's time) and then I stretch and do 15-30 minutes of cardio (freestyle a mixture of JNL Fusion moves with Insanity plus Crossfit--this keeps my body guessing and my mind motivated; I burn more calories this way versus being on an elliptical machine for the same amount of time)

7am= drink 2 large glasses of water + make a big green drink (protein, chocolate almond milk, kale, romaine, parsley, lemon, cayenne, spirulina, greens powder, 1-inch slice of ginger, lucuma, maca, Goji berries, banana

7:15am= wake up kids for school and help them get ready, make their lunches

8am= drive kids to school

8:15am= catch up on the day's news online, check email, social media, and start working

11am= eat pre-workout meal (a common meal is quinoa pasta with marinara sauce and spinach)

12:40pm= pre-workout drink of water and glutamine and BCAA's

1-2:30pm= workout

2:45pm= high protein drink (coconut water, blueberries, protein powder, acerola cherry)

3pm= shower, put on sunscreen on face (Tizo), under eye cream (Priori), facial day cream (Priori), makeup

3:15pm= 1 tablespoon of peanut, cashew, or almond butter; spend time with kids

4pm= work

5:30pm= dinner (a common meal is an avocado and kelp noodles with marinara sauce), CLA + EGCg (or a digestive aid capsule) combo

6-9pm= work

9pm= water + scoop of protein, and source of healthy fat like a tablespoon of flax or a tablespoon of chia seed oil (this helps sustain me through the night and helps prevent muscle breakdown as I sleep)

Health & Fitness Questions

What sports do you participated in for fun?
Cross Fit, scuba diving, pole dancing, rock climbing.
……

How long have you been playing those sports?
Started all of them within the last three years, although my first rock climbing stints happened back in tenth grade.
......

What got you started in that sport?
Thought they looked fun and I wanted to learn new things.
......

What is your biggest accomplishment in your sports? Include fun sports and any athletic career.
I was afraid of the water because I'm not the greatest swimmer so going on multiple scuba diving trips was big for me. For Cross Fit I tied in first place (the other person was a male) doing as many rounds as possible of things like box jumps, walking lunges, wall balls. I have super strong legs so I think that may have played a role ☺ And I think my knock-knees help make me a better jumper!
......

How do you motivate yourself and stay motivated?
I think back to the domestic attack and that now I have three children on my own to look after. My children give me reason to push forward everyday. If I feel like crying, they are my reminder for me to mop up my tears and keep going. I count my blessings and am grateful for them all. They humble me. I am in a good position and have no right to complain. People from all walks of life motivate me, whether it be a fellow fitness professional that keeps me on my toes or a person that doubts me--that keeps me focused on the finish line even more!
......

What are some of the main foods you would include in your shopping list to maintain a lean and muscular physique?

Blueberries, avocados, coconut oil, raw nuts, lentils, flax, chia, kale (but really a wide range of veggies), coconut water, oatmeal, quinoa, ginger, lemon, fresh herbs.
......

What is the most challenging thing you deal with about consistently staying in top shape?
Being a chef and personal trainer at the same time! Talk about will power! I taste everything I make for customers and that includes super yummy desserts. I end up eating so many leftovers since raw food is free of preservatives and other nasties, and so it may not keep as well in the fridge as other foods.
......

Please describe your normal diet. What do you eat in a typical day to stay in shape?
Breakfast: green smoothie with protein powder.
Snack: veggies + hummus.
Lunch: quinoa with veggies.
Snack: Protein drink.
Dinner: Avocado, kelp noodles.
Before bed: protein drink.
......

What type of exercises do you include in your routine to stay in shape?
Combo of weight training and cardio. Cardio for me usually consists of freestyle plyometrics, jump rope, and Crossfit moves. I've also been doing Pilates recently with good results.
......

What tips do you recommend for eating out at restaurants to make sure we don't gain too much weight/fat?
Ask your sever what the dish is made of down to the nitty gritty. Ask what type of oil and sweetener they use. Ask them for substitutions. Many servers don't have a clue about healthy eating so you need to know what ingredients are

suitable for you so that you can look for them or request them. Don't take the menu they give you at face value. The best vegan meal I've ever had outside home was at a restaurant known for their high meat-based creations.

Some kitchens are more than happy to accommodate you however they can. Other than this, tell servers as soon as you sit down not to bring the bread basket if carb-binging is your weakness. Aim for roasted, sautéed methods vs fried or grilled. Grilled is usually advised as the better route and while it can indeed lower fat content on the food, cooking at high heat can sometimes create toxins (think grilled steak).
……

What exercises do you recommend for getting a bigger, rounder and fuller butt?

1. Glute Bridge Raise: Lie back on the floor and bend knees while keeping feet flat on floor. Raise your hips, squeeze for 5 seconds, and slowly lower hips back towards floor. Repeat 12 times.
Ramp it up: Place a barbell across your hips (place where comfortable as it can hurt if right on bone!).
2. Single Leg Step Ups: Find a bench or wooden box and step up with one leg and step back down. Repeat on same leg for 15 times and switch legs. Repeat circuit 3 times.
Ramp it up: Strap on ankle weights.
3. Sumo Squat: Stand with legs just wider than shoulder-width apart and feet pointing slightly outwards. Keeping firmly on ground and holding a kettle ball or dumbbell with both hands, slowly squat until weight touches ground. Keep back straight and chest up. Raise up to original position. Repeat 15 times.
4. Hamstring Curl with Exercise Ball: Lie on your back and place heels on an exercise ball. While pressing your heels into the ball raise your hips off the floor until all your bodyweight is resting on the upper back and shoulders. Hold this position and then roll ball towards your body by bending

your legs back and pulling the ball in with your heels. Push the ball away by straightening your legs. Repeat 20 times.
What are your top tips for developing toned and defined arms? Specific exercises, diet advice, etc.
......

What are your top tips for losing unwanted body fat? Specific exercises, diet advice, etc.
Keep your meals in moderation. Find out ideal portion sizes because this if often an eye-opener for people. I can't offer supplement recommendations but I personally use EGCg in combination with CLA and a digestive enzyme. Avoid any and all fad diets.

Do weight training 3-5 days a week and hit cardio right after each session.
......

What are your top tips for developing toned and defined arms? Specific exercises, diet advice, etc.
Like other exercises, choose ones you enjoy and mix it up with different workouts. Diet plays a huge role. If you want a defined look, body fat needs to decrease and weight lifting intensity should progressively increase with subsequent workouts.
......

What are your top tips for staying motivated on a fitness plan?
Think back to the reasons you started on your fitness journey. Imagine yourself in the body you desire and feel how it would feel to get there.

Do whatever it takes to stay motivated. Switch sports or routines, pump up the music, alternate gyms, find a workout buddy that's in the same shape or better than you.
......

What is your training routine like? Please include a few details.
My workouts vary quite a bit. Here's a typical chest day:

-flat bench press.
-incline dumbbell press.
-dumbbell flys.
-pullovers.
-dips.
-close grip push-ups.
......

What is the best way to get started in your industry?
Research the best teachers and coaches in the field and seek them out. Go learn from them.
......

What is the best way towards becoming a personal trainer?
Find out exactly what the job entails and ask yourself if you have enough passion to do it for at least a month for free. Find out which organization you want to become certified through and find out what your local gyms require as job prerequisites. There are a handful of online done-in-a-weekend certification "programs" that cost a few hundred dollars but the certificate won't mean anything to most employers. Do your research because you're about to invest in time and money.
......

Have you suffered any injuries? What injuries?
I tore a chest muscle years ago during the heaviest lifting period in my life. I also fell on my ankle, for which the cartilage is still damaged more than five years later.
......

What things do you currently do in your training that is key to your success?

I switch things up, whether it be exercise, sport, or interval. Not only does it keep me more engaged but it keeps my body guessing and developing all around. Plus the spikes with interval training help boost metabolism quite a bit.
......

Isn't it hard to stay fit? How do you manage that?!
Keeping fit is what keeps me sane. Honestly. I have so much on my plate but if I don't keep with a physical activity routine, I become miserable, lethargic, cranky, less creative, less motivated. Keeping fit gives me the energy I need to handle my busy life and gives me a lot of confidence.
......

Business Questions

Tell us about your first entrepreneurial experience as a kid or older.
As a kid I had zero exposure to entrepreneurship. Out of dozens and dozens of relatives, I know of an aunt and uncle who had a candy shop, which they later sold. That was it. Everyone else was working for someone else, doing the 9-5 thing. Business is new to me but I made the decision to get into it and learn the ropes. So here I am. I'm growing from here on in.
......

What is the most difficult part of starting your business?
Learning who to trust and find out what the best resources are for helping me reach my goals.
......

What do you consider to be success as a business owner or entrepreneur?

Living the life you dream.
......

What's your least favorite part about being a business owner or entrepreneur?
The loneliness, bookkeeping, taxes, no health insurance.
......

What's the biggest thing you struggle with as a business owner or entrepreneur?
Running a one-woman show can be quite lonely, so I really value networking with my colleagues and meeting new people.
......

How do you think running a business or being an entrepreneur has made you a better person?
Wow, so much! It has helped me to view the world differently and understand human behaviour more. I am more aware of myself and more attentive all around.
......

How did you arrive at running this business? What path brought you here?
One of my thoughts during what I thought were my final breaths as I was being choked by my husband, was "this isn't fair. I didn't get to do everything I wanted to do." That moment inspired me to find out what I want in life and take action immediately.
......

What was the most difficult part of starting your business?
Starting it all from square one alone with little emotional support.
......

What do you do on a daily basis to grow as a person/business person/entrepreneur?

I network with people and research a ton online. I'm always busy catching up on new trends and am on a webinar training almost daily.
......

What's unique about the service that you provide?
I offer the both of best worlds being a raw chef and personal trainer. I also use my own struggles to help strengthen my clients so that they don't make the same mistakes I did.
......

What entrepreneurial hacks have you developed to stay focused and productive in your day-to-day?
I make sure I stick to my workout routine because fitness and my business run parallel to one another. I self-talk about "how bad I want it", "keep pushing on", "2 more reps"...the talk I give myself in the gym is the same talk I often use as I develop my business.
......

Do you have any of your own branded products? If so, what are they?
Chica Momma raw vegan food.
......

Mixed Questions

What would be your ultimate achievement in any area of your life?
To become a professional speaker so that I can serve even more people.
......

If you could be any character in fiction, who would you be?

Super Woman.
......

At present, what is your biggest challenge, and what are you doing to manage this challenge?
Raising three children on my own. I manage by keeping my eye on the prize, that being the life I desire for them and myself.
......

What things do you believe differentiates you from your contemporaries?
I have gone through deep personal struggles that have allowed me to gain such insight on not only how people can lead healthier lives, but how to dig deeper into someone's life so that they can really optimize their results.
......

Have you ever experienced a breakthrough, and if so, what led to it?
The empowerment I received by standing up to abuse. It took SO much for me to press charges and testify in court against the man I was in a relationship for so many years. But doing that led me to a whole new life I never imagined I'd experience. I am in a good position. I am blessed. Life is great!
......

Who has been the biggest influence on your life? What lessons did that person teach you?
My husband, for teaching me what NOT to do.
......

Do you have a saying or motto that you live your life by?
"If it doesn't challenge you, it doesn't change you."
......

Where do you draw your inspiration from?
My children push me everyday. And just the drive to see my dreams a reality. I set my bar high.
......

Made any mistakes that helped or hurt you in a way that you would like to share?
I don't regret many things in my life because all the mistakes make me who I am today. But I would advise not committing to a serious relationship at 17 or 18 years old. Take the time and find out what you want out of life and what things make you happy. I would tell my 17 year old self to forget the boyfriend and instead move to New York to study and take in everything that city has to offer. I find NYC amazingly inspiring and encourage others to find the same for themselves.
......

What were your biggest personal battles and how did you confront them?
Being super shy and not being able to express my opinions, feelings, and knowledge with other. Then I realized people do want to hear from me and that my word is valuable. I'm still trying to overcome this.
......

What were the most difficult decisions you had to make during your lifetime? Why?
Leaving a 10-year marriage and starting a new life as a single mom of three children. I was comfortable in being married, even though there was abuse, for a long time. And there were, and still are, questions of how I'm going to carry on and what will happen next and what will the future bring? It was scary, a risk, and took a huge leap of faith for me.
......

If you could paint a picture of any scenery you've seen before, what would you paint?

A beach scenery with blue skies, bright warm sun, turquoise water, white sand, very little evidence of human life.
......

What are some goals you are still trying to accomplish?
Becoming a naturopathic doctor or holistic nutritionist; working with certain top coaches; reaching the level of success I envision with my business.
......

What are the most important lessons you've learned in life?
To be honest and to only compete with yourself. To not harbour ill feelings towards anyone.
......

What are you proudest of in your life?
Having three healthy, happy, loving children.
......

How do you set your goals?
I envision my dreams and then I layout an action plan that I feel will best get me there.
......

What else would you do if you weren't in your current line of work?
Dental hygiene or naturopathic doctor.
......

Do you believe in the Law of Attraction?
Only since this year, yes. I always thought it was hokey pokey stuff but I've experienced it first hand and I am trying to better understand the power behind it and figure out how I can make it work in my benefit.
......

What's your favorite food?
My green drink of about 21 different ingredients.
......

What would we find in your refrigerator right now?
Kale, parsley, ginger root, homemade almond milk, apples, spirulina, lettuce, French beans, buckwheat sprouts, homemade raw vegan macaroons, apple juice, flax, chia, vitamin D drops, grapes, quinoa, barley powder, greens powder, coconut meat, almond pulp, Irish moss.
......

If you had the opportunity to get a message across to a large group of people what would your message be?
Education is power. No matter what field you're in, being educated better arms you. You have to be able to stand up for yourself. The great thing about education is that no one can take it from you.
......

Where do you see yourself in 5 years?
Living the life I dream with my children.
......

What are you best at?
Educating myself.
......

What books do you like to read?
Business, Fitness, Self-Improvement, Humour.
......

What is your favorite type of music?
Jazz (especially Latin Jazz), 90s R&B.
......

Describe your parents, what are they like?

They're a solid couple, been married for about 35 years now. My mom is from Peru and my pops is from Malaysia so they spoke English at home, hence is why I can't speak Chinese. I can't tell you how many looks of shame I've gotten in my life for not knowing my "own language" (*gasp). I understand and speak more Spanish than anything.

My parents are non-traditional Chinese so I've been fortunate, if you want to call it that, to be able to do many things I wanted growing up or at least without such harsh restrictions. I had many friends with belt-strapping, 4 hours a day homework, no TV except Saturdays type of parents.
......

What were your dreams as a child and did you achieve any of them?
I wanted to be a paediatrician because I loved kids and was always intrigued by how the human body functioned. I didn't end up getting a medical degree. But I do have 3 beautiful children at home that I can play with and I am a holistic health professional so I get to dip into my human body function fetishes. I am glad I'm not a medical doctor at this stage in my life because I couldn't bear prescribing many existing drugs to patients on a daily basis.
......

Tell us a time in your life that was a time you'll never forget?
Being choked unconscious, stabbed, and told, "I'll kill you" by my husband.
......

What things do you find yourself doing that you said you'd never do?
Public speaking. And more of it.
......

What are some qualities that you value in a person?

Honesty, Respect, Passion, Integrity, Compassion.
......

Where did you grow up and what was it like?
I was born and raised in Edmonton, Alberta, Canada. As a Chinese girl growing up there in the 80s and 90s there were definite challenges. Even though Edmonton is the capital city, I was one of maybe ten Oriental kids in the entire school of kindergarten to sixth grade. Everyone was pretty much friends at that time but I did experience racism.

Then in grade 7 onwards it really hit. Kids hung out according to their ethnic background and more of a divide was created. In high school there were "doors" according to ethnicity. For example, Italians had their territory at the back doors of the school.

Since then, Edmonton has experienced explosive growth due to the oil and construction industry and now there are way more people from different countries. Put it this way, a Chinese kid in second grade wouldn't stand out like a sore thumb like I did growing up.
......

Name 5 of your favorite movies.
Sin City, American Me, Home Alone, Pretty Woman, White Chicks (so cheesy, I know, but it was hilarious).
......

What TV shows do you like?
I cancelled TV at least 4 years ago. Too much money for too much junk. My time is better spent elsewhere.
......

What do you enjoy doing on a Sunday afternoon?
Heading to the local vegan cupcake joint and chilling by the waterfront with my kids.
......

You are stranded in the Amazon rain forest. What 3 items would you want to have with you and why?
A bag of coconuts because I can drink the water and eat the meat; A gun with plenty of extra ammo to shoot any jealous animals (sorry, PETA); A machete to open my coconuts, use as a backup weapon for my gun, and to hack down branches and other brush in my way.
......

Is there anything in particular that you wish you could do over? What is it?
Not get into a serious relationship at 17 years old and instead move to NYC to study and soak up everything the city has to offer.
......

What personality traits in your mind are best suited for your job, career, etc?
Hardworking, driven, professional, respectful, excellent listener, compassionate, motivated, dedicated, transparent, honest.
......

What is your favorite drink?
Fresh coconut water.
......

What is your favorite color?
Pink and purple-it's a tie.
......

Name a movie that touched you in some way.
"White Chicks" tickled my funny bone.
......

When in life have you felt most alone? Why?

I would say when my fiancée (at the time) was incarcerated and I was at home and responsible for relocating our stuff from city to city on my own. I was 18 at the time. But in reflection, I was alone during my entire marriage really. I felt like no one understood what I was going through and I had no one to open up to about the abuse I suffered. I was good at making things look gravy from the outside but I'd go home and cry until I couldn't anymore.
……

What would be impossible for you to give up?
My workouts and healthy food.
……

Why would someone not want to work with you?
I take a holistic approach to optimal health and some people just want the magic pill that will fix their problems in a week. But these type of clients are the ones who fall back into old patterns and habits just as fast as they think they have figured out the solution. Quick fixes are just a bandage. I work with someone from many different angles for the best results—this takes time. It requires guidance, desire, commitment.
……

What activities did you enjoy in school?
Nothing that had to do with physical activity hahaha. I avoided it from very early on because I was super shy and no one wanted me on their team. Yes, I was THAT kid.
……

What kind of child were you?
Painfully shy.
……

If you could be a superhero, what would you want your superpowers to be?
To read people's minds; To be transported anywhere in the world with a touch of my ring.

······

How do you want to be remembered?
A dedicated mother who turned her adversities in her favour and empowered others from her own experiences.
······

We all have vices, what are yours?
As much as I'm a go-getter, I'm really just as much a procrastinator. I'm also completely anal about time. I plan my day down to the minute like, "Okay I have 10 minutes to spend in the store, 5 minutes to drive to the café, a maximum of 1 hour to eat, 25 minutes to drive to next meeting..." I can't stand being late.
······

What is one of your favorite quotes?
"Anyone can give up. That's easy. It's about pushing forward at a time when everyone else understands if you can't."
······

What chore do you absolutely hate doing?
Getting on all fours to wash the floors.
······

What is your best feature?
My eyes.
······

What was the last experience that made you a stronger person?
Surviving being beat, choked unconscious, and stabbed by my partner.
······

What makes you uncomfortable, besides these questions?
Sitting for too long, especially in a room with no windows. I don't have ADHD, I just like to keep active and be in natural

environments. Sitting too long kills the blood vessels in the glutes and hams...gotta keep things circulating!
......

If you could change something physical about yourself, what would it be and why?
My knock-knees because they force pressure on my ankles the wrong way and now I have ankle issues. Plus my boot heels become slanted within a month of buying them from the uneven pressure placed on my heels as I walk.
......

Besides money, what are your favorite ways to compensate people?
Free products or food.
......

When was the last time you tried something new?
Yesterday. I've had Pilates on my bucket list for years and I did a class yesterday for the first time ever. I fell in love with the reformers that I went back to the studio an hour later for another one hour session!
......

How would you describe yourself in three words?
Hardworking, soft-spoken, inspiring.
......

What is one thing you are not?
Mean-spirited.
......

Do you think crying is a sign of weakness or strength?
Both.
......

What makes you angry?

I don't get angry really. Upset yes, at my kids leaving a mess and at ignorant people like those who toss their cigarette butts out the window while driving.
......

What makes you laugh?
My kids, myself, some angry people (it's funny but not funny...they look silly with what they say or do but I feel sorry for them for having all that inner negativity.
......

What are you afraid of?
Being disabled or dead and leaving my children without a mother; bugs; what lies beneath the deep sea.
......

What would be the first thing you would do if today was your last day?
Grab my three kids and hold them.
......

What's your vision of a perfect society?
There'd be zero crime and we were all as pure as we were at birth. We'd live in a super clean environment and there'd be organic fields of fruits and veggies everywhere.
......

What's something you check daily?
Email, social media, the local news, weather, email, did I already say social media?
......

Are you an emotional person?
Definitely not. I'm working on showing more emotion. I find often times how I feel inside doesn't reflect on the outside at all. I've been told by more than one person that I'd make a great poker player.
......

What's your own definition of happiness?
Dreaming my dream and living it out. Being healthy and with my children.
……

Which famous person would you like to interview and which questions would you ask him/her?
Tank, Tyrese, or Joe: "There's this really cool place I'd like to check out and chill on Friday night. Would you like to come with me?"
……

If you could choose to be born with a particular natural skill what skill would it be?
To express myself exactly how I feel inside.
……

What advice would you give someone who wanted to do what you do?
Aim high, set high standards for yourself and seek out the best coaches to help you along. Dream your dream then live it out now and live it out big. Compete with only yourself. Listen to your inner voice because it knows more than you do.
……

While you are watching TV in your home a penguin walks through the door wearing a sheriff's hat and badge. What does he say?
"I'm here to pick up my raw vegan fishcakes."
……

Are there any words of wisdom you'd like to pass along to us?
"If it doesn't challenge you, it doesn't change you."
……

Did you enjoy answering these questions? On a scale from 1 – 10. 1= I hated it. 10= I really enjoyed it.
9.

....

About Jessica

Featured in Cosmopolitan Magazine, Jessica Li, "The Supercharged Fitness Chef", is both a raw food chef and a certified personal trainer based in Toronto.

Working in health care over the last 12 years has given Jessica a unique perspective on the effects of processed foods and a sedentary lifestyle on the aging body.

She is the founder of Women with Integrity, a company that offers holistic lifestyle consulting to busy women entrepreneurs, with a focus on vegan cuisine and fitness.

Jessica is also the visionary behind Chica Momma Health and Juice Bar, which offers raw food classes and meal delivery. She is the author of "High Powered Food and Fitness for the Busy Professional Woman" and is a frequent contributor to various publications.

A portion of all proceeds goes to supporting organizations that provide resources for victims of domestic violence.

Are you ready for your best YOU yet?! Grab your free gifts at www.SuperFitGift.com
Follow on Twitter @superchargedfit

INTERVIEW 7

Elspeth Polt

Personal Information

Full Name:
Elspeth Polt

Age:
26

Location:
Ohio

Relationship Status:
Married

Number of Children:
0

Profession:
Cosmetologist, Personal Trainer, Sponsored Athlete

Educational Background:
Salve Regina University, Newport, RI; Toni & Guy Hairdressing Academy, Cranston, RI

Certifications:
ISSA Personal Training, AFAA Group Exercise
....

General Questions

What are you known for professionally?
I would say I'm most know for being professional and going 'the extra mile'.
......

Tell us about how you got into your line of work.
I have always loved working with and helping people, and beauty and athletics have always been my personal.
......

How long have you been doing what you do?
I have worked in the beauty industry for 7 years, and have been a personal trainer for almost 4 years.

......

What do you enjoy most about what you do?
Seeing the personal growth and happiness of my clients. Changing and enhancing people's lives in a positive way is the greatest gift I could ever ask for.
......

What are you most passionate about professionally? What most excites you about your work & the contribution you can make?
I am most passionate about seeing the personal growth of my clients. I don't want to just apply makeup or write up a training plan- I want to change lives. I want everything I learn or experience be something my clients (and all people!) be able to benefit from. I want them to learn from my mistakes and be inspired by my accomplishments.
......

What's the single most important reason for your success?
Hard work.
......

What do you consider to be your greatest achievement?
Never giving up, and always pushing forward.
......

How do you think women have changed over the years? Regarding business, sports and fitness.
I feel a female's role in these industries have changed dramatically over the years. The stereotypes that existed years ago are constantly being shattered by the perseverance of strong, smart women.
......

Do you think women are competitive with each other? Why? Regarding business, sports and fitness.
I think women can be, but everyone can be competitive.
......

What memorable competitions come to mind in your career?
My first Fitness competition. I was unprepared and had no idea what to expect, but I learned a great deal. It lit a spark in me!
......

What is the number one thing you like best about being into fitness?
The challenge.
......

Is there anything wrong with wanting to portray women athletes, actors, etc as feminine and physically attractive?
Not in my opinion, no.
......

How do you deal with cravings for junk foods, sweets and salty food?
After eating clean for so long, I don't often have cravings. When I do though, I never go hungry! It might not be what I want to eat, but there is always SOMETHING I can eat. I have lots of recipes that are plenty satisfying and healthy that I turn to.
......

Describe a typical day for you, starting from the moment you wake up in the morning.
I usually wake up around 6am and cook breakfast. While I eat breakfast I check and return emails. I take my time because this is my quiet time during the day. Depending on my work schedule for the day I will either train or head into work. After work I usually stop at the grocery and come home and cook

dinner. On the weekends I often travel for work, and it tends to be a little hectic so I like to keep my week nights pretty quiet and just enjoy time with my husband.
......

Health & Fitness Questions

What sports do you participated in for fun?
Volleyball, dance, crossfit, kayaking, running, weight-lifting, softball.
......

How long have you been playing those sports?
I have played volleyball and softball for over 10 years, I have been weightlifting for about 5 years, and the others I do recreationally when I have time.
......

What got you started in that sport?
I started playing softball in 2nd grade along with just about every other girl in my grade (I went to a SMALL school growing up). I continued to play through my senior year in high school. I started volleyball in 6th grade and played year-round all the way through college. After college I was at a loss with what to do with all my new found free time, so I began weight lifting and haven't stopped since!
......

What is your biggest accomplishment in your sports? Include fun sports and any athletic career.
Over the past 4 years or so I have worked very hard to forge my way into the Fitness Industry. I am very proud to say that I am a Dymatize Nutrition sponsored athlete and am an Ambassador for Reebok and FitMark bags (2 of my biggest goals I set for myself). I have also been published in national magazines, (photos and writing), and landed my first cover in December 2012.
......

What competitions have you entered? What were the outcomes?
NPC Jr Nationals 2013 Top10 Bikini ANPC Jr USAS 2013 3rd place Bikini ANPC Kentucky Derby 2013 1st place Bikini AArnold Amateur 2013 Top 10 Bikini ANPC Jr Nationals 2012 4th place Bikini AArnold Bikini Amateur, March 2012: 2nd place BikiniNPC Kentucky Muscle, November 2011: 1st place Bikini NPC Ohio and Great Lakes, September 2011: 3rd/ 5th place Bikini NPC IFBB Cleveland, Ohio Nationals competitor, September 2011 NPC Mike Francois Class, May 2011: Top 10 BikiniNPC Paradise Cup, October 2010: 3rd Place BikiniINBA Hawaiian Classic, June 2010: 2nd Place BikiniNPC Stingrey Classic, April 2010: 2nd Place Bikini
......

How do you motivate yourself and stay motivated?
The way being healthy makes me feel! I feel healthy, strong, and confident when I'm maintaining a healthy lifestyle. When I feel this way everything else in my life is more positive. Being an athlete I will always love sports of any form. I love the challenge, the comradary, and competition. Overall fitness has enriched my life in so many ways- I can't imagine my life without it.

What are some of the main foods you would include in your shopping list to maintain a lean and muscular physique?
Lean proteins, healthy fats, veggies, fruit, spices, healthy carbs, stevia, Kevita, apple cider vinegar, unsweetened cocoa, mustard.
......

What is the most challenging thing you deal with about consistently staying in top shape?
Making sure I have time in the day to work out, work, and spend time with family. Balance is key!
......

Please describe your normal diet. What do you eat in a typical day to stay in shape?

Example diet: Meal Plan*You will be eating 5-6 meals a day, every 2-4 hours. There are 3 specific options for each Meal. For each meal there is one "easy and quick" option in case you don't have time to cook. Many of the recipes can be made in larger servings so you can freeze for later in the week, or share with your family.

Meal 1: Option 1: 1 serving Kashi crunch cereal, 1 cup 1% milk, 1/2 c berriesOption 2: 1 Protein PancakeOption 3: 2 egg muffins plus I/2 c melon or 1 grapefruit

Meal 2: Option 1: protein shake (1 scoop protein) * If post workout, add 1/2 c berries or 1/2 banana. Option 2: Chocolate covered strawberries/ choc pudding with strawberriesOption 3: Eggs Florentine wrap

Meal 3: Option 1: 3 oz turkey cutlets with 1/2 c broccoli and 1/2 c roasted root veggiesOption 2: Lentil Stew (aprox 1 c) Option 3: 3-4 oz chicken steak, 1/2 csweet potato fries, and 1/4 c ketchup

Meal 4: Option1: 1 c 1% cottage cheese, 1/4 c salsa, 1 rice cake (2 if eating Kroger brand) Option 2: Black bean burrito Option 3: Bahn Mi Wrap

Meal 5: Option 1: salmon with dill sauce Option 2: chicken Provençal Option 3: lettuce rolls*Optional Meal 6: *Optional* "Dessert": Option #1: "Icecream" 1 scoop whey protein, ½-1 c water, stevia, cinnamon, dash of sea salt, 1 tbs unsweetened cocoa powder: mix together and freeze for 1 hour. Option #2: Protein Crepe: 1/4-1/3 c egg whitesStevia dropsDash of salt1 tbs unsweetened Hershey's cocoa powder½ scoop whey isolate protein (I recommend chocolate) *mix together and pour over heated and sprayed (with Pam) skillet*will cook quickly top with 1 tbs P2B peanut butter and roll up! Option

#3: Tea! I love Apple Cinnamon with Stevia Drops- taste like cider!

A total beginner is about 35 pounds overweight. She doesn't really know where to start. What tips can you give her to follow the right track?
Take it one step at a time. Write down mini goals to get you on track to your ultimate goal. Have patience and be persistent.
......

What tips do you recommend for eating out at restaurants to make sure we don't gain too much weight/fat?
Be picky! Request no butter, sauces on the side, Ect...It's your meal and you're paying for it- it needs to be prepared the way you want it.
......

What exercises do you recommend for getting a bigger, rounder and fuller butt?
Squats!
....

What are your top tips for losing unwanted body fat? Specific exercises, diet advice, etc.
Consistent clean eating, a mixture of resistance training and cardio, sleep, low amounts of stress, and a positive attitude.
......

What are your top tips for staying motivated on a fitness plan?
-Write your goals down. -Make a plan of action to get you to that goal. -Track yourprogress. -Find things you enjoy and are motivated by.

What is your training routine like? Please include a few details.

I train about 5-6 days a week, varying up my training every 4 weeks or so to keep my body guessing and fight boredom.

Here is a sample workout: Plyo: week 1-3: 3x. Week 4: 4x Rest 30 sec between circuit sets. Rest I min between circuits after completing all sets.
Set 1: Plyo lunge 30 sec.Jump squat 30 secMountain climbers 30 sec High knees 30 sec
Set 2: Box jump 30 sec Toe taps on bench 30 secHop squat 30 sec Burpee with a Pushup 30 sec
Set 3: mountain climbers: 20 sec on, 10 sec rest 8x (4 min total) *1 time only.
……

What is the best way towards becoming a personal trainer?
Search the different certifications and find which best suits you. I recommend ISSA.
……

What things do you currently do in your training that is key to your success?
Taking a rest day. I used to never take one, but your muscles need time to recover. Taking 1-2 days off has helped my overall physique and health immensely.
……

Isn't it hard to stay fit? How do you manage that?!
It something that I truly enjoy. I am an athlete at heart and will always enjoy the challenge. There are definitely days that are simply 'off' but I remind myself that doing my best will be different every day.
……

Business Questions

Tell us about your first entrepreneurial experience as a kid or older.
I have always followed my heart and have always had that feeling deep in my gut telling me to shoot for the moon.
......

How have your entrepreneurial motivations changed since you first started?
They are constantly evolving.
......

What do you consider to be success as a business owner or entrepreneur?
How many lives I touch in a positive way.
......

What's the biggest thing you struggle with as a business owner or entrepreneur?
Finding balance.
......

How do you think running a business or being an entrepreneur has made you a better person?
It has made me jump out of my comfort zone and become a much stronger and more confident person.
......

What do you do on a daily basis to grow as a person/business person/entrepreneur?
Continue my education.
......

What's unique about the service that you provide?
I think what sets me apart is my strong work ethic and compassionate attitude.
......

What entrepreneurial hacks have you developed to stay focused and productive in your day-to-day?
I am persistent and reliable.
......

Do you have any of your own branded products? If so, what are they?

Mixed Questions

What would be your ultimate achievement in any area of your life?
Raising a happy family while maintaining a career that enriched my life.
......

At present, what is your biggest challenge, and what are you doing to manage this challenge?
Learning how to build my brand and reach a wider audience. I have a message I feel people can relate to and am reaching out to as many people as I can.
......

What things do you believe differentiates you from your contemporaries?
I think the beauty of this industry is that we are all a little different. We may be promoting the same thing (living a happy, healthy life), but our stories are different and will make people connect differently.
......

Have you ever experienced a breakthrough, and if so, what led to it?
Yes, of course. As I learn and grow I often have that 'ah ha!' moment where everything seems to just click. It usually follows a mistake or failure. I find I do my best thinking after the fall.
......

Who has been the biggest influence on your life? What lessons did that person teach you?
I have been very blessed to have had many positive and encouraging mentors throughout this journey. I am a very determined and hardworking person, but the support from my family, friends, and mentors has been invaluable in my successes (and breakthroughs during more challenging times).

Do you have a saying or motto that you live your life by?
Be so good they can't ignore you. Steve Martin.
......

Where do you draw your inspiration from?
Everything! Clients, mentors, peers, nature, books I'm reading, ect...inspiration will show up unannounced where you least expect it- that's what makes it so special.
......

Made any mistakes that helped or hurt you in a way that you would like to share?
Of course! I make mistakes every day, often multiple times, but I try and learn from them and move ahead.
......

What were your biggest personal battles and how did you confront them?
My self esteem and eating battles- something that many women struggle with. The first step of recovery is admitting the problem, then taking action. Easier said than done, but I work every day trying to make myself a better, more balanced, individual.
......

What were the most difficult decisions you had to make during your lifetime? Why?
To leave college to pursue cosmetology.

......

If you could paint a picture of any scenery you've seen before, what would you paint?
Lake Winnipesaukee, where I grew up.
......

What are some goals you are still trying to accomplish?
Overall, my goal is to continue to learn, grow, and evolve with each phase of my career/ life. Specifically: -Create an after school program for middle school and high school girls focusing on the importance of self-esteem with a focus on the benefits of athletics and the arts (2 things that have helped, and continue to help), me grow and find confidence. -Continue my writing- I would love to have my own column in a nationally published magazine. -Grow as a fitness model. Earn my Pro Card in NPC Bikini. -Travel! This Industry has given me the chance to travel throughout the US, and I plan to continue traveling and connecting with people all over).
......

What are the most important lessons you've learned in life?
Listen to your heart, not what others say or think.
......

How do you set your goals?
I am constantly setting goals as I grow and evolve. I set my goals and work backwards on how I plan to achieve them.
......

What else would you do if you weren't in your current line of work?
I would work in the Art History field.
......

What are your religious beliefs/spiritual beliefs?

I believe in love, equal rights for everyone and the freedom to believe in whatever God or religion you believe in.
......

What is your diet like?
I eat clean year-round, 5-6 meals a day every 2-4 hours. My meals are filled with lean proteins, healthy fats, veggies, fruits, and health carbs.
......

What's your favorite food?
Almond butter.
......

What would we find in your refrigerator right now?
Eggs, turkey, chicken, fish, LOTS of fresh veggies, grapefruit, Kevita, Bragg's Apple Cider Vinegar, Greek yogurt, red wine, berries, almond butter, and avocado.
......

If you had the opportunity to get a message across to a large group of people what would your message be?
To go after your dreams! Don't let your fear be bigger than your faith!
......

Where do you see yourself in 5 years?
Building my brand and developing my after school program for middle and high school girls.
......

What are you best at?
Working hard!
......

What books do you like to read?
I read a variety, but historical fiction is my favorite.
......

What is your favorite type of music?
Again, I listen to a variety, but country is my favorite.
......

Describe your parents, what are they like?
My parents are wonderful. They are incredibly hardworking, honest, non judging people. I was raised in a very caring and supportive home, and am beyond grateful for my upbringing.
......

What were your dreams as a child and did you achieve any of them?
I wanted to do everything and travel everywhere! I'm slowly checking off the list).
......

Tell us a time in your life that was a time you'll never forget?
My younger years playing softball when my dad was my coach: some of my favorite memories from my childhood.
......

What things do you find yourself doing that you said you'd never do?
Public speaking! I used to get soo nervous!
......

What are some qualities that you value in a person?
Honesty, work ethic, compassion.
......

Where did you grow up and what was it like?
I grew up in a small town in NewHampshire. I went to a K-12 public school and graduated with only 38 kids! I played sports, was involved in student council, and other school activities and truly enjoyed my years there. I grew up going to the lake everyday in the summer, skiing in the winter- and naturally,

like every small town kid, day dreamed constantly about leaving and traveling the world). Now I can't wait to get back!
......

Name 5 of your favorite movies.
Now and Then. Legally Blonde. Breakfast at Tiffany's.
Clueless.
Beauty Shop.
......

What TV shows do you like?
I'm a sucker for comedy sitcoms and the Real Houswives Reality shows.
......

What do you enjoy doing on a Sunday afternoon?
Going for a hike and grilling out on our patio.
......

You are stranded in the Amazon rain forest. What 3 items would you want to have with you and why?
The Bible, to read and keep my faith.
......

What personality traits in your mind are best suited for your job, career, etc?
Patience, flexibility, readability.
......

What is your favorite drink?
Water with lemon and chai tea.
......

What is your favorite color?
Blues and purples.
......

Name a movie that touched you in some way.

I'm not really a movie person. If I do watch them they have to be comedies.
......

What would be impossible for you to give up?
Going after my dreams!
......

Why would someone not want to work with you?
That's a good question!
......

What activities did you enjoy in school?
Art, gym, clothing and textiles class, history.
......

What kind of child were you?
Quiet, but focused. I was shy, but played sports and was involved in numerous class activities.
......

If you could be a superhero, what would you want your superpowers to be?
I would want to fly!
......

How do you want to be remembered?
As honest, caring, reliable, and genuine.
......

We all have vices, what are yours?
I hate cleaning my car! I'm a dirty bird, as my husband says.
......

What is one of your favorite quotes?
Anything from Og Mandino, but this is one of my favorites: "Realize that true happiness lies within you. Waste no time and effort searching for peace and contentment and joy in the

world outside. Remember that there is no happiness in having or in getting, but only in giving. Reach out. Share. Smile. Hug. Happiness is a perfume you cannot pour on others without getting a few drops on yourself."
......

What chore do you absolutely hate doing?
Vacuuming.
......

What is your best feature?
My caring disposition.
......

What was the last experience that made you a stronger person?
Life is constantly challenging me to become a better and stronger person. Working in customer service I am challenged to continuing my education, improving my skills, and providing a better experience.
......

If you could change something physical about yourself, what would it be and why?
I am constantly challenging myself physically as an athlete- I would not say it's so much as something I want changed, but more of how I wish to improve.
......

Besides money, what are your favorite ways to compensate people?
Making them feel empowered and beautiful.
......

When was the last time you tried something new?
Last week! I tried crossfit for the first time!
......

How would you describe yourself in three words?

Honest, caring, Genuine.
......

What is one thing you are not?
Rude.
......

Do you think crying is a sign of weakness or strength?
I think crying is a natural way of releasing emotion.
......

What makes you angry?
I try not to get angry, but we all have our breaking points.
......

What makes you laugh?
Pretty much anything- I'm a giggly girl :)
......

What are you afraid of?
The dark ha-ha.
......

What would be the first thing you would do if today was your last day?
Kiss my husband. Hug my family.
......

What's your vision of a perfect society?
World peace. Cliché, I know, but it's true. Love is all we need.
......

Is it possible to lie without saying a word? How?
Yes, actions speak louder than words.
......

What's something you check daily?
My phone.

......

Are you an emotional person?
Yes.
......

What's your own definition of happiness?
Being at peace with yourself. When you are at peace with yourself you can fully enjoy and experience all the beauty and love life has to offer.
......

Which famous person would you like to interview and which questions would you ask him/her?
Hmm that's a hard one! There are just too many to pick- authors and artists intrigue me. I want to know their creative drive, what inspires them, their thought process...it fascinates me.
......

If you could choose to be born with a particular natural skill what skill would it be?
To sing! I am just mesmerized by beautiful voices.
......

What advice would you give someone who wanted to do what you do?
I would say 'Go for it!' I love what I do, and would certainly encourage anyone thinking of entering either profession- training or cosmetology.
......

While you are watching TV in your home a penguin walks through the door wearing a sheriff's hat and badge. What does he say?
Have you been watching Billy Madison writing these questions??
......

Do you have any secrets you want to share with the few of us reading this? We won't say anything....promise!
Eat real food, stay active with something you enjoy, find balance, love yourself.
......

Are there any words of wisdom you'd like to pass along to us?
Always have faith in yourself. You are much stronger than you could ever think.
......

Did you enjoy answering these questions? On a scale from 1 – 10. 1= I hated it. 10= I really enjoyed it.
I really enjoyed it. 10.

....

About Elspeth

Hello! My name is Elspeth or simply just Elle, and my mission in life is to live it to it's fullest! I want to help people live a healthier, happier life both physically and mentally. We all deserve to be the best version of ourselves, but sometimes we need a little help getting there, and that's where I come in.

Being a military spouse has moved me around the country, forcing me to learn how to adapt to new surroundings quickly, and to never take anything for granted. Instead of dwelling on the hardships of moving, I used my somewhat nomadic lifestyle to create opportunities and racked up a few job titles and certifications along the way.

I am a licensed cosmetologist (TIGI trained since 2007), an ISSA certified personal trainer, and AFAA certified group exercise instructor, a sponsored athlete, a National level Bikini competitor, a published writer, and aspiring Beauty entrepreneur. I've created a lifestyle for myself that allows me to create beauty from the inside out in both myself and the people I come in contact with. Bottom line, when you do what you love, you truly never 'work' a day in your life!

I work as a personal trainer, hair and makeup artist, and model myself. It may seem as though I wear many hats, but in reality all aspects of my life blend together very cohesively, enhancing one another. For example: I have been a hair stylist & makeup artist for almost 7 years now: 4 years ago one of my clients introduced me to weight lifting and fitness competing...I was hooked from the get-go!

I became certified in personal training and started competing myself. After competing in a few shows I thought "I would love to do hair and makeup for this!"..and so a new venture was paved! I am now the Assistant Manager for the Liquid Sun Rayz Beauty Team and we travel throughout the country providing beauty and tanning services for competitors. As my interest in the Industry grew I had a need to further educate myself and others: enter Dymatize Nutrition!

They became my amazing sponsor, and my career as a spokesmodel began. I began blogging and working more events, connecting with people from literally all around the world. Words can't describe the inspiration I find in meeting people from all walks of life, from all over the world, and how much I've learned from merely traveling and connecting with people!

From here, my modeling has begun to blossom, this year landing my first ad in a National magazine and my first cover. I also became an Ambassador for ReebokONE, (an online community for Fitness Professionals) and or FitMark Bags: two companies that I greatly admire and am so grateful to be apart of.

As you can see each stepping stone in my life has played a role in what is to come. In my life beauty and fitness, (and of course furthering my education) go hand and hand. They are what make me feel strong, beautiful, and empowered and these emotions translate to the clients and companies I work with.

This, I whole heatedly believe, is what makes both myself and my clients successful. I truly believe every person has the right to feel beautiful: mentally, physically, and emotionally. And it is my mission to give them the knowledge to do so. I love living a fit healthy lifestyle while at the same time looking and feeling beautiful, and more important, I aspire to educate and inspire others to do the same. We all deserve to be the best versions of ourselves!

Credits:
My Sponsors: Dymatize Nutrition and Liquid Sun Rayz.
ReebokONE
FitMark Bags

Photographers: Harry Grigsby of LHGFX and James Patrick

Where you can find me! I constantly post healthy recipes, workouts, general health advice & beauty tips.
ReebokONE:http://www.reebok.com/elspeth.polt
Dymatize: http://www.dymatize.comLook under "Featured Athletes"
Facebook: Elspeth Polt
Twitter: elspeth_polt
Instagram: ELSPETH_POLT
Website:http://www.elspethpolt.com

INTERVIEW 8
Dr. Marisa R. Silver

Personal Information

Full Name:
Dr. Marisa R. Silver

Location:
Jericho, New York

Relationship Status:
Married

Number of Children:

1
Profession:
Doctor of Chiropractic Medicine, Personal trainer, business owner

....

General Questions

What are you known for professionally?
I am known for giving each and every patient that I take care of my very best that I have to offer.
......

Tell us about how you got into your line of work.
I always enjoyed and excelled at helping others. I always had a thirst for knowledge and compassion for others. I knew that alternative medicine was for me at a young age. I always wanted to know the why behind the question not just the answer.
......

How long have you been doing what you do?
I have been a chiropractor and personal trainer for the past 13 years. I have been involved in physical fitness since I was a child. I have been a business owner for the past 10 years.
......

What do you enjoy most about what you do?
I enjoy helping others. There is nothing more satisfying then having a patient come in to your office with a complete decrease in their cervical (neck) range of motion with associated pain and discomfort. At the end of the treatment they are no longer in pain and have increased their range of motion.

I still get a euphoric feeling when treating patients, this is when I know I made the right choice for my profession. I feel a similar satisfaction in personal training. Clients come to me physically overweight and mentally defeated. The best reward is helping them achieve their fitness goals and assist them in returning to a positive mental attitude.
......

What are you most passionate about professionally? What most excites you about your work & the contribution you can make?
I am passionate about making a difference in one's life. I have the ability to change someone's life and in many aspects, I have increased an individuals life span by educating them on the importance of diet and exercise.
......

What's the single most important reason for your success?
The main reason for my success is passion. I truly believe in what I am doing and it shows in every breath I take.
......

What do you consider to be your greatest achievement?
My greatest achievement is owning a private wellness center when most have gone corporate.
......

How do you think women have changed over the years? Regarding business, sports and fitness.
I think women are more respected than in recent years. I feel that when we speak we are not only looked at as a female but as an authority in our discipline.
......

Do you think women are competitive with each other? Why? Regarding business, sports and fitness.

Women are very competitive with each other in everything that we do. I feel that it's only natural an educated woman wanting to be the best is healthy and normal. If you were to ask a man this question he would say testosterone: as a woman I say estrogen. Its all about hormones.
......

What is the number one thing you like best about being into fitness?
Fitness has become my way of life. It is not something that I think about. With obesity on the rise, I am fortunate that this epidemic will never affect me or my family. I will always keep an eye on my family's health.
......

Is there anything wrong with wanting to portray women athletes, actors, etc as feminine and physically attractive?
I think that women can be attractive inside and out. I feel that women can be feminine as well as confident.
......

How do you deal with cravings for junk foods, sweets and salty food?
I believe that you might be in the mood for a certain type of food. But I don't believe that there is anything chemical that causes one to desire a particular flavor or taste. There are, however, psychological motivations that can initiate a desire for specific foods. It's important to be aware of those motivations and keep them in check so as not to over indulge.
......

Describe a typical day for you, starting from the moment you wake up in the morning.
I wake up by the sound of my son's voice in the morning. My son and I go downstairs and the fun begins. I put on the TV for him and start to make coffee as I make my son pancakes. We then proceed to get dressed and my husband drives my son to

school as I leave to go to the office. My lunch break consists of me driving to pick up my son from school to take him home. From there I drop him off at home where I have someone at my home to watch him. I continue to go to the office. I am generally at the office until 8:30 pm.
......

Health & Fitness Questions

What sports do you participate in for fun?
Fitness training, running.
......

How long have you been playing those sports?
20+ years.
......

What got you started in that sport?
My grandfather was incredibly fit and athletic.
......

How do you motivate yourself and stay motivated?
I'm a health conscious person; my motivation comes from continuing this philosophy.
......

What are some of the main foods you would include in your shopping list to maintain a lean and muscular physique?
I have lean protein every day. I believe it is important to include vegetables in your daily diet as well as for strength of the bones. My regimen also includes daily vitamins.
......

What is the most challenging thing you deal with about consistently staying in top shape?
Sometimes I wonder if I am pushing my body too much. I think about my joints such as my hips and shoulders and the activity level that I put them through on a daily basis. I am concerned about degenerative joint disease (DJD) and wonder not how but when I am going to feel the consequences of my activity level.
......

Please describe your normal diet. What do you eat in a typical day to stay in shape?
I start off every morning with a protein shake. I try to switch up the fruits I use for variety. I have a low fat Greek yogurt for lunch which is followed up with a healthy dinner which usually consists of a lean protein and a large salad. I also drink at least 6 bottles of water throughout the day.
......

What type of exercises do you include in your routine to stay in shape?
I'm a chiropractor as well as a personal trainer. There are days that I can see 10 personal training clients in a row. I like to do some of the basic core exercises with them. On any given day I can do 1000 crunches, 100 bicep and tricep exercises. I do 100 push ups a day and do a variety of low impact cardio vascular exercises to maintain endurance.
......

A total beginner is about 35 pounds overweight. She doesn't really know where to start. What tips can you give her to follow the right track?
To anyone who is going start an exercise routine, I always suggest to get a doctor's clearance. Once you have clearance, you should seek out a certified personal trainer that has a good reputation.
......

What tips do you recommend for eating out at restaurants to make sure we don't gain too much weight/fat?
Do not eat the bread.... Do not eat the bread. Always ask how the food is prepared. Ask for the food to be prepared without butter and salt. If the meal comes out as a large portion you do not have to eat it. Just because the chef decided that was a good portion does not mean that you have to eat it.

I suggest either asking the waiter to only give you half the portion and wrap it up before it leaves the kitchen. Skip dessert. Trust me you will thank me. Most restaurant desserts range from 450 -1000 calories. This is probably more calories than your meal was.
......

What exercises do you recommend for getting a bigger, rounder and fuller butt?
I think squats are a great way to increase the muscularity of the buttock muscles. It is important to develop the Gluteus Maximus properly so that a round look is achieved rather than a square look. Hamstring curls are also a good exercise as well as lunges.
......

What are your top tips for developing toned and defined arms? Specific exercises, diet advice, etc.
I like to exercise with 3-5 lb. weights to develop definition. Anything more than that will cause a larger look but a less defined appearance. I do 2 sets of 12 repetitions of bicep curls. 2 sets of 12 repetitions of tricep push backs.

I think the deltoid muscle is just as important as it is the muscle that encompasses the shoulder and can be seen in every direction. I do deltoid raises in anterior, medial and posterior directions for development. Of course, it is equally important to have a low caloric diet so that the muscles

striations show rather than a puffy look of extra adipose tissue.
......

What are your top tips for losing unwanted body fat? Specific exercises, diet advice, etc.
To start to lose unwanted body fat you must start to reduce your caloric intake. Cardio vascular exercises are an easy way to burn off extra calories. Basic exercises such as bicep curls or tricep push backs can be done with an added lower extremity exercise such as knee bends at the same time to burn off more calories.
......

What are your top tips for gaining lean muscle mass? Specific exercises, diet advice, etc.
To gain lean muscle, diet plays a crucial role. One must eat lean meats and not processed foods. You should avoid foods that contain saturated fats and fructose corn syrup. To gain muscle mass and achieve a muscular appearance on average size women, I would recommend using 8-12 lb. weights with less repetitions and more sets. To gain lean muscle, it is important to fatigue your muscle rather than build endurance, which is what you do with lighter weights and more repetitions.
......

What are your top tips for improving breasts lift and shape? Specific exercises, diet advice, etc.
To improve muscularity around your breasts, you have to start with the pectoral muscles. These are the muscles that lie underneath the breast. When these muscles are developed, it will promote the appearance of higher and firmer breast tissue. Chest flies are a great exercise to enhance Breast tissue. Push ups will also add to the development of the pectoralis major and minor muscles. Of course diet plays an important role, consuming lean meats, fruits and vegetables into your diet are essential for any training program.

What are your top tips for staying motivated on a fitness plan?
A great method for continuing motivation is to see results and feel energized. It is common to lose motivation every now and again, you are even allowed to take some days off, but it is important to remember what your goals are and to stick with them.

What is your training routine like? Please include a few details.
My training routine consists of mostly endurance training. I train with my clients so I am constantly moving and burning calories. I focus on upper extremities, core and the lower extremity. I like my body to look well balanced and proportioned.

What is the best way to get started in your industry?
The best way to get started is by becoming educated. I don't just mean getting certified, I mean reading about exercise physiology on your own time. Don't make it a profession, make it a life style.

What is the best way towards becoming a personal trainer?
I suggest every personal trainer become certified.

What things do you currently do in your training that are key to your success?
The key to my success is changing up the workouts. If I see a training client looking at the clock or their watch then I know I am not doing my job. I also have grown very close to my clients. It's not just about weight loss. It's about quality of life and that's what I think sets me aside from others in the

industry. I have been told I have the energy of a machine, sometimes that good but sometimes you can't turn me off.
……

Isn't it hard to stay fit? How do you manage that?!
I don't think it's hard or difficult to stay fit because I made it a life style not an activity. If you are truly committed to health and fitness it should be a gift that you want to give to others and not something that you have to manage.
……

Business Questions

Tell us about your first entrepreneurial experience as a kid or older.
My first experience as a child was working for my father. He was in the textile industry and owned his own company for 50 plus years and I would spend many summers and vacations working for him. He taught me the importance of controlling your own destiny. He instilled in me that success comes with many responsibilities. Even when you are sick or don't feel like going to work if you own the company, you show up no matter what and lead by example.
……

What is the most difficult part of starting your business?
The most difficult part about starting a business is looking toward the future. Let's be honest; it's nice to get a guaranteed pay check. When you own your own business; if you don't work you don't get paid. If you are out sick you don't get paid. There are no sick days, no personal days and no maternity leave and no health insurance.
……

How have your entrepreneurial motivations changed since you first started?

Unfortunately, the more successful you are the more that you want out of life. I am now motivated to achieve more than what I initially set out to do.
……

What do you consider to be success as a business owner or entrepreneur?
I feel that being a successful business owner is not just being financially sound, but it's being satisfied with yourself and the decisions that you make. What I do and say impacts other people, so I am constantly trying to encourage others to make better and healthier choices.
……

What's your least favorite part about being a business owner or entrepreneur?
The hardest part about being a business owner was having a child. I gave birth on a Monday and went back to work the next week. It was very difficult and painful, but when you are a business owner you can't just call out sick.
……

What's the biggest thing you struggle with as a business owner or entrepreneur?
My most significant struggle is finding time for my family. I work very long hours and unfortunately when you own your own business it does come home with you. It's a difficult balance to manage, and it's something that I am still working on.
……

How do you think running a business or being an entrepreneur has made you a better person?
I have respect for others that work as hard as I do. I respect business owners such as myself because although it might look exciting it's definitely a sacrifice.
……

How did you arrive at running this business? What path brought you here?
I always wanted to be a business owner. I actually had my company name in my head while I was still in chiropractic school. I was always involved in physical fitness, the combination of the two was a natural progression.
......

What do you do on a daily basis to grow as a person/business person/entrepreneur?
To grow as a person and a business owner, I try to accommodate my patients and grow with their needs and wants.
......

What's unique about the service that you provide?
I think what is unique is the personal touch and attention that I give my clients. I think that this is something that is overlooked these days.
......

Mixed Questions

What would be your ultimate achievement in any area of your life?
To be on a nationally syndicated television program promoting health and wellness.
......

At present, what is your biggest challenge, and what are you doing to manage this challenge?
My biggest challenge is trying to juggle being a successful business owner without sacrificing my family life. It's a difficult task that demands constant arranging so that no one feels second.

......

What things do you believe differentiates you from your contemporaries?
I feel that my compassion for others separates myself. I truly care for each person that walks through my office and I am still able to give my very best. When the time comes that I am not excited to start my day is the day I need to rethink my profession.
......

Who has been the biggest influence on your life? What lessons did that person teach you?
My husband has been the biggest influence in my life. I know that sounds like a cliché but it is true. He has taught me that every cloud has a silver lining and he always shows me the good in people. He truly is a gift to my life.
......

Do you have a saying or motto that you live your life by?
My motto is If you are not giving up, it means you are succeeding.
......

Where do you draw your inspiration from?
I feel that we were all put on this earth for a purpose. Mine was to help people meet their physical and emotional potential.
......

Made any mistakes that helped or hurt you in a way that you would like to share?
The mistakes that I have made in business are the most common ones. I have trusted the wrong people and have gotten burned.
......

What were your biggest personal battles and how did you confront them?
Juggling all my life responsibilities along with my businesses on a daily basis. Having a supporting husband makes it easier to handle. Mostly, it's important to push on no matter what.
......

If you could paint a picture of any scenery you've seen before, what would you paint?
A happy family holding hands walking on the beach.
......

What are the most important lessons you've learned in life?
The most important lesson I have learned is to never give up and to keep reaching for your dreams. It's the dreamers in life that succeed.
......

What are you proudest of in your life?
I am proudest of being a chiropractor and having a beautiful son and being happily married.
......

How do you set your goals?
I set my goals every 6 months. I have a vision board and I look at it every day.
......

What else would you do if you weren't in your current line of work?
Wall street..... I think I would get a rush being on the trading floor competing with men.
......

Do you believe in the Law of Attraction?
I definitely believe in the law of attraction I have a vision board in my bed room. It reminds me every day of my goals

and dreams. If you put out positive energy it will come back to you magnified.
......

What is your diet like?
I don't believe in the word diet I like to think of it as adopting a healthy life style. Same as question 24.
......

What's your favorite food?
Chicken.
......

What would we find in your refrigerator right now?
You would find lots of different types of yogurt and fruit. And I always have a pre made salad available at all times.
......

If you had the opportunity to get a message across to a large group of people what would your message be?
We should live life to the fullest. We really have a short stay on this earth and we should be kind to others and make every day count.
......

Where do you see yourself in 5 years?
Doing what I'm doing now just on a grander scale.
......

What are you best at?
I am best at motivating people and making people feel comfortable.
......

What books do you like to read?
I like to read self-help books and motivational books.
......

What is your favorite type of music?
I like music that has feeling. I love anything that has piano and the violin.
......

Describe your parents, what are they like?
My parents are both highly intellectual and head strong. That's where I get it from.
......

What were your dreams as a child and did you achieve any of them?
I wanted to be a veterinarian, like every other child. Instead I am a Dr. of the spine.
......

Tell us a time in your life that was a time you'll never forget?
My father had heart surgery this year and went through an extremely difficult recovery process.
......

What are some qualities that you value in a person?
I value honesty and integrity.
......

Where did you grow up and what was it like?
I grew up in Roslyn, New York. It is a beautiful suburb on Long Island. It was a wonderful place to be raised. I acquired many values and a sense of community.
......

Name 5 of your favorite movies.
Stealing Home, A Chorus Line, The Natural, Field of Dreams, Willy Wonka and the Chocolate Factory.
......

What TV shows do you like?
Modern Family, Big Bang Theory, 60 Minutes, Dateline.

......

What do you enjoy doing on a Sunday afternoon?
Spending time with my family. They are the root of my survival.
......

You are stranded in the Amazon rain forest. What 3 items would you want to have with you and why?
A bottle of Water, GPS and a snake bite kit. Why: Hydration, directions and protection.
......

Is there anything in particular that you wish you could do over? What is it?
No, my actions have lead me where I want to be now.
What personality traits in your mind are best suited for your job, career, etc?
You have to have patience and be compassionate.
......

What is your favorite drink?
Pineapple juice.
......

What is your favorite color?
Purple.
......

Name a movie that touched you in some way.
Stealing Home.
......

When in life have you felt most alone? Why?
When my father had heart surgery, I would just watch him breath and realize how fragile life is.
......

What would be impossible for you to give up?
It would be impossible for me to stop working out. It is in my blood.
......

Why would someone not want to work with you?
I tend to push and I don't understand what it means when someone says they can't do it, that just makes me want to push more.
......

What activities did you enjoy in school?
I enjoyed science, history and especially creative writing classes.
......

What kind of child were you?
I was a happy child that always liked to please others.
......

If you could be a superhero, what would you want your superpowers to be?
I would like to be a super hero that can read people's minds, have super speed to get things done and be able to fly to get from one location to the next as fast as possible.
......

How do you want to be remembered?
A female version of Jack LaLane, his energy was contagious.
......

What is one of your favorite quotes?
Live life to the fullest; this is not a dress rehearsal.
......

What chore do you absolutely hate doing?
Folding laundry, I never know where the missing socks go, it's a laundry mystery.

......

What is your best feature?
My ability to connect with people and my abs, of course.
......

What was the last experience that made you a stronger person?
My father's heart surgery.
......

What makes you uncomfortable, besides these questions?
Nothing.
......

If you could change something physical about yourself, what would it be and why?
I would love to be taller. My husband is 6'7".
......

Besides money, what are your favorite ways to compensate people?
Telling them two simple words: "Thank you" It seems to be a lost art these days.
......

When was the last time you tried something new?
I tried to dive last week. It was an exhilarating experience.
......

How would you describe yourself in three words?
Compassionate, loving, strong.
......

What is one thing you are not?
Shy.
......

Do you think crying is a sign of weakness or strength?
Neither, it's a necessary emotion for coping with life's experiences.
......

What makes you angry?
Laziness.
......

What makes you laugh?
My son telling a joke.
......

What are you afraid of?
Failing.
......

What would be the first thing you would do if today was your last day?
Kiss my son and my husband.
......

What's your vision of a perfect society?
A society that does not judge others. And is kinder to one another.
......

What's something you check daily?
My email and my horoscope.
......

Are you an emotional person?
Yes.
......

What's your own definition of happiness?

Accomplishing the goals I set for myself and coming home to a loving family.
......

Which famous person would you like to interview and which questions would you ask him/her?
Ann Frank. I would ask her if she believes in God.
......

If you could choose to be born with a particular natural skill what skill would it be?
Extreme athletic ability.
......

What advice would you give someone who wanted to do what you do?
Stay in school, become educated and explore as many opportunities as possible.
......

Are there any words of wisdom you'd like to pass along to us?
Never give up, even in the face of adversity.
......

Did you enjoy answering these questions? On a scale from 1 – 10. 1= I hated it. 10= I really enjoyed it.
10.

....

About Marisa

Dr. Marisa R. Silver Is the owner of In The Zone Personal Fitness and Silverspine Chiropractic & Heath. She is a Doctor of chiropractic medicine, certified nutritionist and personal trainer. She is currently a contributing author for multiple fitness and nutrition books located on amazon com. She has a fitness television program on Cablevision Long Island.

She can be contacted drsilver@bodybysilver.com and the website is www.bodybysilver.com

INTERVIEW 9
Elizabeth Kallam Turner

Personal Information

Full Name:
Elizabeth Kallam Turner aka Kally O'Mally

Age:
44

Location:
Sacramento, CA

Relationship Status:

Divorced

Number of Children:
None (2 awesome canine companions)

Profession:
Health Care Administration, Published Songwriter, Yoga Teacher

Educational Background:
Bachelor's Degree from Florida State University
Associate of Arts from Miami Dade Community College New World School of the Arts.

Honors & Awards:
Miss Coral Springs, 1992
Miss Homestead, 1993
....

General Questions

What are you known for professionally?
My work with the University of California, Davis, my yoga instruction and my music.
......

Tell us about how you got into your line of work.
Making music is my passion. As a child I preferred the stereo to the television. To this day I can pull a melody out of thin air and I don't feel whole and healthy unless I'm expressing my creativity through music. I fell into academic healthcare job. I had actually seen TLC's "Trauma in the ER" and an episode they had filmed at UC Davis.

When we moved to California, we purchased a house in the same neighborhood as the hospital so it made sense that I would work there and not commute. Music and healthcare are actually fairly closely related and I enjoy the academic environment. I fell in love with yoga in early 2000 when I started practicing at Yoga Loka in Sacramento. In 2005 I began teaching yoga as a second job and on average have taught more than 160 classes a year since then.
......

How long have you been doing what you do?
Making music is my most natural gift and I've been singing solo and with groups since elementary school. At the same time, it's hard to make a living making music unless you're well connected, so I took a day job with the University of California, Davis Department of Anesthesiology and Pain Medicine, where I work directly for the Chair as his executive assistant.
......

What do you enjoy most about what you do?
I absolutely love making music. I love all aspects of it, the meticulous and repetitive nature of practice all the way through to producing a CD or new song. I get great mental stimulation and satisfaction from the process. But when the listener or a reviewer tells me how much they enjoy it, that just really makes my day.... I enjoy teaching yoga almost as much as I love making music.

The human body is a powerful instrument of energy and working with students on how to marry strength, balance and flexibility is extremely rewarding. I get enormous pleasure from watching students improve and fall in love with the postures. They make me proud.
......

What are you most passionate about professionally? What most excites you about your work & the contribution you can make?
Being on the ground floor and making my own way. It takes longer and it takes great patience, but when people light up because they like my music it's incredibly rewarding. And because I'm a little older and because I've worked so hard to get to where I am, the fruit tastes all the sweeter. Music and yoga are also similar in the contributions they make, they bring people together and uplift the spirit. They both have the power to heal and make our lives better and brighter.
……

What's the single most important reason for your success?
Self actualization. Achieving my full potential.
……

What do you consider to be your greatest achievement?
Just getting to this point in my life. Working this hard requires great focus and discipline and it's very exciting to see my goals coming to fruition, my music being licensed for different projects and good reviews coming in, but in the end, to wake up in the morning and have another beautiful day to work on what I love doing is my greatest achievement. Talk to me after I've won a Grammy.
……

How do you think women have changed over the years? Regarding business, sports and fitness.
I can't speak for all women but I can tell you that my mother pushed me to be independent, to obtain my education and delay childbearing and marriage until I was sure of the direction I wanted to grow in. She herself was remarkable for a woman as she was a Florida Highway Patrol Officer in South

Florida during a time when there were very few women troopers.

I credit her with giving me good fitness habits as well. She was a long distance runner and she would encourage me to get out of the house and run with her, though I hated it at the time, I love it now. I'm in the gym or yoga studio on an almost daily basis and feel that being strong and healthy is intrinsic to living a vibrant and fulfilled life.
......

Do you think women are competitive with each other? Why? Regarding business, sports and fitness.
I do think that women are competitive on the surface, but once you break the top layer, women are very supportive and want to see each other succeed. When it comes to the modern woman, we're creating the paradigm rather than coming from an established set of rules that men have had in place for many years.

It's fresh territory for us so in some ways we're learning how to behave and how to appropriately support each other. Sheryl Sandberg's book Lean In and the Lean In groups that she's spearheading are a great example. If we can move towards mutual support we have a much better chance at succeeding all the way around. It would do us well to not forget that we've only had the right to vote since 1920.
......

What memorable competitions come to mind in your career?
I was Miss Coral Springs 1992 and Miss Homestead 1993 in the Miss America Pageant System. The pageant's I won helped me pay for college.
......

What is the number one thing you like best about being into fitness?

Feeling healthy, feeling good!
……

Is there anything wrong with wanting to portray women athletes, actors, etc as feminine and physically attractive?
Rather than focusing on portraying women as feminine and physically attractive, we should portray them as they are, intelligent, unique, diverse, complicated and valued. I think we should keep the image of women focused on radiant health with an appropriate range of body types.

We run into trouble, serious trouble when the media continually portrays the ideal image as a sleep deprived, bone thin woman that looks like a strong wind could blow her over. I also think it's extremely important to show a wide range of diversity and inclusion. America is a beautiful collection of all types and that's something we should celebrate.
……

How do you deal with cravings for junk foods, sweets and salty food?
I indulge and remember the law of diminishing returns, which means that the first taste is always the best. Each bite thereafter you don't taste as much, so I savor the first few bites and then stop.
……

Describe a typical day for you, starting from the moment you wake up in the morning.
I wake up at 6am, grab some coffee, check my email, maybe create a little music while my mind is clear or write. I generally just mess about in the mornings until about 7:45 when I jump in the shower. I'm at work by 8:30.

I'm so lucky in that my home is 4 minutes on foot to my house so I go home for lunch or a break in the middle of the day. I'm home by 5:10 and in yoga or the gym by 6:30. I'll typically

find some time to work on my voice and guitar during the evening as well. After yoga or the gym I love to have salad and a beer and am usually in bed and out by 10, 10:30.
......

Health & Fitness Questions

What sports do you participated in for fun?
Weight lifting, bicycling and yoga.
......

How long have you been playing those sports?
Yoga since 2000, Weight lifting started in earnest in 2010.
......

What got you started in that sport?
With yoga it was a natural curiosity. With weightlifting it was the desire to have strong bones as I age.
......

What is your biggest accomplishment in your sports? Include fun sports and any athletic career.
I absolutely love teaching yoga. Memorizing the dialogue, focusing on the physiology and helping people realize their potential is my biggest accomplishment.
......

What competitions have you entered? What were the outcomes?
I'm not competitive with regard to sports, but keep an eye out for me at this year's Grammy's.
......

How do you motivate yourself and stay motivated?

It's easy. I love it. I love the feeling I get from working out and I love feeling strong in my body. It's easy to embrace something that feels so good and is so good for you.
......

What are some of the main foods you would include in your shopping list to maintain a lean and muscular physique?
Chocolate. I Hop Cinn-a-Stack pancakes. Just kidding. I love salads. My main shopping list includes lots of spinach, cranberries, almonds, sourdough breads and pasta, tomatoes, greens. I'm lucky in that I love veggies, but I crave the bad stuff for sure!
......

What is the most challenging thing you deal with about consistently staying in top shape?
Sitting a desk during the day and ageing. I think the sitting is worse though than the ageing.
......

Please describe your normal diet. What do you eat in a typical day to stay in shape?
I eat what I want and don't restrict my eating. I don't like feeling uncomfortably full and if I'm going to eat something sugary or sweet I do it early in the day so I can burn it off throughout the day.
......

What type of exercises do you include in your routine to stay in shape?
Full routine of weights, 30 to 40 minutes on the Stairmill 3-4 times a week and 3 days of yoga per week.
......

A total beginner is about 35 pounds overweight. She doesn't really know where to start. What tips can you give her to follow the right track?

Work at your edge and work hard. Keep at it and don't judge, just do and keep doing. If you judge you're more likely to quit, if you accept that it's a lifestyle change and focus on how much better you'll feel overall with time, you're more inclined to stick it out. But I see too many women at the gym not really working at their edge. Instead of doing 50 or 80 lb leg extensions they'll do 20 lbs and not really get to the point where the burn comes in. You've got to get to that point where you're cursing when you finish those last few reps and if you can't finish them, you go back for them. Muscle growth takes time but it's so worth it.

What tips do you recommend for eating out at restaurants to make sure we don't gain too much weight/fat?
I typically look for lower fat items and will only have few bites of things that I know aren't healthy. Bikram yoga is great for detoxing the body and the thing is, once you feel good, you don't typically like to do things or eat things that are going to take that feeling away.
......

What exercises do you recommend for getting a bigger, rounder and fuller butt?
Lunges, squats and the stairmill. The key is to give it a good squeeze during the lift.
......

What are your top tips for developing toned and defined arms? Specific exercises, diet advice, etc.
Do a variety of arm exercises, push ups and pull ups are of course great, but challenging. The biggest key is to make sure the weights are heavy enough to give you a challenge but not so heavy that you can't do the workout. If I'm doing 20 reps, those last 5 are a total pull my hair out bear.
......

What are your top tips for losing unwanted body fat? Specific exercises, diet advice, etc.

Don't drink and of course avoid the sugars and the fats. Once you've developed a strong muscular body, the control of the top layer of fat seems like it's much more dependent on food intake.
......

What are your top tips for gaining lean muscle mass? Specific exercises, diet advice, etc.
I drink a protein shake when I'm lifting. It's much harder to make substantial gains for a woman than a man, which is why women don't have to worry about getting bulky. That and lift at your edge.

What are your top tips for improving breasts lift and shape? Specific exercises, diet advice, etc.
Lol...implants.
......

What are your top tips for staying motivated on a fitness plan?
Imagine yourself at 50, 60, 70 and 80 and then see if that's a vibrant and active picture or one that tends towards immobility. Gravity is a bitch and it's a constant force on the body, I want to be teaching my yoga class and standing on my head when every hair on my head has gone grey. I want to be mobile and still reeling in the beauties that life has to offer well into my old age. I won't be able to do that if I ignore my physical instrument.
......

What is your training routine like? Please include a few details.
Sweaty...very sweaty. Whether it's yoga or the gym I love to really sweat. Yoga is 90 minutes in a room heated to about 105 degrees. 26 postures and two breathing exercises that addresses every organ, muscle and joint in the body and every system of the body. When it's the gym I typically will lift weights for 40- 45 minutes and then do some cardio. I try to

mix up my legs and arms as recovery is more challenging if I do large muscle groups at the same time.
......

What is the best way to get started in your industry?
One of the best ways to become a yoga instructor is to find a studio that resonates with you and then decide on what type of certification you want and work towards your goal. There are 200 hrs, 500 hr and all sorts of different styles of certification. Get some knowledge about which style you prefer and then get to work. My teaching developed out of my disciplined practice and love for the yoga, it was a very natural and organic progression that started about 5 years after I began my practice.

What is the best way towards becoming a personal trainer?
Get the training, education and experience you need and lead by example.
......

Have you suffered any injuries? What injuries?
No real injuries.
......

What things do you currently do in your training that is key to your success?
Consistency. It's a part of my daily habit.
......

Isn't it hard to stay fit? How do you manage that?!
It's simple, but not easy. It's simple in that you know what you have to do, but not easy in that its work. Luckily, the benefits are so visible and palpable to me that I don't have any problem being motivated to work out. In fact, I wish I had more time to spend in the gym or at the yoga studio.
......

Business Questions

Tell us about your first entrepreneurial experience as a kid or older.
Ha! I ran a backyard circus where I got the neighborhood kids to participate in skits or show off their talents. I got their parents to come and charged them money for tickets. It was quite good!
……

What is the most difficult part of starting your business?
Overcoming the financial hurdles, making music is expensive and so is living in California. I have never ascribed to the starving artist theory and have always worked to support my music habit. Getting the money together to get my LLC and Business license set up, manufacturing the CD, etc., those were all challenging, but once I got those things accomplished, I've started to see some great things happening.
……

How have your entrepreneurial motivations changed since you first started?
I see even greater possibilities. The world we live in today offers so many opportunities for good musicians to emerge if they're able to pull together the right tools. I'm very excited about the successes I've had in licensing my music and looking forward to making this business my full time job.
……

What do you consider to be success as a business owner or entrepreneur?
If I can make enough money doing what I love to retire on, I will feel personally successful.
……

What's your least favorite part about being a business owner or entrepreneur?
The anxiety that goes along with waiting for your break, other than that it's great.
......

What's the biggest thing you struggle with as a business owner or entrepreneur?
Understanding the full framework of the music business is a big challenge, and in order to succeed you have to tackle what you don't know in order to stand a chance at being heard or rising above the white noise.
......

How do you think running a business or being an entrepreneur has made you a better person?
Without a doubt, owning and running your own business sharpens you and keeps you on edge. You become more aware of opportunities, your strengths, your weaknesses and if you want to succeed you'll be inspired to improve.
......

How did you arrive at running this business? What path brought you here?
I've been a musician since I was a small child. I'm prolific as a producer and can write new music at an impressive pace. I realized that in order for me to be viable in the market place, I needed to take care of, and understand the business side of the music business. Now that I've gotten a bit of a foothold and am starting to license some music, I'm excited and feeling quite optimistic about the growth of my business.
......

What was the most difficult part of starting your business?
Coming up with the initial collateral to establish the business.
......

What do you do on a daily basis to grow as a person/business person/entrepreneur?
I keep my eye on quality. Quality musicianship, quality interactions and prompt responsiveness to requests. I also expect great things.
......

What's unique about the service that you provide?
There are not very many female producers who are both multi-instrumentalists and technological whizzes. I got lucky in that my brain is highly adaptable to new technologies, so when I get into the studio or online to work with my tracks or communicate, I feel incredibly blessed to have the natural talent and technological abilities to bring my dreams to fruition.

What entrepreneurial hacks have you developed to stay focused and productive in your day-to-day?
While it's not much of a hack, living right across the street from my day job is huge. My commute time is 4 minutes door to door on foot. Living so close is a huge benefit to my productivity. I've adopted some habits that enable me to pull it all together. People are amazed when they find out how much I do, but I couldn't accomplish nearly as much if my life weren't designed this way.
......

Do you have any of your own branded products? If so, what are they?
I have 3 full length CD's on the market and two instrumental singles. I also created Kalyco Covers, which are cool seat covers designed to fit the common Steelcase office chair.
......

Mixed Questions

What would be your ultimate achievement in any area of your life?
I'd love to win a Grammy or 5, which is really about validation isn't it? The pinnacle for me would really be to know that folks are enjoying my music and to be able to support myself fully with that endeavor.
......

If you could be any character in fiction, who would you be?
Nancy Drew. I read all of those books voraciously as a child and still adore them. Nancy had it going on!
......

At present, what is your biggest challenge, and what are you doing to manage this challenge?
Keeping a balance with all of my obligations. I currently work 7 days a week and have for several years. I teach yoga on Saturday and Sunday, but I love it so much, it doesn't feel much like work. That said, it is work and the reality is that I need to ensure that while I'm working hard to achieve my dreams, that I'm not missing out on the beauty of being in touch with and aware of my daily life. I try to enjoy myself as much as possible no matter what I'm doing, consistently put forth my best effort and savor the beautiful moments.
......

What things do you believe differentiates you from your contemporaries?
My ability to handle so many different aspects of my business from the sound engineering, producing and putting together workable graphics, to playing the tambourine, I often surprise myself with my abilities. I'm very, very thankful for this ability to grasp and accomplish the tasks I take on.
......

Have you ever experienced a breakthrough, and if so, what led to it?

I break through all the time and think it's important to be open to possibilities and circumstance. I like the phrase "success is when preparation meets opportunity." The preparation part for me, means growing in all areas. Learning how to run a business and all that entails, learning cutting edge music technologies and how to apply them in my works, and being a diligent and hard worker in my job with the University.
……

Do you have a saying or motto that you live your life by?
I try to live in a state of gratitude. I'm not always successful but I find ways to come back to being grateful. If I'm out on a walk, I try to notice what's beautiful and give thanks. I make gratitude my home base. No matter what's happening on the field of play, I'm aiming to get back to home base and that state of thankfulness. It's so important to remember how transient life is and how our circumstances are ever changing, so I don't want to focus too much on external or material things. I try to focus more on being aware and awake.
……

Where do you draw your inspiration from?
Other great musicians, artists, orators and storytellers….dancers, people who laugh a lot and are happy. We have more than enough pain in this world that needs to be healed, so I like to focus on how I can bring more healing energy, music, joy & art into people's lives.
……

Made any mistakes that helped or hurt you in a way that you would like to share?
I'm sure I made mistakes along the way. I'm really happy with my life and the way that things have evolved, so mistakes and all my only advice is to not quit and don't be afraid to fail. If you have a dream then cultivate your talents, skills and abilities continuously and don't quit. It may take you 5 years,

10, 15 or even 20, but you'll never ever achieve your dream if you don't at least try. When you have a "failure" don't judge it so much as to try to learn what happened and not repeat the same mistakes.
......

What were your biggest personal battles and how did you confront them?
I had terrible struggles with self worth and self esteem. I felt like a burden to my family and really struggled through my childhood on many levels. I joined the US Air Force at 16. I took the recruiter to my home and had my parents sign the papers. I turned 17 in basic training and was living in England at 18. It was rough. Luckily for me, I was a late bloomer and things started to shift for me as I got into my twenties.
......

What were the most difficult decisions you had to make during your lifetime? Why?
Asking for a divorce was definitely one of my lowest points. I don't believe that anyone goes into marriage lightly and there's a sense of personal failure when you know you can no longer go on in the same relationship paradigm with your spouse. But at that point the damage was insurmountable on my part. It was incredibly difficult and painful and I took a long time to come to the conclusion that there was no turning back. It was one of my darkest times as an adult.
......

If you could paint a picture of any scenery you've seen before, what would you paint?
The LA Coastline... I love the way the mountains meet the water in Southern California and as a bona fide water baby, that coastline calls my name!
......

What are some goals you are still trying to accomplish?

I'm still working hard on getting my name out there and solidified in the Americana Music Genre. I don't come from a musical family, I come from a working class family and as such, getting my foot in the door has been much more of a challenge. Luckily I have a wonderfully supportive community of folks who have heard and purchased my music and that is very exciting.

The production tools that are available to me are amazing, so I'd like to master more of the sound engineering aspects of what I do. The more I work on the material, the more it opens up to me, which is exciting and keeps me engaged and excited for the future.
......

What are the most important lessons you've learned in life?
Be open, be yourself, be genuine, get your butt to yoga. Be compassionate, but have good boundaries.
......

What are you proudest of in your life?
My musical compositions and my yoga teaching.
......

How do you set your goals?
My goals setting process is internally driven in that when I want to accomplish something it knaws at me until I get it finished. There will be no turning back though there may be slight shifts in direction. I become very clear sighted and energized when I'm working on a project. I'm already gearing up for the next CD and looking forward to the projects I'm gonna work on. Just you wait!
......

What else would you do if you weren't in your current line of work?

If I couldn't make music I'd be a painter. After my divorce I couldn't sing. I literally could not make a sound that worth throwing in the trash. It was as if the wind had been knocked out of me. But I'm such a creative person that I couldn't just sit around and watch TV, so I painted. My mother was a painter and I think that music and paint are similar artistically. I really enjoyed working with mixed media on canvas. I like bright large colorful abstract work with lots of texture. Yummy.
……

What are your religious beliefs/spiritual beliefs?
I believe that God's most basic form is the energetic form and that exists everywhere.
……

Do you believe in the Law of Attraction?
Absolutely. Like attracts like, which is why it is so important to practice good mental health hygiene. I don't think folks are taught enough about how to live happily. We're taught to achieve and succeed materialistically (sort of) and then we're faced with marketing messages designed to instill a desire for their product, but we're not really given a framework on how to life abundantly and positively despite less than perfect circumstances.

For me books like, Julia Cameron's The Artist's Way and Deepak Chopra's works are really valuable for instilling good positive mental health habits. The more you practice feeling good, the more you feel good! Energy is powerful and whichever way you direct your mental energy and thoughts will grow, so better to direct them onto positive wavelengths that will bear fruit as opposed to depression or allowing negativity to permeate your experience.
……

What is your diet like?

I love my veggies and salads. I strive for a balanced diet but am not radical about watching every calorie...see the answer to the next question!
......

What's your favorite food?
Chocolate.
......

What would we find in your refrigerator right now?
Creamer, leftover pizza, beer, mushrooms, spinach, shredded cheddar.
......

If you had the opportunity to get a message across to a large group of people what would your message be?
Be love. Be compassion in action.
......

Where do you see yourself in 5 years?
I'd like to see my music doing well in the music licensing marketplace. I'd like to see my business expand and my song catalog grow significantly. I'd like to be out and about performing interesting shows - maybe open for Lyle Lovett.
......

What are you best at?
Making music, making people laugh and smile and being a supportive person.
......

What books do you like to read?
It depends. If I'm on a flight or vacation, something funny like Janet Evanovich or Carl Hiasen - something to make me laugh. Otherwise I'm more inclined to read trade oriented books and self help type of stuff. Psychological thrillers are great too, but I don't have much time for reading for enjoyment these days.

......

What is your favorite type of music?
World musics, classical.
......

Describe your parents, what are they like?
My parents were both cops. We had a lot of guns around our household growing up. They were strict and they worked a lot. They made sure we had what we needed but they were very intent on encouraging us to get our education and have good jobs with benefits.
......

What were your dreams as a child and did you achieve any of them?
My dreams were to be a great musician and yes, I'm achieving them.
......

Tell us a time in your life that was a time you'll never forget?
I had a Spinet piano when I was in junior high school and I used to pray to God to let me wake up in the morning knowing how to play that piano perfectly. I would get up in the morning and go and sit at the piano and wait for it to all come together and I got kind of pissed when after doing this for weeks nothing happened.

The funny thing when I was in college at Florida State, I bought a chord wheel from the music store and I was working on classical repertoire in the practice room when I pulled out this chord wheel. I sat down at the piano and started to play. I finally really understood the piano and how it worked. I thought back to that fervent prayer I had made and chucked at the thought that came into my head, "God answers your prayers, just not always on your timeline."
......

What things do you find yourself doing that you said you'd never do?
I never thought I'd play the bass. I rock the bass, it's my favorite instrument to play.
......

What are some qualities that you value in a person?
Honesty, hard work, open-mindedness and compassion. I have great respect for people who are even tempered and kind.
......

Where did you grow up and what was it like?
I grew up in Homestead, FL. Homestead was a super interesting place to grow up. It's highly agriculturally oriented and extremely diverse. It's about 30 minutes from Homestead down to Key Largo.
......

Name 5 of your favorite movies.
We Were Soldiers, A Beautiful Mind, Bourne Identity Series, Casino, Fargo *I'm not a super movie buff... but I love really good movies with great plots or mindless funny stuff.
......

What TV shows do you like?
Law & Order, CSI, Nashville.
......

What do you enjoy doing on a Sunday afternoon?
Swimming in a pool or the ocean and enjoying life.
......

You are stranded in the Amazon rain forest. What 3 items would you want to have with you and why?
My ipad (to capture images and sounds and spark creativity) a good pair of king boots and a mosquito net.
......

Is there anything in particular that you wish you could do over? What is it?
There used to be things that I wished I could do over, but now I see where I am to be the culmination of everywhere I've been and all that I've done thus far, so I actually wouldn't change a thing because I'm pretty happy now and things are looking really bright.
......

What personality traits in your mind are best suited for your job, career, etc?
Risk taking, ingenuity, creativity and a bit of an OCD mindset.
......

What is your favorite drink?
Tossup between coffee, diet coke and beer.
......

What is your favorite color?
Green.
Name a movie that touched you in some way.
Yentl. I fell in love with Mandy Patankin that year... he's amazing!
......

When in life have you felt most alone? Why?
My high school years were burly. I was awkward and bullied and generally depressed. My life at home was extremely difficult and I wasn't at all optimistic about how things would turn out for me.
......

What would be impossible for you to give up?
My guitars/music.
......

Why would someone not want to work with you?

I'm easy-going and enjoy collaboration, but I can hear in an instant if something is not working. I'll make a cut if I have to and do my best to spare feelings, but the music comes first and sometimes that means being a shrewd taskmaster and producer. I'm not afraid to embrace that role.
......

What activities did you enjoy in school?
Chorus, music classes & my English classes.
......

What kind of child were you?
Creative, active and deeply thoughtful, part monkey. You couldn't get me out of the trees on a nice afternoon.
......

If you could be a superhero, what would you want your superpowers to be?
The ability to ease suffering for those who want or need it.
......

How do you want to be remembered?
I want to be remembered as a great songwriter and musician.
......

We all have vices, what are yours?
I'm a friend of the pineapple.
......

What is one of your favorite quotes?
"Policy should serve the people." Winston Churchill.
......

What chore do you absolutely hate doing?
Dusting.
......

What is your best feature?

My brain.
......

What was the last experience that made you a stronger person?
My divorce and subsequent rebound relationship.
......

What makes you uncomfortable, besides these questions?
People being mean to their children and people being mean in general. Seeing people in a state of suffering is tough and Sacramento has a significant homeless issue so you see folks around here struggling a lot.
......

If you could change something physical about yourself, what would it be and why?
I would have my nose fixed. I broke it on the bottom of Dr. Kalbac's swimming pool when I was in my early twenties and then I broke it again years later and the cartilage inside still isn't right. I'd have it set and reduced.
......

Besides money, what are your favorite ways to compensate people?
Trade a form of work if possible, or help promote their work. In this day and age to recommend and promote the work of another is nearly just as tangible as money in some instances.
......

When was the last time you tried something new?
I try new things all the time. It's part of being a technophile. I love technological advancements and developments. Working with my ipad in the studio was amazing!
......

How would you describe yourself in three words?
happy, talented, hardworking.

......

What is one thing you are not?
A mathematician.
......

Do you think crying is a sign of weakness or strength?
Neither, it's a need for stress relief.
......

What makes you angry?
Mean or inconsiderate folks.
......

What makes you laugh?
Funny videos or photos I find online, funny stories and funny things in general. I love to laugh and think that laughter is integral to good health. When I was going through my divorce I would intentionally seek out funny things to make me laugh more, despite the fact that I didn't feel much like laughing. More often than not, I'd find stuff that was just hilarious, crazy things on YouTube, or shows....that's how I found out about Demitri Martin.
I got into the habit of sharing the funny things I find on my Facebook and Twitter accounts so that my friends could laugh too and there are times that they come up with some brilliant comments that are as funny as the content itself. It makes life wonder funny!
......

What are you afraid of?
I really dislike going downhill fast. I finally learned how to snow ski about 5 years ago and I really can enjoy the intermediate slopes at a nice medium pace, but I intensely dislike going downhill super fast, like right on the edge of out of control. No mountain biking or black diamond ski trails for me.
......

What would be the first thing you would do if today was your last day?
Have sex.
......

What's your vision of a perfect society?
One where basic needs are met, incarceration rates are low, abundance is high and our concern for our natural environment is a driving force in how we plan and navigate our lives.
......

Is it possible to lie without saying a word? How?
I'm not so sure that it's possible to lie without saying a word, but it is surely possible to deceive without saying a word.
......

What's something you check daily?
My teeth. I want to keep my teeth as long as I can so I make sure to brush and floss.
......

Are you an emotional person?
I'm a thoughtful person. Emotion without thought behind it can be very draining energetically, so while I feel my emotions, I intentionally refrain from acting when I feel "emotional". My preference is to give things time, to see how things play out, and to make decisions from a place of calm. I'm an uplifting type of person, though for sure. I believe in enjoying this life, it's the only one we've got and it will be gone in a flash, so I try to come from my highest place in all situations. That's not to say that I succeed though and I'm just as prone to the occasional misstep as anyone. But that's where a good strong yoga practice comes in; it pulls you back to your center.
......

What's your own definition of happiness?

Living a satisfied life where I spend more time giving thanks for and reveling in the beauty of my days than I do wanting something different.
......

Which famous person would you like to interview and which questions would you ask him/her?
I have several I'd love to chat with, Dolly Parton, K.D. Lang, Barbara Streisand, Allison Krauss and I could keep going on down the list. For Dolly our discussion would surely revolve around songwriting process and vocal process. She's an outstanding musician so I'm curious about her artistic process. Same thing for Barbara Streisand, but I'd love for her to talk about her vocal technique and what exercises she uses to maintain her vocal flexibility.

With K.D., and Allison Krauss I'd add questions about the business component. Shadowland is one of my favorite CD's as was Dolly's the Grass is Blue. They're all great artists whom I admire and there are soooo many more. I've had some dreams where I went motorcycle riding through the Keys and Everglades with Sheryl Crow and in another dream Willie Nelson gave me piano lessons....(which was crazy cool). Hah!
......

If you could choose to be born with a particular natural skill what skill would it be?
I was born with it and I wouldn't change a thing. My ability to innately understand how a song works and how music works feels like an incredible blessing. I've been extremely lucky to have encountered some incredible experiences along my path as a result of that gift and it continues to grow as I age. And I'm still at the tip of the iceberg. I get great satisfaction in learning new instruments or software and exploring how sound and rhythm come together to create something we remember.
......

What advice would you give someone who wanted to do what you do?
Follow your own path, find your own voice, don't try to sound like anyone else. Learn as many instruments as you can and write, write, write. Write the good songs, write the bad songs, don't judge, just keep doing and keep writing. Listen to those who have gone before and pay attention to those formulas for songwriting as they work for a reason.

Get a voice teacher, get a music teacher, take care of yourself, get plenty of sleep and treat people right. Enjoy the small pleasures as much as you do the big ones. Don't give up on your passion as there are many ways to achieve your dreams, the only question is which path do you want to take. Have confidence and stay the course. Music is a tough business but there are lots of opportunities for those who have the knack.
......

While you are watching TV in your home a penguin walks through the door wearing a sheriff's hat and badge. What does he say?
"Those brownies were medicated." If there's a penguin in a sheriff's hat with a badge at my door, there's a problem!
......

Do you have any secrets you want to share with the few of us reading this? We won't say anything....promise!
No secrets to tell...
......

Are there any words of wisdom you'd like to pass along to us?
Be happy. Be love. Be an inspiration to yourself and others by becoming the highest version/vision of yourself. Don't judge, forgive. Have fun. Sing and dance. Walk prayerfully and have an attitude of gratitude. Do these things and you'll see the

colors of your life turn brighter and experience the manifestation of great things rather than a state of want. ......

Did you enjoy answering these questions? On a scale from 1 – 10. 1= I hated it. 10= I really enjoyed it.
9.

....

About Elizabeth

http://www.kallyomally.com
http://www.audiosparx.com/KallyOMally
My commercial music licensing agent's page.
http://www.facebook.com/kallyomally77
http://www.sactv.com/reviews/2013-0430-kally.htm   Recent press

INTERVIEW 10
Kellie Davis

Personal Information

Full Name:
Kellie Davis

Age:
33

Location:
California

Relationship Status:
Married

Number of Children:
2

Profession:
Writer/Fitness Coach

Educational Background:
BA in English

Honors & Awards:
Magna Cum Laude, Sigma Tau Delta Honorary English Society, Golden Key International Honor Society
....

General Questions

What are you known for professionally?
Professional Writer/Fitness Coach.
......

Tell us about how you got into your line of work.
After moving to Arizona and facing a dwindling teacher's market, I decided it was time to begin my own writing business. A few of my clients where fitness professionals and having helped them create content for their own business I realized that my passion for fitness could really work well with my writing career.

I began following many well-known fitness bloggers and started my own fitness blog. Over the course of a year or so, things really took off and soon I was being contacted by major websites to contribute content. My blog (as well as my co-author's blog) also led to a book deal.
......

How long have you been doing what you do?
I always like to say I've been writing my entire life, but I've only been writing as a paying career for four years. Prior to that I was an English teacher. As far as fitness goes, I started coaching clients a little more than a year ago. As with writing, I've always heavily immersed myself in the fitness world and have been in the weight room since I was a teen.
......

What do you enjoy most about what you do?
Above anything, the most enjoyable part of my career is the connections I make with people from every part of the world. The stories of courage, triumph, and passion that I hear on a daily basis are what keep me going. I meet some of the most incredible women and men who have amazing stories to tell.
......

What are you most passionate about professionally? What most excites you about your work & the contribution you can make?
I love witnessing the personal growth of both my clients and colleagues. It's amazing to watch their personal journey, and to then reflect back as to where they began. Though I work as a fitness coach, I want to empower women to create positive changes in their lives so they can see what they are capable of. It's a process of healing and nurturing from the inside out.

It's great to see the self-love, self-discipline, and self-appreciation that develops over the course of our time together. As a writer, nothing gives me more satisfaction than to receive emails and notes from people whom my work touched. That's the beauty of the written word. It has a lasting impact on the lives of people with whom I may have otherwise never connected.
......

What's the single most important reason for your success?
My family putting their faith and trust in me. Everyday I wake up knowing that everything I do impacts the lives of my husband and children. That's what drives me forward and allows me the security to take risks, explore, and sometimes fail.
......

What do you consider to be your greatest achievement?
In business, definitely publishing Strong Curves with Bret Contreras.
......

How do you think women have changed over the years? Regarding business, sports and fitness.
So many more women are now on the forefront of the sports and fitness business. We have more of an authoritative presence and are making great headway when it comes to how women are perceive in the fitness business. You see so many women in the by-lines of men's fitness and health magazines, as sports broadcasters, and in administrative position within the sports and fitness industry. It's all a wonderful thing to see.
......

Do you think women are competitive with each other? Why? Regarding business, sports and fitness.
Everyone has a competitive edge, but most often I think it's more of a competition within ourselves than it is with those who surround us.
......

Is there anything wrong with wanting to portray women athletes, actors, etc as feminine and physically attractive?

Not at all. Some of my favorite photos or interviews of women sports figures are when they are dressed up or wearing swimwear. I don't think we should veil the fact that women are power and beautiful.

How do you deal with cravings for junk foods, sweets and salty food?
I honestly don't get cravings anymore. I used to be a huge sugar addict, but I learned to control it and don't think too much about junk food.
......

Business Questions

Tell us about your first entrepreneurial experience as a kid or older.
My friend and I used to set up yard sales with our own things. We probably made two dollars total over the course of five yard sales, but it was a fun venture. I am sure everything was overpriced.
......

What is the most difficult part of starting your business?
Having the confidence to know I was doing the right thing. I always second guess my decisions or doubt my own capabilities. I think in general this is an issue for women in many different types of business.
......

How have your entrepreneurial motivations changed since you first started?
Yes, definitely. When I first started writing I just wanted to be a ghost writer—the quiet observer who didn't ever sit in the

spotlight. Now I am front and center. It's still a bit intimidating for me, but I'm slowly getting used to the role.
......

What's your least favorite part about being a business owner or entrepreneur?
I never clock out. Things don't get done when I am away and I can't just check out at 5 PM. I am always thinking about work even when I'm not working. New strategies, new marketing plans, new products.
......

What's the biggest thing you struggle with as a business owner or entrepreneur?
Finding new business is never an easy thing. When you have great skills, products, or services, they don't matter if you don't have customers or clients.
......

How do you think running a business or being an entrepreneur has made you a better person?
I didn't expect the type of personal evolution that I went through when I began things. I've grown so much as a business woman and I never expected myself to be in this position.
......

Mixed Questions

If you could be any character in fiction, who would you be?
I guess it would be Daisy Buchanan. I think she is the total opposite of me, so it would be nice to live life through her lens for a short while.

......

At present, what is your biggest challenge, and what are you doing to manage this challenge?
It's tough trying to balance work and life. I don't want to be married to my job. I love spending time with my kids, being with them when they wake up and picking them up from school. I just don't ever want to be disconnected from the part of my life that really matters.
......

What things do you find yourself doing that you said you'd never do?
Everything my mother did that I said I would never do.
......

Where did you grow up and what was it like?
I lived in Colorado until I was 9 and then moved to Florida. Both areas were small communities with not a whole lot to do. I spent a lot of time outdoors getting dirty and exploring.
......

What TV shows do you like?
Oh, this will be embarrassing. I watch way too much TV. Breaking Bad, Walking Dead, Dexter, Nurse Jackie, and Shameless.
......

What do you enjoy doing on a Sunday afternoon?
I work in the garden on the weekends.
......

You are stranded in the Amazon rain forest. What 3 items would you want to have with you and why?
A machete, a compass, and a canteen.
......

What is your favorite drink?

Coffee in its many forms.
……

What is your favorite color?
Green of various shades.
……

Name a movie that touched you in some way.
The Secret Life of Bees—both the book and the movie. The relationships the women in that story had were captivating. No matter how distant they grew or how much they disagreed, they were always there for each other. In the end, their bond was the most powerful and most intimate I'd ever seen in a book/movie.
……

When in life have you felt most alone? Why?
After 9/11 I lost my job. I was in college, didn't know how I would pay rent or put food in the fridge. My family lived elsewhere, my brother was off at war. I felt like things had become completely undone.
……

What kind of child were you?
I was very shy, apprehensive, and unobtrusive in every sense. I didn't really find my voice or my confidence until I was an adult.
……

How do you want to be remembered?
As a kind, loving, generous, and thoughtful person.
……

We all have vices, what are yours?
Coffee in its many forms.
……

What chore do you absolutely hate doing?

Laundry is the pit of my demise. I never feel accomplished with it. At least when you scrub a bathroom it stays that way for a few days. But when you finish the laundry more appears instantaneously.
......

What is your best feature?
My eyes. I have green eyes and long eyelashes, which isn't all too common.
What is one thing you are not?
Deceptive.
......

Do you think crying is a sign of weakness or strength?
It depends. I think having strong emotions is a good thing, but crying to get away with something is a different story.
......

What makes you angry?
Lack of integrity.
......

What makes you laugh?
My kids, all the time.
......

What are you afraid of?
Letting people down.
......

What would be the first thing you would do if today was your last day?
Kiss my family fervently.
......

What's something you check daily?
My calendar and my email.
......

Are you an emotional person?
When it comes to my family, yes. But when it comes to business, no.
……

What's your own definition of happiness?
Looking forward to the day when you wake up.
……

What advice would you give someone who wanted to do what you do?
Just own it. Go forward with confidence and never be afraid to take a risk.

……

About Kellie

Kellie Davis is a freelance writer and blogger turned fitness coach living in Northern California. She published short fiction and essays in anthologies and literary magazines before starting a full time career as a health and fitness writer. She currently works as a contributing author to several online fitness publications, and also runs corporate blogs in the health food industry.

In addition to writing, Davis helps women all over the world achieve optimum health as a fitness and nutrition coach.

She runs MotherFitness : www.motherfitness.com, is the co-owner of Get Glutes : www.getglutes.com and the co-author of Strong Curves: A Woman's Guide to Building a Better Butt and Body :   www.barnesandnoble.com/w/strong-curves-bret-contreras/1111318681

INTERVIEW 11
Teiler Robinson

Personal Information

Full Name:
Teiler Robinson

Age:
21

Location:
Washington, DC

Number of Children:
0

Profession:
Founder and Editor-in-Chief of FAQTOR Fashion Book and Jett-Set Fashion, Founder and Creative Director of Rich Girls Society, Founder and Blogger for Billion Dollar Girl
....

General Questions

What are you known for professionally?
I am known for my work in the fashion industry.
......

Tell us about how you got into your line of work.
I've always had a great love for fashion, both high and street fashion. I preferred to watch Fashion Files on "E!" instead of cartoons and always had a copy of Vogue growing up.
......

How long have you been doing what you do?
I've been a published Journalist for almost 8 years now. I've had Jett-Set Fashion for more than 3 years. FAQTOR, Rich Girls Society and Billion Dollar Girl are my newest additions to my growing empire.
......

What do you enjoy most about what you do?
I love to create. Whether it is a story, editorial or piece of clothing. Being able to express myself in an art form so diverse and interesting is the greatest joy.
......

What are you most passionate about professionally? What most excites you about your work & the contribution you can make?

Being able to see my work coming to life and knowing that other people are ENJOYING what I am giving them excites me greatly. Style is eternal so the things that I create make a contribution that will last forever.
......

What's the single most important reason for your success?
Passion.
......

What do you consider to be your greatest achievement?
My journey is still fresh so I really can't answer that just yet... If I had to choose something, the first 8 years however, I guess creating FAQTOR because my dream is to have a top fashion and culture magazine.
......

What is the number one thing you like best about being into fitness?
It keeps me healthy and gives me a body that I can be proud of at the same time! It is also a great stress reliever and can be a lot of fun too.
......

Is there anything wrong with wanting to portray women athletes, actors, etc as feminine and physically attractive?
Not at all. Especially in the industry that I am a part of. I feel that women should be portrayed as beautiful. It is great to be a female. Embrace it.
......

How do you deal with cravings for junk foods, sweets and salty food?
I don't deprive myself at all. I have to realize that moderation is key, but if I want a cupcake, I'll have one.

......

Describe a typical day for you, starting from the moment you wake up in the morning.
I wake up, shower, get dressed (best part), go to the office for about 9 hours if I do not have any special events. Then I will probably go out with some friends and enjoy the city. Come home, work on a few more things and watch a little TV. I have a few shows that I am addicted to, so I try to get caught up. I then like to read a few fashion magazines before I really get into bed.
......

Health & Fitness Questions

What sports do you participated in for fun?
Ballet.
......

What are some of the main foods you would include in your shopping list to maintain a lean and muscular physique?
Boneless chicken, fish, "Naked" juice, a lot of water and juice and green vegetables like asparagus or spinach.
......

Please describe your normal diet. What do you eat in a typical day to stay in shape?
I TRY to get around to have breakfast. I have to admit that I don't always get to, which isn't good. But when I do, I like to have egg white omelettes or something with carbs like a bagel to jumpstart the day. If I am on the go, I may drink a Naked juice smoothie instead because it is actually pretty filling and PACKED with vitamins. For lunch I like Panini's or some sort

of sandwich or a really good salad. For dinner, I like to have fish or shellfish. I am a big seafood fan.
......

What type of exercises do you include in your routine to stay in shape?
Squats, crunches, Yoga and Pilates.
......

A total beginner is about 35 pounds overweight. She doesn't really know where to start. What tips can you give her to follow the right track?
Do not be discouraged of you do not see instant results. Get motivated and find a fitness routine that works for YOU. IF you need help, see a nutritionist or a personal trainer. You will see results, I promise.
......

What tips do you recommend for eating out at restaurants to make sure we don't gain too much weight/fat?
Do not deprive yourself of what you want. But if you are actively dieting, try looking at the low-cal options or requesting smaller portions.
......

What exercises do you recommend for getting a bigger, rounder and fuller butt?
Squats!
......

What are your top tips for developing toned and defined arms? Specific exercises, diet advice, etc.
Lifting light weights and yoga.
......

What are your top tips for losing unwanted body fat? Specific exercises, diet advice, etc.

Running is your best friend. That will shed weight from your overall body. Whether it is an outside jog or a run on the treadmill. Also, reducing the amount of fatty foods you take in. Boneless chicken (baked or grilled) and fish will help with this.
......

What are your top tips for staying motivated on a fitness plan?
Always remember that you want to be fit and healthy. Leave yourself little notes and forms of inspiration.
......

Have you suffered any injuries? What injuries?
Yes. I am actually injured right now. I have an awful back spasm that is as hard as a bone. It is horribly painful and makes inhaling deeply very difficult. I can't wait for it to heal.
......

Isn't it hard to stay fit? How do you manage that?!
I make sure I work it in to my schedule. The way that I look and feel means a lot to me. If I am sluggish, I can't properly do my job. I have made it a part of my life.
....

Business Questions

Tell us about your first entrepreneurial experience as a kid or older.
I had a thing for sewing purses and wallets. They were awful though! I then ran the Photography and literary magazine in 7th grade and attempted to start a line of lotions and body washes with one of my friends.
......

What is the most difficult part of starting your business?

Knowing where and how to start from scratch with little experience. I didn't know what to expect, I just knew that I loved it.
......

How have your entrepreneurial motivations changed since you first started?
Yes they have.
......

What do you consider to be success as a business owner or entrepreneur?
Having a brand that is recognizable and functioning. The money will come in time.
......

What's your least favorite part about being a business owner or entrepreneur?
Taking all of the responsibility, especially during the bad times.
......

How do you think running a business or being an entrepreneur has made you a better person?
I am more vocal about my opinions and what I want. I have learned a lot that I never would have learned if I did not choose this path. I am also a MUCH more confident person.
......

How did you arrive at running this business? What path brought you here?
I had a desire to see something different in the industry but I wanted to do it myself and do it my way. I just have an entrepreneurial soul.
......

What was the most difficult part of starting your business?

Starting from scratch with just a domain and a vision. No one to guide me, I just had to go through a lot of trial and error.
......

What do you do on a daily basis to grow as a person/business person/entrepreneur?
I continue to learn and improve.
......

What's unique about the service that you provide?
For starters, I am 21 with a functioning global fashion brand, something that most people do not expect to see in someone so young. Besides that, I work with creative people around the world to provide a unique and universal experience.
......

Do you have any of your own branded products? If so, what are they?
Yes I do. Rich Girls Society is my luxury "street wear" collection that is inspired by my image and ties into my overall brand.
......

Mixed Questions

What would be your ultimate achievement in any area of your life?
Being a top Fashion Editor and Icon, globally known and well respected.
......

If you could be any character in fiction, who would you be?

A mix of Blair Waldorf and Serena Van Der Woodsen, LOL! Successful and overachieving but a free spirited and fun-loving girl.
......

At present, what is your biggest challenge, and what are you doing to manage this challenge?
Finding enough hours in the day to maintain everything. I manage with proper scheduling a great team to help me.

What things do you believe differentiates you from your contemporaries?
My ability to form a fashion brand with various ventures under its umbrella that still maintains global brand awareness. I've developed a fashion collective, bringing visionaries from around the world to help create something that will be HUGE in the future.
......

Do you have a saying or motto that you live your life by?
"Study the greats and become greater" –Michael Jackson (my lifelong hero).
......

Where do you draw your inspiration from?
The decade of my childhood. I grew up in the 90's where fashion (street fashion in particular) was at its most diverse. People weren't afraid to be themselves. I am also VERY inspired by traveling.
......

What were your biggest personal battles and how did you confront them?
Becoming confident in myself and knowing that I could become recognized for doing great work. I just had to believe in myself and understand that there was room in the industry for me.
......

If you could paint a picture of any scenery you've seen before, what would you paint?
Flying into Los Angeles for the first time. The sky was almost pitch black and that skyline with those lights is forever burned into my brain.
......

What are some goals you are still trying to accomplish?
Becoming bigger, better and greater.
......

What are the most important lessons you've learned in life?
Be a leader.
......

What are you proudest of in your life?
Going after what I want and not allowing anyone to stop me. Learning to not be afraid.
......

How do you set your goals?
I think about what I feel I want to do next, like what just feels natural and exciting at that point and then I write them down and go for it.
......

What else would you do if you weren't in your current line of work?
Television host (which I still plan on doing in the future). It would have to be something expressive and fun. My brain and my soul do not like "average".
......

What are your religious beliefs/spiritual beliefs?

I do not have a "specified religion". I believe in God and I believe in a higher power. Something greater than what we could ever comprehend.
......

Do you believe in the Law of Attraction?
Yes, I do.
......

What is your diet like?
I like to try new and different foods. I like to have fun but not go overboard on unhealthy foods.
What's your favorite food?
ANYTHING made with potatoes, OMG. French fries especially. That's soooo bad but very true.
......

What would we find in your refrigerator right now?
Bagels, last night's Chinese food, Naked juice, asparagus. I need to go grocery shopping today!
......

If you had the opportunity to get a message across to a large group of people what would your message be?
Believe in yourself. Do not let negative words or actions from bad people, especially bullies, bring you down. I was bullied for being an overachiever and at times it made me want to stop and blend in with the masses. Luckily, I learned better. Be fierce, stand out, be a leader, and be bigger than what is average or expected. Shine bright and do NOT dim your light for ANYONE. Inspire, aspire, be inspired and have no fear.
......

Where do you see yourself in 5 years?
Running a major fashion corporation, designing a high fashion collection and inspiring people around the world.
......

What are you best at?
Writing.
......

What books do you like to read?
I love a good fiction book with a great story line, historical non-fiction, and of course anything artistic, like, photography or architecture books.
......

What is your favorite type of music?
Electronica in many forms: acid jazz, nu jazz, lounge, house, trance and music that reminds me of the beach like Jack Johnson or Tahiti 80. I also love R&B, a little bit of hip-hop and Michael Jackson, of course.
......

What were your dreams as a child and did you achieve any of them?
I wanted to be in fashion, music and film. Yes, I have achieved some of them, but I am still very early in my path so I have much more to do.
......

Tell us a time in your life that was a time you'll never forget?
May 2010, starting Jett-Set Fashion. I was SO inspired and imaginative. Graduating from high school was another great time and going to Fashion Week for the first time.
......

What things do you find yourself doing that you said you'd never do?
Waking up before 10.
......

What are some qualities that you value in a person?
Honesty, kindness, creativity and a great sense of humor.

......

Where did you grow up and what was it like?
I grew up in Pittsburgh during the 90's. It was very cultured and fun. I loved seeing the huge paintings on the sides of homes and buildings. We have the Warhol museum there and downtown was always so full of life and people. I miss the loud music coming from cars and all of the mom and pop stores there.
......

Name 5 of your favorite movies.
Breakfast at Tiffany's, Titanic, Night Shift, The Hunger Games and Some like it hot.

What TV shows do you like?
Scandal, Gossip Girl, Pretty little liars, I am currently getting into Twisted, The Young and The Restless, Sex and the City and I watch a few Reality Shows as well.
......

What do you enjoy doing on a Sunday afternoon?
Sleeping late, eating my favorite foods, hanging out with my friends, reading fashion magazines and enjoying the outdoors.
......

You are stranded in the Amazon rain forest. What 3 items would you want to have with you and why?
A cell phone to call for help, a Birkin bag to motivate me of why I need to survive and get help, and a cute pair of rain boots to help me make it through all of that wet terrain.
......

Is there anything in particular that you wish you could do over? What is it?
Nope. Everything is for a reason.
......

What personality traits in your mind are best suited for your job, career, etc?
Creativity, confidence, a sense of humor is nice because there isn't enough of that sometimes and passion.
......

What is your favorite drink?
Lemonade in all flavors (non-alcoholic) and I like a cranberry or pineapple with vodka here and there. I also like Champagne when celebrating.
......

What is your favorite color?
Pink. I love to wear a lot of black though.
......

When in life have you felt most alone? Why?
High School. I was miserable most of the time. I needed to stay to myself to stay out of the circle of drama. I was developing my writing skills and figuring out who I wanted to be. I was a cheerleader and in the performing arts but outside of those things and Student Government once in a while, I stayed to myself. I HATED school so much.
......

What would be impossible for you to give up?
Fashion.
......

Why would someone not want to work with you?
I honestly have no idea, haha. Maybe I'm a perfectionist.
......

What activities did you enjoy in school?
Cheerleading, theatre and chorus.
......

What kind of child were you?

Very loving, sweet, shy and artistic.
……

If you could be a superhero, what would you want your superpowers to be?
Invisibility and the ability to jump to different places in 2 seconds.
……

How do you want to be remembered?
As one of the biggest fashion icons, philanthropists and visionaries. Someone that was unafraid, bold and fierce. I want to break records and make history.
……

We all have vices, what are yours?
Sugar ☹
What is one of your favorite quotes?
"In order to be irreplaceable, one must be different" –Coco Chanel.
……

What chore do you absolutely hate doing?
All of them, I'm so bad.
……

What is your best feature?
Physically, I guess my eyes or long legs and Spiritually, I am very compassionate.
……

What makes you uncomfortable, besides these questions?
Nothing, just these questions. Just kidding, I am still very shy so I hate talking on the phone to strangers sometimes. It always feels so awkward.
……

If you could change something physical about yourself, what would it be and why?
Nothing. I am who I am.
......

Besides money, what are your favorite ways to compensate people?
Inspiration.
......

When was the last time you tried something new?
Yesterday, it was a crazy roller coaster. I believe the next new thing will be alligator...apparently it tastes like chicken.
......

How would you describe yourself in three words?
Creative, adventurous, funny.
......

What is one thing you are not?
Weak.
......

Do you think crying is a sign of weakness or strength?
Strength. It takes a strong person to let out their emotions.
......

What makes you angry?
Bullies.
......

What makes you laugh?
I could not possibly sum that up into a simple answer. I find myself laughing a LOT.
......

What are you afraid of?
Failure.
......

Is it possible to lie without saying a word? How?
Yes, if you let someone believe something false when you know it isn't true.
......

What's something you check daily?
My email and the weather.
......

Are you an emotional person?
Yes.
......

What's your own definition of happiness?
Feeling free, laughing, feeling safe and secure.
......

Which famous person would you like to interview and which questions would you ask him/her?
I would interview Pharrell and ask him about his favorite places to travel and gain inspiration. I admire his artistic work and would love to get inside of his brain!
......

If you could choose to be born with a particular natural skill what skill would it be?
Superior sewing.
......

What advice would you give someone who wanted to do what you do?
Be confident and work hard. Do your homework and learn about the industry.
......

While you are watching TV in your home a penguin walks through the door wearing a sheriff's hat and badge. What does he say?
Nothing, he just stands there and stares while I laugh hysterically.
......

Do you have any secrets you want to share with the few of us reading this? We won't say anything....promise!
I have to crack my hips every single morning, which is kind of gross to some people but I can't help it. I am also extremely double-jointed. I can basically jump rope with my arms and do all sorts of crazy tricks.
......

Are there any words of wisdom you'd like to pass along to us?
Live your life with no fear. Be courageous, have faith in yourself and love life! Don't let anyone stop you or dictate your life. Have fun and express yourself.

Did you enjoy answering these questions? On a scale from 1 – 10. 1= I hated it. 10= I really enjoyed it.
10! It was such a great mix of insightful and fun questions.

....

About Teiler

Jett-Set Fashion- http://www.jettsetfashion.com
FAQTOR Fashion Book- www.faqtorfashion.com
　Billion Dollar Girl- www.imthebilliondollargirl.com

INTERVIEW 12

Rhonda Shear

Personal Information

Full Name:
Rhonda Shear

Age:
58

Location:
St. Petersburg, FL

Relationship Status:

Married
Number of Children:
2 Step Children, 3 Grandchildren

Profession:
Actress/Comedian/Designer

Educational Background:
Loyola – Bachelors in Communications

Honors & Awards:
Recent:
Winner of 2012 Ernst & Young Retail and Consumer Products Category, Florida

Winner of HerRoom.com "Undies Awards" 2011 & 2012 for Best Leisure Bra

Winner of HerRoom.com "Undie Awards" 2012 for Select Hi-Cut Brief

Winner of "Best Female Presenter" 2011 Moxie Awards by ERA

Winner with Ahh Bra for Best Long Form Infomercial 2012 Moxie Awards by ERA

Winner of 2012 Enterprising Women Award

Winner of 2012 Best Product Award at HSN

3rd Place Winner of 2012 WPO's of Top 50 Fastest Growing Women Led
Companies

Winner of Treasure Coast International Film Festival Visionary Award

3rd Place Winner in 2012 Stevie Awards as Most Innovative Company of the Year
Winner of 2012 Gulf Coast Business Review Entrepreneur of the Year

Winner of Tampa Bay Business Journal's Businesswoman of the Year 2012: Entrepreneur of the Year

Finalist 2012 Women in Business Stevie Awards

Past:
Miss Louisiana USA
Miss Louisiana World
Miss Hollywood
Miss LA Press Club
Miss Golden Globes
Best B-Movie Actress (Prison A Go-Go)
....

General Questions

What are you known for professionally?
Many people remember me from my years in Hollywood appearing on shows, on stage as a stand-up comedian and as the Friday night hostess of USA: Up All Night. Others know me from my line of intimate apparel, Rhonda Shear Intimates, now sold in over 30 countries and on shopping channels including HSN, QVC:UK/Germany/Italy, TSC: Canada, and many more. My infomercial on the Original, Authentic Ahh Bra sold over 30 million units worldwide!
......

Tell us about how you got into your line of work.
I took my entertainment background and designed what I couldn't find in the intimate apparel market. The line was

picked up by HSN and grew from there. I love what I do to make women comfortable and confident with beautiful, quality intimates!

How long have you been doing what you do?
Part of me has always been designing as a New Orleans beauty queen, actress, but I finally launched my vision as a line in 2003.
......

What do you enjoy most about what you do?
I love hearing from women who have found comfort or confidence wearing Rhonda Shear Intimates. For me it is all about enhancing assets and feeling great at any size or age.
......

What are you most passionate about professionally? What most excites you about your work & the contribution you can make?
I am passionate about helping other women! I frequently speak to women's business groups, donate to shelters, and am involved in several local charities including ACS: Making Strides and Pace School for Girls.
......

What's the single most important reason for your success?
Determination! I have heard people tell me I can't do something time and time again, and that makes me even more driven to do it. I keep my blinders on in business and design from my needs and those of my customers instead of looking to other brands for inspiration.
......

What do you consider to be your greatest achievement?
I would say starting a successful business and finding love later in life.
......

How do you think women have changed over the years? Regarding business, sports and fitness.
I think women are amazing! We work hard, play hard, nurture families and relationships, and help each other. Women are more educated and active in business than ever before and I think it is great!
……

Do you think women are competitive with each other? Why? Regarding business, sports and fitness.
Yes, some women are very competitive, but so many raise each other up too. I think you hear women thanking those around them when they succeed. I love to see women succeed in reaching their goals whatever they may be!
……

What memorable competitions come to mind in your career?
I won dozens of beauty queen titles growing up and competed throughout my Hollywood career for parts on shows and in films and now I compete with other brands worldwide. My trick is to catch attention, then show them my talent. You have to be memorable to be remembered in a sea of talent.
……

What is the number one thing you like best about being into fitness?
I work out to feel good. For me it isn't about dress sizes anymore, I just want to be comfortable and healthy.
……

Is there anything wrong with wanting to portray women athletes, actors, etc as feminine and physically attractive?
Interesting question… I think women want to look good without being objectified.
……

How do you deal with cravings for junk foods, sweets and salty food?
Chips are my weakness... I try to keep healthy options on hand instead of the naughty stuff.
......

Health & Fitness Questions

What sports do you participated in for fun?
I love dancing! I also enjoy yoga – I even used to do mime!
......

How long have you been playing those sports?
I have been a dancer since childhood, and was athletic growing up as the "Shape Spa" girl in New Orleans – I was even on the cover of Muscle & Fitness years ago.
......

What got you started in that sport?
Competing in pageants really got me going as a dancer.
......

What is your biggest accomplishment in your sports? Include fun sports and any athletic career.
I have not competed professionally in athletics but definitely interviewed a ton of amazing athletes!
......

How do you motivate yourself and stay motivated?
Staying motivated can be tough as I have gotten older, but it is so important to continue to take care of your health. I plan on staying in business and continuing to start new projects, and to do those things well, I have to take care of myself!
......

What is the most challenging thing you deal with about consistently staying in top shape?
I have been every size between a 2 and a 12 and honestly as a woman my body is constantly changing. The toughest thing may be to mentally accept those changes and adjust.
......

Please describe your normal diet. What do you eat in a typical day to stay in shape?
I eat what I always have, but try to eat smaller portions, drink more water, and drink less of other things.
......

What type of exercises do you include in your routine to stay in shape?
My trainer pushes me to work more by incorporating exercises that I enjoy, changing up our routine and encouraging me to keep going.
......

A total beginner is about 35 pounds overweight. She doesn't really know where to start. What tips can you give her to follow the right track?
She needs to know that it takes hard work, and doesn't happen overnight. Stick with it and maybe find a friend to help you stay motivated!
......

What tips do you recommend for eating out at restaurants to make sure we don't gain too much weight/fat?
Drink less... Eat in when you can, and don't obsess over every little calorie; just know that tomorrow you may want to push a little harder.
......

What exercises do you recommend for getting a bigger, rounder and fuller butt?
I have always been a curvy girl, and have actually even created some intimates designed to lift and shape the derriere. You can't change your body type totally-its genetics, but you can do squats and lunges to tone up and shape the booty.
……

What are your top tips for losing unwanted body fat? Specific exercises, diet advice, etc.
Whatever you do you have to stay hydrated and get the sweat pumping and heart rate up to lose a lot. In the meantime, dress for your shape! Check out shaping apparel, shapewear, and flattering silhouettes for your body now.
……

What are your top tips for improving breasts lift and shape? Specific exercises, diet advice, etc.
Wear the correct size and shape of bra, try sleeping in a bra, and work the muscles that tone that area. My "girls" are plenty big, but many women just don't have as much breast tissue. I believe any shape is beautiful, and you shouldn't force your body to be something it isn't. Often when women lose weight it is from the breasts and derriere first as these tissues are made largely of fat.
……

What are your top tips for staying motivated on a fitness plan?
Find a buddy who motivates you whether it is a trainer, lover, or friend, it's a lot harder to cancel a workout if isn't just you it affects.
……

What is your training routine like? Please include a few details.
I switch up the routine to target different areas and keep it interesting.

......

What is the best way to get started in your industry?
I approached it in the same way I do any endeavour – catch their attention and show them my talent. You can be super-hot and unknown if you don't get out there, take advice and adjust to meet clients' needs.
......

What is the best way towards becoming a personal trainer?
I have never been a personal trainer, but love working with them! Have a positive personality, be in it to help people and set realistic goals and schedules for each of your clients. Not all trainees are looking for the same things or able to work at the same pace.
......

What things do you currently do in your training that is key to your success?
I just want to be comfortable and feel good. I know I won't be a size 2 again but I can still look good at any age or shape.
......

Business Questions

Tell us about your first entrepreneurial experience as a kid or older.
I have always been a creative soul and wanted to do things differently. I broke the mold with my approach to many projects.
......

What is the most difficult part of starting your business?

Getting started and pacing projects can be hard for me – I want to do it all... now!
……

How have your entrepreneurial motivations changed since you first started?
I have realised that I have to stay true to my vision and really believe in everything I put out there with my name on it. If I wouldn't wear it- I won't produce it!
……

What do you consider to be success as a business owner or entrepreneur?
Success isn't all about the awards, it is more about having a team that gets it done and allows for growth. You have to keep at it... who know what you could accomplish if you don't give it your all?
……

What's your least favorite part about being a business owner or entrepreneur?
I am not a numbers person. I luckily have a husband/business partner who is very savvy with that part of the business which leaves me free to do what I love- create!
……

What's the biggest thing you struggle with as a business owner or entrepreneur?
I have struggled with pacing new projects. It is easy to get excited and want to go a million directions at once, but it is important to focus on what you know works and test other things in small quantities to see what new ideas will work.
……

How do you think running a business or being an entrepreneur has made you a better person?
I have learned a lot about people, about an industry I came into knowing very little about, and about giving back.

......

How did you arrive at running this business? What path brought you here?
So many things I learned from costumers and wardrobe stylists in Hollywood have inspired my designs. That and my own ever-changing body have helped drive my line.

What was the most difficult part of starting your business?
I had to invest a lot to get started, but if I can't believe in myself, how can I expect anyone to? It worked out and the business has seen a lot of growth and success since then!
......

What do you do on a daily basis to grow as a person/business person/entrepreneur?
I take time to get to know my team and discover their talents. I believe in having the right people in the right positions leads to a happier, more productive work place.
......

What's unique about the service that you provide?
Intimate apparel is very personal. Every great outfit starts with the perfect undergarment and I want women to look and feel great at any size and age.
......

What entrepreneurial hacks have you developed to stay focused and productive in your day-to-day?
Find a great team that you trust to bring your vision to life. As a business grows it is nearly impossible to do everything yourself and it is really important to take a step back and look at the big picture.
......

Do you have any of your own branded products? If so, what are they?
Visit the new www.RhondaShear.com to view all the latest!

......

Mixed Questions

What would be your ultimate achievement in any area of your life?
Finding love and creating a successful business later in life.
......

Who has been the biggest influence on your life? What lessons did that person teach you?
My mother always pushed me to be better, dress better, and never take no for an answer!
......

Where do you draw your inspiration from?
Every experience can be inspiring and even small moments can become big ideas!
......

Made any mistakes that helped or hurt you in a way that you would like to share?
Mistakes happen in life; it is what you do next and how you learn from them that matters!
......

What were the most difficult decisions you had to make during your lifetime? Why?
Making moves. Moving to LA changed my life in showbiz and moving away from LA allowed me to grow as a business owner.
......

If you could paint a picture of any scenery you've seen before, what would you paint?

Nothing is more calming than looking out over the water!
......

What are some goals you are still trying to accomplish?
I'm looking forward to writing a book and branching into fragrance and cosmetics!
......

What are the most important lessons you've learned in life?
I've learned to keep my blinders on and do what feels right, for me.
......

How do you set your goals?
I make a decision and act on it... Put a stake in it and make it happen!
......

What else would you do if you weren't in your current line of work?
I would probably still be in LA acting and preforming stand-up.
......

What philosophy do you live your life by?
Live, love, work, and play hard!
......

If you had the opportunity to get a message across to a large group of people what would your message be?
Be who you are, not who you think others want you to be.
......

Where do you see yourself in 5 years?
Right here in Florida, working away at new projects!
......

What are you passionate about personally? What do you really enjoy? What can't you stop talking about?
I always love helping women and children! Both personally and through business I just love to see people succeed!
......

What is your favorite type of music?
Music you can dance to!
......

Describe your parents, what are they like?
Hard working, driven people.
......

What things do you find yourself doing that you said you'd never do?
Going to bed occasionally before 2am.
......

What are some qualities that you value in a person?
Kindness, intelligence, honesty and generosity.
......

Where did you grow up and what was it like?
I grew up in New Orleans and it was fabulous!
......

What do you enjoy doing on a Sunday afternoon?
Hanging out with my 4 dogs and relaxing at the house, or taking the boat out!
......

You are stranded in the Amazon rain forest. What 3 items would you want to have with you and why?
My Ahh Bra, a phone that can reach the nearest rescue helicopter, and some bug spray I guess.
......

What personality traits in your mind are best suited for your job, career, etc?
Humour, drive, and creativity.
......

What is your favorite drink?
What's the occasion?
......

What is your favorite color?
I'm really into purple these days.
What would be impossible for you to give up?
My dogs, they make me so happy!
......

What activities did you enjoy in school?
Dancing and teasing boys.
......

What is one of your favorite quotes?
Behind every great woman, is a great behind!
......

Besides money, what are your favorite ways to compensate people?
Goodies! I love sharing my product with family and friends!
......

When was the last time you tried something new?
I am always trying new things.
......

What is one thing you are not?
Patient – I like things to happen fast!
......

Do you think crying is a sign of weakness or strength?
I think it is a sign of crying... depends on the situation.

......

What makes you angry?
Copycats.
......

What makes you laugh?
Life.
......

Is it possible to lie without saying a word? How?
Yep- lies of omission, right?
What's something you check daily?
My health; I'm a hypochondriac.
......

Are you an emotional person?
It depends as a comedian I can keep it together in the toughest crowd but I feel very deeply about those I love.
......

If you could choose to be born with a particular natural skill what skill would it be?
Singing! I love to dance, but was never a very good singer.
......

Did you enjoy answering these questions? On a scale from 1 – 10. 1= I hated it. 10= I really enjoyed it.
That was a lot of questions...

....

About Rhonda

Rhonda Shear has been breaking the mold since her beginnings as a New Orleans beauty queen, during her brief stint in politics, as Hollywood actress/sex symbol, touring as a stand-up comedienne, and now as the entrepreneur behind Rhonda Shear Intimates and the Ahh Bra!

After appearing on countless shows and shoots, in films and hosting USA: Up All Night for over 450 episodes, Rhonda knows all about costuming, enhancing her own assets, and capturing the attention of audiences around the world.

She uses this experience along with her own ever changing body as inspiration for her award winning line of intimates, sleepwear, shapewear and apparel. She has always said about her curves:
"I'm a good girl, trapped in a bad girl's body!"

Rhonda encourages women to find an Ahh Moment by embracing curves and expecting more from their lingerie drawers! She prides herself in personally designing and selling quality, comfort, fit, and color in a wide variety of intimate apparel solutions sized from XS to 3X.
"Behind every great woman is a great behind!"

Building on Rhonda Shear Intimates' international acclaim Rhonda plans to launch a new line of fragrance & beauty products, expand Rhonda Shear Intimates' presence in retail, and even write a book within the next year!

Websites:
www.RhondaShear.com
http://www.ShearEnterprises.com

Media inquiries please contact:

MarieCrane@sheatenterprises.com

Sales inquiries please contact:
Sales@shearenterprises.com
GlobalSales@shearenterprises.com

INTERVIEW 13
Sherry Ann Boudreau

Personal Information

Full Name:
Sherry Ann Boudreau

Age:
45

Location:
Vancouver, BC

Relationship Status:
Married

Number of Children:
Four

Profession:
Sheriff/Personal Trainer/Group Fitness Instructor

Educational Background:
Cosmetology Degree / Grade 12 Graduate / Justice Institute of BC Sheriff Recruit Graduate

Honors & Awards:
2003CNBF Fitness Champion, 2003 Ms Exercise World, 2005 BC Fitness Champion, 2010 GNC North American Fitness Champion

Certifications:
BCRPA Certified Personal Trainer, BCRPA Certified SFL Group Fitness, Zone Certified Meal Planner, DotFit Certified Coach, IFBB Fitness Pro
....

General Questions

What are you known for professionally?
Elite Trainer/IFBB Fitness Pro.
......

Tell us about how you got into your line of work.
I started teaching group fitness and competing in Amateur fitness shows and moms would often ask me how they too can look as fit as me.
......

How long have you been doing what you do?

Since 1994.
......

What do you enjoy most about what you do?
Helping others get fit ,healthy and happy.
......

What are you most passionate about professionally? What most excites you about your work & the contribution you can make?
Giving people the tools to shape their bodies and helping them to make healthy eating choices while maintaining balance.
......

What's the single most important reason for your success?
I am passionate about my teachings and don't always help for money.
......

What do you consider to be your greatest achievement?
I helped a husband and wife lose over 100 pounds together and kept it off. Now the husband is pursuing a career in Personal training. It so wonderful to see them work out together and help others around them do the same.
......

How do you think women have changed over the years? Regarding business, sports and fitness.
Women are much more involved in the business world. There are increasing numbers of working moms that have personal training businesses out of their home while still managing to raise their children and take care of their homes. As a matter of fact, they seem to be bringing in the same amount of monies in half the amount of time. Professional sports and personal training are becoming a money making career.
......

Do you think women are competitive with each other? Why? Regarding business, sports and fitness.
Not that I have witnessed. Fit moms that I have met seem to really support each other and share information on blogs, meetings or at events.
......

What memorable competitions come to mind in your career?
Ms Exercise World was my first pro event and I went in hoping to just place in top 5, never expected to walk away the winner.
......

What is the number one thing you like best about being into fitness?
It keeps people guessing your age.
......

Is there anything wrong with wanting to portray women athletes, actors, etc as feminine and physically attractive?
No, I think it's important to show other woman that you can be both strong a sexy in a very classy and fit way.
......

How do you deal with cravings for junk foods, sweets and salty food?
I always have a cheat meal once per week to stave off any cravings that build up during the week. Most of the time my diet is quite balanced so I don't often crave junk foods.
......

Describe a typical day for you, starting from the moment you wake up in the morning.
Wake up eat breakfast then go to work. After work I go to the gym and work out. I usually teach a class or train a client or

two. Weekends I get up and do a work out and then spend the day with my family, During completion season I add a morning cardio and practise my routine on weekends.
......

Health & Fitness Questions

What sports do you participated in for fun?
None.
......

How do you motivate yourself and stay motivated?
I keep a food/workout journal and take monthly pictures. I have a trainer who specializes in training Pro Fitness Girls so he keeps me on track.
......

What are some of the main foods you would include in your shopping list to maintain a lean and muscular physique?
Chicken Breast, Tilapia, Tuna, Flank Steak, Quinoa, Yams, Asparagus, Leafy Lettuce, Oatmeal, Egg Whites and Almonds.
......

What is the most challenging thing you deal with about consistently staying in top shape?
Age! Being in your forties can be a struggle against imbalanced hormones.
......

Please describe your normal diet. What do you eat in a typical day to stay in shape?
Breakfast: Oats, Egg Whites.
Snacks: Protein Shake, Almonds.
Lunch: Flank, Yams, Asparagus.
Snacks: Protein Shake, Almonds.
Dinner: Chicken Breast or Tilapia, Quinoa and Salad.
......

What type of exercises do you include in your routine to stay in shape?
Split Body workouts lifting heavy during off season and lifting to failure lighter weights during contest prep.
……

A total beginner is about 35 pounds overweight. She doesn't really know where to start. What tips can you give her to follow the right track?
Three to Four Days of week of 30 minute cardio sessions followed by 30 minutes of Weights
Eat every two to three hours, 5- 6 small meals consisting of lean meats, greens, complex carbs and healthy fats.
……

What tips do you recommend for eating out at restaurants to make sure we don't gain too much weight/fat?
Design your own plate. Most restaurants allow you to ask for foods separately.
……

What exercises do you recommend for getting a bigger, rounder and fuller butt?
Dead lifts, steps ups, lunges and squats.
……

What are your top tips for developing toned and defined arms? Specific exercises, diet advice, etc.
Push ups, Triceps dips super setting with Dumb bell arm exercises like curls and kickbacks.
……

What are your top tips for gaining lean muscle mass? Specific exercises, diet advice, etc.
Hire a nutritionist to design a diet based on your own needs and body composition.
……

What are your top tips for staying motivated on a fitness plan?
Day to day and documentation.
......

What is your training routine like? Please include a few details.
Mon to Fri 1/2 hour of weights followed by 45 minutes of cardio.
......

What is the best way to get started in your industry?
Start competing in amateur bikini shows.
......

What is the best way towards becoming a personal trainer?
Start off as a group fitness instructor so that you can build a clientele from the participants that come to your classes.
......

Have you suffered any injuries? What injuries?
Yes, I was rear ended a year ago while sitting a stop light. I was sitting in an awkward twisted position when a girl hit me doing about 40 km. It pulled all my muscles on the left side of my neck and back. I have been doing rehab since then but find my age is not allowing me to heal as fast as I would have in my twenties. I still suffer headaches and a bit of muscle imbalance but I never let those ailments get in my way. I still train but maybe not lift as heavy as the past.
......

What things do you currently do in your training that is key to your success?
Group training is where it's at these days. I always send out work outs and meal plans at the beginning of each season to keep my clients motivated.
......

Isn't it hard to stay fit? How do you manage that?!
Staying fit is a priority without thought. There are so many health benefits that keep me going day to day. I plan on being around to meet my great grandchildren.
......

Mixed Questions

What would be your ultimate achievement in any area of your life?
Raising 4 healthy great children with good morals and respect for everyone.
......

If you could be any character in fiction, who would you be?
Wonder Woman, strong confident happy and healthy! A role model to all ages.
......

What things do you believe differentiates you from your contemporaries?
I believe in Karma and I live my life every day being true to myself and others.
......

Who has been the biggest influence on your life? What lessons did that person teach you?
My step father was my biggest influence. He instilled in me honesty, integrity and respect.
......

Do you have a saying or motto that you live your life by?
Start today tomorrow never comes.
......

Where do you draw your inspiration from?

Fit Moms.
......

If you could paint a picture of any scenery you've seen before, what would you paint?
A white sandy beach with a blue ocean.
......

What are the most important lessons you've learned in life?
Think before you speak.
......

What are you proudest of in your life?
My children.
......

How do you set your goals?
One day at a time.
......

What else would you do if you weren't in your current line of work?
Own my own Group Fitness Studio.
......

What are your religious beliefs/spiritual beliefs?
Believe in God.
......

Do you believe in the Law of Attraction?
Absolutely.
......

What is your diet like?
90 % Clean.
......

What's your favorite food?

Hamburger.
......

What would we find in your refrigerator right now?
Egg Whites, Chicken, Quinoa and a whole lot of lettuce.
......

If you had the opportunity to get a message across to a large group of people what would your message be?
Treat others as would want to be treated and keep smiling.
......

Where do you see yourself in 5 years?
Vancouver Island.
......

What books do you like to read?
I don't read my mind is too busy to concentrate.
......

What is your favorite type of music?
I love the 70' and 80's but Techno works too.
......

Describe your parents, what are they like?
Irresponsible.
......

What were your dreams as a child and did you achieve any of them?
Always wanted to be a hairdresser and I did achieve that.
......

What are some qualities that you value in a person?
Blunt and honest.
......

Where did you grow up and what was it like?

Foster Care and it was not too memorable.
......

Name 5 of your favorite movies.
Blade, Twilight Series, 40 year old Virgin, Forgetting Sarah Marshall, Wizard of Oz.
......

What TV shows do you like?
Cougar Town and Rules of Engagement.
......

What do you enjoy doing on a Sunday afternoon?
Hanging out with my family watching movies.
......

You are stranded in the Amazon rain forest. What 3 items would you want to have with you and why?
Lip Gloss, Scrunchie for hair and my hoodie.
......

What personality traits in your mind are best suited for your job, career, etc?
Confident, easy to get along with but stern.
......

What is your favorite drink?
Margarita.
......

What is your favorite color?
Red.
......

Name a movie that touched you in some way.
Notebook.
......

When in life have you felt most alone? Why?
As a child, my parents separated and neither wanted the responsibility of children.
......

Why would someone not want to work with you?
Very hyper and talk a lot.
......

What activities did you enjoy in school?
P.E. and English.
......

What kind of child were you?
Social Butterfly and very hyper.
......

If you could be a superhero, what would you want your superpowers to be?
I would like to be incredibly strong.
......

How do you want to be remembered?
As always being happy and smiling.
......

We all have vices, what are yours?
Stubborn.
......

What is one of your favorite quotes?
Keep Smiling.
......

What chore do you absolutely hate doing?
Laundry.
......

What is your best feature?
Eyes.
......

What was the last experience that made you a stronger person?
Sheriff Recruit Academy.
......

What makes you uncomfortable, besides these questions?
Conflict.
......

If you could change something physical about yourself, what would it be and why?
Thicker and longer hair.
......

Besides money, what are your favorite ways to compensate people?
Pass on my high energy and positivity.
......

When was the last time you tried something new?
I just joined a Dragon Boat team. I have never done this before.
......

How would you describe yourself in three words?
Energetic, Kind, Positive.
......

What is one thing you are not?
Affectionate.
......

Do you think crying is a sign of weakness or strength?

Neither, it's cleansing.
......

What makes you angry?
Negative people.
......

What makes you laugh?
Judd Apatow movies.
......

What are you afraid of?
Death.
......

What would be the first thing you would do if today was your last day?
Lock myself inside my home with my family.
......

What's your vision of a perfect society?
Caring and respect.
......

Is it possible to lie without saying a word? How?
Not sure.
......

What's something you check daily?
My weight.
......

Are you an emotional person?
No.
......

What's your own definition of happiness?
Balance.
......

Which famous person would you like to interview and which questions would you ask him/her?
Jennifer Anniston – What is your daily regime?
......

What advice would you give someone who wanted to do what you do?
Get signed up and start today.
......

While you are watching TV in your home a penguin walks through the door wearing a sheriff's hat and badge. What does he say?
Howdy.
......

Did you enjoy answering these questions? On a scale from 1 – 10. 1= I hated it. 10= I really enjoyed it.
8.

....

About Sherry

http://www.sherryboudreau.com

INTERVIEW 14
Nicole Busch

Personal Information

Full Name:
Nicole Busch

Age:
36

Location:
Los Gatos, CA

Relationship Status:
Married

Profession:
Personal Stylist/Image Consultant

Certifications:
Certified Personal Stylist, Certified Personal Trainer

....

General Questions

What are you known for professionally?
I am known for helping women transform their wardrobe, which helps build confidence and give them more self-esteem. I empower women!
......

Tell us about how you got into your line of work.
I had run a boot camp in Columbus Ohio and at the end of my 6-week camp I noticed that the participants were still dressing in their bigger clothes. I decided to have a fashion show using my boot campers. I coordinated clothes, hair and makeup for "models".

It was such a magical moment. I felt so complete. After that I moved to Chicago and worked part time at Bebe to learn the business. One year later my husband and I moved to California. I knew I wanted to merge my three passions- fitness, fashion and helping people. I enlisted in school to become a certified personal stylist and here I am! Nicole Blair Wear was born!
......

How long have you been doing what you do?
3 fabulous years.
......

What do you enjoy most about what you do?
I love the interaction with my clients and the moment when they realize just HOW spectacular they are!
......

What are you most passionate about professionally? What most excites you about your work & the contribution you can make?
Building confidence and self-acceptance. Its one of the best gifts you can give someone! I love meeting a client for the first time and taking them from meek to chic!
......

What's the single most important reason for your success?
I would have to say that I am approachable. It has opened so many doors for me. Also, I am a hard worker.
......

What do you consider to be your greatest achievement?
Being able to practice what I preach and having repeat clients.
......

How do you think women have changed over the years? Regarding business, sports and fitness.
I think women have more on their plates. I think they are more competitive and are more fearless. The down side of that is I feel because they take on so much that they tend to put themselves last. This is where I come in.
......

Do you think women are competitive with each other? Why? Regarding business, sports and fitness.
Yes I do. I'm not really quite sure why. I never knew just how competitive I was until my husband pointed it out (thank you

lol) I think competition can be a great quality but I also believe in lifting women up and supporting them.
......

What memorable competitions come to mind in your career?
I attended an event in New York for Style For Hire. It was for stylists and we had to put together outfits. Being surrounded by so many talented and creative people I knew I had to bring my A game. It forced me to dig deep and rise to the occasion. It was one of the most memorable times in my career.
......

What is the number one thing you like best about being into fitness?
Pushing myself to the limit.
......

Is there anything wrong with wanting to portray women athletes, actors, etc as feminine and physically attractive?
No I don't think so. I personally find the woman's body to be such a beautiful thing and to be able to show it off as both feminine and strong is an honor.
......

How do you deal with cravings for junk foods, sweets and salty food?
I believe in moderation. If I have a craving for ice cream I eat it, I just make sure that I don't go over board.
......

Describe a typical day for you, starting from the moment you wake up in the morning.
A typical day consists of coffee ASAP! Post to my social media outlets, check email, get a list of my TTD for the day, make a green smoothie, shower, workout, shower again, check in with clients, quick lunch with my husband, and then work. Work

can consist of pulling for a client, personal shopping, cleaning out a clients closet, putting together outfits etc. Then I stop by my office, connect, network, more emails, set up appointments, then dinner and time to connect with my husband.

Health & Fitness Questions

How do you motivate yourself and stay motivated?
Never settle. I remember as a child if I got a good grade my Dad would say good job now try to get better next time. I think I learned early on that I could always do better.
......

What are some of the main foods you would include in your shopping list to maintain a lean and muscular physique?
Spinach, kale, fish, chicken, eggs, sweet potatoes, buffalo, brown rice, acai, blueberries, apples, oatmeal to name a few.
......

What is the most challenging thing you deal with about consistently staying in top shape?
Knowing your sliding scale. It's hard to stay in tiptop shape and socialize and entertain. So I have a sliding scale- it keeps me in check.
......

Please describe your normal diet. What do you eat in a typical day to stay in shape?
Green smoothie in AM (green apple, kale, spinach, cucumber, handful of bananas, parsley, acai), Salad for lunch chicken with some type of protein on organic greens, dinner consists of protein, brown rice and veggies. In between I drink water with lemon, and have a piece of fruit and/or protein bar and greek yogurt.
......

What type of exercises do you include in your routine to stay in shape?
I love to lift. If I could do legs all day long I would. I enjoy squats, lunges, and any type of plyometrics.
......

A total beginner is about 35 pounds overweight. She doesn't really know where to start. What tips can you give her to follow the right track?
As long as she has no ailments-I believe in walking on a consistent basis. I also think it's important to have clients add things to their diet vs. cutting out. For instance I encourage my clients to get more veggies. Eat your veggies and protein first then eat your "snack or junk food" This is a different approach but I have found it works.

If I say never eat pizza again, then my client is going to want pizza. But if that client typically eats 2 slices and instead they have a salad with veggies and protein then they may only eat ½-1 slice. They don't feel deprived. Over the next few weeks they will see a change and slowly take those fattening foods out of their diet.
......

What tips do you recommend for eating out at restaurants to make sure we don't gain too much weight/fat?
Ask to have your meal grilled no butter and have them box up half of your meal BEFORE they bring it to the table.
......

What exercises do you recommend for getting a bigger, rounder and fuller butt?
Lunges and squats. I love jump squats. It's a great way to lift your tush. Plyometrics.
......

What are your top tips for developing toned and defined arms? Specific exercises, diet advice, etc.
Eat clean, low fat, low sugar. Triceps dips, bicep curls (try different angles).
......

What are your top tips for losing unwanted body fat? Specific exercises, diet advice, etc.
Up your cardio and try to get in as much lean protein and fresh veggies as you can. Eat your complex carbohydrates before 2pm and stay active.
......

Business Questions

What is the most difficult part of starting your business?
Not knowing where to begin or having someone to bounce ideas off of. It really meant having faith in myself.
......

How have your entrepreneurial motivations changed since you first started?
I look at the big picture. I realize how networking is so important and I want to keep challenging myself.
......

What do you consider to be success as a business owner or entrepreneur?
Clients who have achieved success based on my work, personal growth and a booming business.
......

What's your least favorite part about being a business owner or entrepreneur?
Not having someone to bounce ideas off of internally.
......

What's the biggest thing you struggle with as a business owner or entrepreneur?
Turning my brain off. I feel there is always something to do and I would work 24/7 if I could. Trying to find that balance has been difficult.
......

How do you think running a business or being an entrepreneur has made you a better person?
It has made me stronger and more mature. I see the value and have more respect for businesses and their owners.
......

What do you do on a daily basis to grow as a person/business person/entrepreneur?
Personally I try everyday to be a better person, to give more, love more and see the positive in every situation!
As a business, I try to focus on networking and connecting people. To stay cutting edge, grow my business and remain grounded.
......

What's unique about the service that you provide?
Typically people hire me to help them with clothes, but really it is SO much more than that. I look at my clients' wardrobe and how they dress as a painting. If you have ever gone to an art gallery and looked at an artists work, you are interrupting what that artist is saying. They are putting their thoughts, ideas and love into this painting. The same rules apply when dressing a client. I am HELPING them tell their story to the world through clothes. I teach self-expression and allow my client to feel comfortable enough to express just who they are.
......

What entrepreneurial hacks have you developed to stay focused and productive in your day-to-day?
Early on I worked from home and would turn on my TV hours later I was still watching it. So I decided to put a sticky note on my TV with the initials NBW (Nicole Blair Wear). Any time I wanted to turn it on it would reinforce that if I truly wanted to be successful wasting hours in front of the TV would not help. Another hiccup I found was getting lost on Facebook. So I would set a timer and allow 15 minute breaks throughout my day to play however I liked be it TV, Facebook, chat with a friend then it was back to work.
......

Do you have any of your own branded products? If so, what are they?
Not yet but that is in my future!
......

Mixed Questions

What would be your ultimate achievement in any area of your life?
To have a successful business, marriage, friendships, give back (pay it forward) and enjoy life all while doing what I love.
......

If you could be any character in fiction, who would you be?
I think in the past I would have said Julia Roberts from pretty woman (minus the prostitution part) in some ways it was the modern day fairy tale, rags to riches theme. Now after owning my business I'd say Wonder Woman. She was strong, powerful, fearless, inspiring and defined herself. I remember

as a little girl wanting to be her! (I guess some things never change).
......

At present, what is your biggest challenge, and what are you doing to manage this challenge?
I am working on a project very near and dear to me, stay tuned. Finding the time and motivation to take on this project has been hard. However, I just moved into office space and I am looking forward to uninterrupted time to spend on this project.
......

What things do you believe differentiates you from your contemporaries?
Great question! My gift for gab. As you can see I have quite the sense of humor. Which I think helps set me apart. I believe in finding the positive in every situation AND humor in any situation! Life is what we make of it- lets have fun, look and FEEL great and laugh.
......

Have you ever experienced a breakthrough, and if so, what led to it?
Personally and professionally I have. I was introduced to a life coach and have been working with her for a little over a year and a half. She helped me "get out of my own way" and to recognize when I start to "sabotage" myself. This has been eye opening to me and I can see when I am fearful, this comes into play. Now I can recognize this behavior and ask myself what is really going on!
......

Who has been the biggest influence on your life? What lessons did that person teach you?
I have been fortunate to have 3. My grandmother, mother and father. As a child I spent a lot of time with my grandmother.

She cooked, cleaned, took care of my grandfather and was an overall inspiration.

My father worked hard, played hard and climbed the corporate ladder. He introduced me to the finer things in life, taught me to work hard and strive for this.

My mother definitely influenced me the most. She was a single parent, worked hard and yet always had time for us kids. Family was a priority for her. She managed to work 12-hour shifts, pick me up and take me to gymnastics, be the mother and father of the household all the while enforcing rules and loving me unconditionally. My mother is a strong woman who never gave up and is still to this day my biggest cheerleader.
......

Do you have a saying or motto that you live your life by?
Several. "A woman is like a tea bag; you never know how strong it is until it's in hot water." –Eleanor Roosevelt
And my all time favorite- "Everything happens for a reason!"
......

Where do you draw your inspiration from?
My gut. I go by what "feels" right to me.
......

Made any mistakes that helped or hurt you in a way that you would like to share?
I used to think that I made a ton of mistakes, now I view it as it's all a part of my journey and has led to the next chapter in my life.
......

What were your biggest personal battles and how did you confront them?

I really struggled in school. I have always had a hard time reading and retaining. I later found out that I am dyslexic and have ADD.
My junior year of High School I dropped out, I was struggling so much. My Mom sat me down and said you have to get your GED or go back to high school you will not sit at home and live off of me. You will get a job and pay rent until you figure out what you want to do. I realized as much as I struggled I couldn't quit.

I went and received my GED, worked full time and entered cosmetology school. I later graduated the top of my class. Now I look back on that "mistake" and realize it was part of the plan. I'm where I am today because of these battles. I had a very difficult time in styling school, but I knew just how bad I wanted it. I made arrangements with my teacher, studied as best as I knew how and never gave up!
......

What are some goals you are still trying to accomplish?
Make my brand a household name.
......

What are the most important lessons you've learned in life?
Be kind to people, never burn a bridge- you never know when you may have to cross that bridge again.
......

What are you proudest of in your life?
Starting my own business!
......

How do you set your goals?
I'm great at big picture; I struggle with the smaller ones. I try to connect the dots to see what my next steps are to get to the bigger picture.

......

What else would you do if you weren't in your current line of work?
I think I'd be in real estate. I love homes and the art of negotiating appeals to me.
......

What are your religious beliefs/spiritual beliefs?
I was raised Roman Catholic. I'm intrigued by certain parts of Buddhism. After reading Dalai Lamas book The Art of Happiness I had a new outlook on life. I have a strong faith and relationship with God. I also try to follow the 3 R's
-Respect for self
-Respect for others
-Responsibility for all your actions

Most of all, give love. It's one of the hardest to follow but only good can come of it. If you are angry, hurt, disappointed, jealous give love. If you are giving LOVE it makes it harder to be mad, sad, jealous etc.
......

Do you believe in the Law of Attraction?
YES very much so. I believe what you put out to the universe you get back. Negativity breed's negativity, positivity breeds positivity!
......

What is your diet like?
80% clean 20% cheat ☺
......

What's your favorite food?
Sushi.
......

What would we find in your refrigerator right now?

Eggs, spinach, yogurt, milk, creamer, left overs.
……

If you had the opportunity to get a message across to a large group of people what would your message be?
Pay It Forward!! It's good for your soul.
……

Where do you see yourself in 5 years?
In 5 years I see myself living in my dream house, visiting my family, managing a booming bi-coastal business, and becoming a fashion designer.
……

What are you best at?
Connecting with people.
What books do you like to read?
Does Facebook count?
I'm not a big reader but when I do its something inspirational or have a strong message.
……

What is your favorite type of music?
Pop, top hits.
……

Describe your parents, what are they like?
My father was a strong, quiet man, a man of very few words, but when he spoke, you listened.
My mom is loving and particular.
……

What were your dreams as a child and did you achieve any of them?
To marry someone rich and live in a mansion, be happy.
Somewhat. I don't live in a mansion, but I am the happiest I have ever been. My husband is my biggest supporter and I want for nothing.

......

Tell us a time in your life that was a time you'll never forget?
I lost my father when I was 24 years old. He was killed in a plane crash two months after 9/11. It was one of the hardest times in my life. I felt I had lost my "future".
My father climbed the corporate ladder and I didn't get much time with him. When he died, I mourned him but also the life I wanted to have with him.
......

What things do you find yourself doing that you said you'd never do?
I said I would never be a work-a-holic. I am!
......

What are some qualities that you value in a person?
Honesty, loyalty, humor, faith, generosity.
......

Where did you grow up and what was it like?
I grew up In Queens, NY. It was amazing! I had such a great childhood.
......

Name 5 of your favorite movies.
Pay It Forward, Pretty Woman, Bridesmaids, Hang Over and Ever After (the one starring Drew Barrymore).
......

What TV shows do you like?
Seinfeld, The Office, Modern Family, and I hate to admit it but any and all Housewives of _____.
......

What do you enjoy doing on a Sunday afternoon?

Lying on my couch, watching a movie with my husband, snuggled in my robe, surrounded by fresh cut flowers, candles burning and a clean house! Doesn't get better than that!
......

You are stranded in the Amazon rain forest. What 3 items would you want to have with you and why?
A hammock, music, and my friends & family to share in this moment. (But I get dibs on the hammock).
......

Is there anything in particular that you wish you could do over? What is it?
I started to answer this by saying that I wish I could have one vacation with my Dad, but the truth is, things happen for a reason. This is my life and I'm exactly where I'm supposed to be.
......

What personality traits in your mind are best suited for your job, career, etc?
Someone who is detail oriented, creative, passionate and engaging.
......

What is your favorite drink?
Water flavored with fruit (lemon and mint) and coffee.
......

What is your favorite color?
That changes but at the moment HOT pink.
......

Name a movie that touched you in some way.
Pay It Forward.
......

What would be impossible for you to give up?

Shopping.
......

Why would someone not want to work with you?
I'm very particular and sometimes RAW in my delivery. I'm a perfectionist.
......

What activities did you enjoy in school?
PE and art class.
......

What kind of child were you?
I think a good one. Loving, carefree, independent and a little bratty. I practiced applying makeup on my sisters Annie doll.
......

How do you want to be remembered?
As someone who made a difference in someone's life.
......

We all have vices, what are yours?
Shopping.
......

What is one of your favorite quotes?
Keep your head, heels and standards high.
......

What chore do you absolutely hate doing?
Dusting.
......

What is your best feature?
I've been told my smile. I personally love my nails.
......

What makes you uncomfortable, besides these questions?

People with no boundaries.
......

If you could change something physical about yourself, what would it be and why?
I always wanted long, thick hair.
......

Besides money, what are your favorite ways to compensate people?
Thank you cards and gifts. I love to listen to what someone wants and then surprise them with it. One year for Christmas I bought my brother a gift, he said, " I can't believe you remembered!"
......

When was the last time you tried something new?
This past week. I went and played dodge ball at an indoor trampoline place. My new thing is to try something new once a month.
......

How would you describe yourself in three words?
Funny, Smartass, Glam.
......

What is one thing you are not?
Quiet.
......

Do you think crying is a sign of weakness or strength?
I think it depends on the circumstance, but typically I would categorize it as a way to cleanse yourself.
......

What makes you angry?
Rude people.
......

What makes you laugh?
Pretty much anything.
......

What are you afraid of?
The dark and scary movies.
......

What would be the first thing you would do if today was your last day?
Go see my family.
......

What's your vision of a perfect society?
Everyone is nice and helpful.
......

What's something you check daily?
My phone for the time.
......

Are you an emotional person?
Yes.
......

What's your own definition of happiness?
Inner peace, low stress, carefree.
......

Which famous person would you like to interview and which questions would you ask him/her?
God.
What do you think of this world?
......

If you could choose to be born with a particular natural skill what skill would it be?
To be able to sing and be on key.

......

What advice would you give someone who wanted to do what you do?
Go for it! Follow your dreams, learn from the best and then put your touch on it.
......

While you are watching TV in your home a penguin walks through the door wearing a sheriff's hat and badge. What does he say?
Is this a Fashion Faux pas?
......

Are there any words of wisdom you'd like to pass along to us?
Get out of your own way!
......

Did you enjoy answering these questions? On a scale from 1 – 10. 1= I hated it. 10= I really enjoyed it.
10!

About Nicole

Website: http://www.nicoleblairwear.com
Facebook: www.facebook.com/NicoleBlairWear
twitter: @nicoleblairwear
Pinterest: www.pinterest.com/NicoleBlairWear
instagram: Nicole Blair Wear

INTERVIEW 15

Lori Ann Freemire

Personal Information

Full Name:
Lori Ann Freemire

Age:
50 – but I don't look it!!

Location:
Denver, CO

Relationship Status:

Married 28 years

Number of Children:
3 boys

Profession:
Consultant

Educational Background:
MA from Univ. Of Iowa

Honors & Awards:
Lots!

Certifications:
International Trade
....

General Questions

What are you known for professionally?
Being a business growth resource. Helping people grow their businesses and themselves.
......

Tell us about how you got into your line of work.
I was looking for flexibility while raising my sons.
......

How long have you been doing what you do?
1994
......

What do you enjoy most about what you do?
Helping people in a positive way.

......

What are you most passionate about professionally? What most excites you about your work & the contribution you can make?
I am a generous connector. I look for ways to help others in all of my interactions. My initial motivation is not to monetize each interaction, though that usually comes later should that person truly need assistance. I love seeing the excitement when someone finds what they are looking for, personally and professionally.
......

What's the single most important reason for your success?
I believe in giving generously without expectation of return. I love Seth Godin's book "Linchpin." That's what I am.
......

What do you consider to be your greatest achievement?
My family. My sons are truly blossoming into talented young men who are learning who they are and how they can positively contribute to our society. Oh, yeah, and make a buck! My husband and I have also learned how to successfully operate our business together, capitalizing on each's strengths.
......

How do you think women have changed over the years? Regarding business, sports and fitness.
I don't think women have changed. I think the opportunities, demands, options and choices we make are more varied and play a huge role in who we are today. I would have NEVER trained for a ½ marathon even 10 years ago, but did it last year; am doing my second one this summer.
......

Do you think women are competitive with each other? Why? Regarding business, sports and fitness.
Women are competitive especially in business. I don't see competitiveness in fitness in my circles; I see support and encouragement. As for business, there are too many women who are the Lone Ranger, stepping on others to try to get to some higher level rather than truly working with other women collaboratively.
......

What memorable competitions come to mind in your career?
Field Days in elementary school. Hated them. A positive was crossing the finish line in Moab last year after 13.1 miles.
......

What is the number one thing you like best about being into fitness?
We have to take care of our bodies, minds, and spirits to truly be healthy. I have always struggled with my weight, though people look at me (5'3" and 125 lbs) and assume that I don't have issues. My health history and family history are good, but I want to do all that I can to be the healthiest possible.

I have tendonitis in my knees and a neuroma in one foot, so I take care of those little aches and pains with regular chiro checks and special exercises. Being fit helps me feel better about myself, which in turn helps me perform better in every other area of life. I can give generously when I'm in great shape.
......

Is there anything wrong with wanting to portray women athletes, actors, etc as feminine and physically attractive?
Nope. Though, one of my husband's cousins recently got into body-building. She is an adorable, young women who looks like she's in a man's body.

......

How do you deal with cravings for junk foods, sweets and salty food?
Food choices are just that. Choices we make each day. I try to prepare and eat the healthiest food (I love to cook), but we all need to splurge now and then. My son's 13th b-day dinner was last night, and he and I made this ultra-yummy cake. I will nibble on it now and then!
......

Describe a typical day for you, starting from the moment you wake up in the morning.
During the school year which finished last week, I'm up at 6am. We have coffee and check the news. My son gets up at 6:30 and I make breakfast and his lunch. We head to school at 7:30 so he's there by 8 (traffic varies some days). I'm home by 8:30.

My husband and I will either exercise when Spencer gets home (4-5ish) if the evening is open – we'll run, walk or ride bikes. If we have an evening event, then Mike and I will go ahead and run 4-5 miles. If the weather's bad, we'll do P90X in our basement gym. Love Tony Horton! We work on our clients' projects and on our LifeVantage business throughout the day which requires lots of phone calls and online research. Mike usually picks up our son from school at 3:20.

Our lunch is a sandwich, wrap, soup or salad. My husband has Crohn's disease, so we try to keep gluten to a minimum.

Dinner is a balanced meal with some kind of protein, veggies, whole grain rice or pasta. Our guilty pleasure is dark chocolate-covered blueberries or acai berries.

Evenings can be a family dinner, meeting (International Business Circle, city council, LifeVantage, church small

group), or son's team practice. We love to golf also, so that may be on the agenda if the schedule and weather permit.
......

Health & Fitness Questions

What sports do you participated in for fun?
Running, hiking, cycling, golf.
......

How long have you been playing those sports?
Running – 2 years; hiking – on and off over my life; cycling – seriously in last 2 years; golf – seriously last 12 years.
......

What got you started in that sport?
The challenge; love the out of doors; want to prove "I can do it!"
......

What is your biggest accomplishment in your sports? Include fun sports and any athletic career.
Finishing last year's Moab ½ Marathon in 3 hours.
......

What competitions have you entered? What were the outcomes?
We have participated in MANY 5k runs over the years for fun, but now we run for causes and for personal records. We are doing well, getting better, and raising funds for the Crohn's Colitis Foundation.
......

How do you motivate yourself and stay motivated?

Look in the mirror! I feel better when I have exercised. If I want a burger and fries, I know I have to earn it.
......

What are some of the main foods you would include in your shopping list to maintain a lean and muscular physique?
Turkey, chicken, lots of veggies (luv summer), fruits, nuts, whole grains, eggs, Greek yogurt.
......

What is the most challenging thing you deal with about consistently staying in top shape?
My thighs! As we get older, it does get harder to stay lean.
......

Please describe your normal diet. What do you eat in a typical day to stay in shape?
For breakfast, my husband and I have an Advocare meal replacement shake – mocha, really yummy! Lunch is a salad or soup with small sandwich (turkey, egg, chicken salad). Dinner is a meal of meat, veggies/salad, whole grains.
......

What type of exercises do you include in your routine to stay in shape?
P90X has great exercises for upper body strength. I can do way more push ups than ever before. I do believe it's important to mix it up with varied activities to stay motivated, to keep weight in check and to use different muscle groups.
......

A total beginner is about 35 pounds overweight. She doesn't really know where to start. What tips can you give her to follow the right track?
Start walking 15 minutes/day. It takes 3 weeks to develop a new habit, so just start walking and make sure you have a Fitbit or pedometer to track distance, time, etc. Once you start

moving, then start a food journal to make SMALL changes to diet. I can't believe how many people live on sodas. Also, exercise with a buddy – so much more fun and motivating.
......

What tips do you recommend for eating out at restaurants to make sure we don't gain too much weight/fat?
Most menus have a symbol next to the healthier items. But, I always ask. We have several trips this month. I take my own food and then order a la carte if needed (i.e.: for breakfast, get poached eggs and dry whole wheat toast – butter it yourself); get dressings and sauces on the side.
......

What exercises do you recommend for getting a bigger, rounder and fuller butt?
P90X has some great leg and butt-builder exercises!
......

What are your top tips for developing toned and defined arms? Specific exercises, diet advice, etc.
You have to do some kind of weights, push-ups and pull-ups. Again, I love the P90X series because he shows you how to start out when you can't do full extensions.
......

What are your top tips for losing unwanted body fat? Specific exercises, diet advice, etc.
Make sure you do a variety of exercises with good cardio 3x/week. As for food, the less processed food, the better. Make little changes, not a full makeover at once; you'll fall back easily and quickly.
......

What are your top tips for gaining lean muscle mass? Specific exercises, diet advice, etc.

Same as above, but you have to steadily increase the weight you work out with in order to increase muscle mass.
......

What are your top tips for improving breasts lift and shape? Specific exercises, diet advice, etc.
Nope. Don't try to alter what God gave you. Keep 'em healthy; do your monthly checks; wear the right bra during exercise!
......

What are your top tips for staying motivated on a fitness plan?
I like to register for an event so that I have a firm date in mind for my goal.
......

What is your training routine like? Please include a few details.
Decide on an exercise every day. I am building miles right now, so I have to watch how often I run to minimize injury. Running right how is every other day.
......

What is the best way to get started in your industry?
Talk to other women who are doing it.
......

What is the best way towards becoming a personal trainer?
Get certified. Be connected to a good gym or facility.
......

Have you suffered any injuries? What injuries?
Knee tendonitis; neuroma in my foot.
......

What things do you currently do in your training that is key to your success?
Just do it! Attend trainings with my team on Saturdays; make sure I make exercise a daily priority.
......

Isn't it hard to stay fit? How do you manage that?!
Make the time. I put it on my schedule. Each evening, we look at the next day's events and plan accordingly. Sometimes we will get up at 5 pm to exercise.
......

Business Questions

Tell us about your first entrepreneurial experience as a kid or older.
1994. We had just moved to Kansas City and I had two young sons. I had left a wonderful, international job, and knew no one. I started networking (this is pre-internet!) and met a professor-entrepreneur who would become a mentor. I formed a consulting business with his help and then started working with some of his colleagues on some international projects.
......

What is the most difficult part of starting your business?
Keeping balance between raising my sons, my husband's long hours and working for myself.
......

How have your entrepreneurial motivations changed since you first started?
They haven't. I love the flexibility and independence.
......

What do you consider to be success as a business owner or entrepreneur?

Success is doing what you love and paying the bills!
......

What's your least favorite part about being a business owner or entrepreneur?
Rejection. Every now and then, a potential client whom I truly want to help says "no."
......

What's the biggest thing you struggle with as a business owner or entrepreneur?
Time zone differences can make it challenging when I have to take calls in the evening. I don't like to chase people; these days, it seems as though folks don't follow through.
......

How do you think running a business or being an entrepreneur has made you a better person?
Im more compassionate; I'm home for my kids; I can be a healthier person all the way around.
......

How did you arrive at running this business? What path brought you here?
My husband was raised in an entrepreneurial family; we ran that business until we sold it. I had my consulting business; we purchased another one which we then sold so that we could move to Colorado to be near family. We could never be employees again!
......

What was the most difficult part of starting your business?
Making the decision. We have always funded these ourselves, so we made sure we had sufficient savings for at least a year.
......

What do you do on a daily basis to grow as a person/business person/entrepreneur?
I love to read! I have several blogs that I receive each day (John Maxwell, Seth Godin). I also have books and magazines I read.
......

What's unique about the service that you provide?
We work with existing firms who have some kind of obstacle – succession, no profit or very little, need to shift gears in to another market, etc. We become business advisors and coaches many times. Business owners are many times alone, and need that sounding board. Our clients come to us after we have a solid relationship.
......

What entrepreneurial hacks have you developed to stay focused and productive in your day-to-day?
We each have our own office. Chores around the house are done on "breaks." Love online calendars!
......

Do you have any of your own branded products? If so, what are they?
Nope.
......

Mixed Questions

What would be your ultimate achievement in any area of your life?
I'm a people pleaser who believes nothing happens for no reason. We all are here for a purpose. I want to help others find their purpose.
......

If you could be any character in fiction, who would you be?
I like who I am. I'm already taken.
......

At present, what is your biggest challenge, and what are you doing to manage this challenge?
I get pulled in many directions. I love women's leadership and am getting involved in Denver. I have to watch it and not start getting over-committed!
......

What things do you believe differentiates you from your contemporaries?
My interests do cross over into many arenas. I also have an international business background (I speak Spanish). Not on my resume is my 8 years as a First Lady!
......

Have you ever experienced a breakthrough, and if so, what led to it?
Crisis or challenge always helps us see our necessary choices. Moving to Denver was a huge leap of faith personally and professionally but I knew that God wanted us here. We did it and are blessed beyond imagination!
......

Who has been the biggest influence on your life? What lessons did that person teach you?
A former boss. She was my first real boss after college. She was also the worst boss you could have. I learned how NOT to lead and treat others. During that awful year, I built alliances with other co-workers I didn't think possible. To this day, that was one of the best jobs because of all that I learned. Tears and all!
......

Do you have a saying or motto that you live your life by?
"I can do all things through Christ who strengthens me." Philippians 4.13
......

Where do you draw your inspiration from?
God's Word, the Bible.
......

Made any mistakes that helped or hurt you in a way that you would like to share?
Trust your gut. Sometimes you need to listen to you. Other times, you need to get outside advice.

What were your biggest personal battles and how did you confront them?
During the 90s, we had our two oldest boys who were in school. I believed that we were to have another boy. After 4 miscarriages, one of which involved twins, we did have our third, healthy son, just as I was starting a new business!
......

What were the most difficult decisions you had to make during your lifetime? Why?
Quitting a job I loved, selling a business I loved, trying to have that 3rd baby after losing 5.
......

If you could paint a picture of any scenery you've seen before, what would you paint?
A sunset over the snow-capped mountains.
......

What are some goals you are still trying to accomplish?
I want to grow our LifeVantage business to replace our current business, because we have an awesome team we get to work with!

......

What are the most important lessons you've learned in life?
Don't let other people determine your reactions or attitude.
......

What are you proudest of in your life?
I need only look at my husband and 3 wonderful sons!
......

How do you set your goals?
I set some long-range ones without deadlines, but others I just jot down as I go. Heaven is the main one and to bring as many with me as possible!

What else would you do if you weren't in your current line of work?
I would work for a non-profit related to kids in some way.
......

What are your religious beliefs/spiritual beliefs?
I am a Christian; I have always been active in my churches. My family is Christian, Catholic, Jewish and agnostic, but we all get along.
......

Do you believe in the Law of Attraction?
There are no accidents nor accidental encounters. Some people are meant to be together in some kind of relationship.
......

What is your diet like?
Healthy.
......

What's your favorite food?
Really good, homemade soup. Loved the soups in Ireland.
......

What would we find in your refrigerator right now?
Leftovers from last night's b-day dinner – chicken, ribs, wonderful veggie salad, potatoes, one devilled egg, salad fixings, eggs, milk, healthy salad dressings, b-day cake (a rare sighting!).
……

If you had the opportunity to get a message across to a large group of people what would your message be?
What do you truly want to do? What are you passionate about? How can you DO what you are passionate about? How can you make your place in the world better?
……

Where do you see yourself in 5 years?
Right here in Denver with my 3 boys here, two of them out of college and probably married!
……

What are you best at?
Encouraging others. Though it annoys my sons when I say, "Great shot," when we are golfing!
……

What books do you like to read?
Business, non-fiction.
……

What is your favorite type of music?
Christian contemporary, Josh Grobin.
……

Describe your parents, what are they like?
My parents were way young when they married after knowing each other 6 weeks. They divorced 6 years later. Both are stubborn and very driven. They came from horrible, poor families and have succeeded in bettering their lives. Both are

happily remarried. My dad was a career Marine and then worked for United Airlines as a mechanic for 17 years (he followed his dream). My mom went to nursing school after the divorce and has been a hospice nurse. She's tough but tender-hearted.
......

What were your dreams as a child and did you achieve any of them?
I wanted to be an art teacher. I'm lousy at art, but appreciate it (and own a lot of it) but have been a univ. Instructor. I do enjoy teaching. I also studied music and wanted to be a concert pianist. After 4-5 hours/day in a little room my first semester in college, I resolved that I would make music a hobby, not my life.
......

Tell us a time in your life that was a time you'll never forget?
I had a major bike accident at 13. Concussion, hospital, major facial injuries/scars. I'm a bit leary of mountain biking and very cautious on the bike in general. I did learn that looks aren't everything. Fortunately, many scars did heal and I learned that my community really cared about me.
......

What things do you find yourself doing that you said you'd never do?
Moving back to Denver! We change. Life changes. I love it here again.
......

What are some qualities that you value in a person?
Great attitude, generosity, caring, trust.
......

Where did you grow up and what was it like?

My dad was in the Marines, so we lived in CA, Hawaii, WA, NV, NC, and then Denver by the time I was 6. We spent most of my growing up in Denver, near Co. Springs and then back to Denver after California. My parents divorced when I was 5; I grew up with my dad. I had a horrible step-mother, but I did learn how to be strong from that time living with her. I had great friends in CO, and have been re-connecting with many since moving back. I loved living in the mountains outside Co Spgs while I was in elementary and middle school.
......

Name 5 of your favorite movies.
"Iron Lady," "Napoleon Dynamite," the Bourne movies were great, sweet chick-flicks.
......

What TV shows do you like?
NCIS, the news, Jay Leno if I'm up that late!
......

What do you enjoy doing on a Sunday afternoon?
Being with my family outside.
......

You are stranded in the Amazon rain forest. What 3 items would you want to have with you and why?
Food – to sustain my body; Bible – to sustain all of me; cell phone – to get help!
......

Is there anything in particular that you wish you could do over? What is it?
I wish I had had better self-confidence in high school. I would have tried so many more things. My dysfunctional family was a bit of a mess, I had shut down during conflict.
......

What personality traits in your mind are best suited for your job, career, etc?

Willingness to "put yourself out there" and to take risks. Be outgoing and giving. I'm a shy person, but had to learn how to reach out to others. Today, I cannot be in a group that is not interacting. I'll start conversations.
......

What is your favorite drink?
Cabernet and coffee in a tie!
......

What is your favorite color?
Pink – I'm totally girly! Even my 5-fingers are pink.
......

Name a movie that touched you in some way.
"Iron Lady" – loved seeing who Maggie was, and Meryl did an outstanding job. Wish there were more women who followed in Maggie's steps. She was a great role model.
......

When in life have you felt most alone? Why?
There was a stretch when we had just moved to Iowa to take over my husband's family business following his brother's death. We were under huge stress, the business was dying (he turned it around) and my mother-in-law was not the least bit supportive or giving. I didn't have any friends that year and it was a desert time, but I learned a lot about myself.
......

What would be impossible for you to give up?
My morning coffee! (I owned a coffee shop a dozen years ago).
......

Why would someone not want to work with you?
We all have people we rub the wrong way (sand-paper people). I am deadline driven and want organization and follow-through. People have to be accountable – I'm tough on that sometimes.

······

What activities did you enjoy in school?
Spanish club, band.
······

What kind of child were you?
Quiet, introverted. Went through some tough stuff.
······

If you could be a superhero, what would you want your superpowers to be?
Strength to pick anything up.
······

How do you want to be remembered?
As someone who truly cared about others and took the time to invest in them.
······

We all have vices, what are yours?
I love a great glass of wine and dark chocolate. I have to make sure I only drink one or two.
······

What is one of your favorite quotes?
"'For I know the plans I have for you,' declares the Lord." Jeremiah 29.11
······

What chore do you absolutely hate doing?
Doggie poo duty. I had to clean the cat box while growing up. Hated it. I'll clean toilets any day!
······

What is your best feature?
My smile. Years of orthodontics helped!
······

What was the last experience that made you a stronger person?
Helping a friend through a tough marital issue.
......

What makes you uncomfortable, besides these questions?
Having to confront someone with a difficult question. Had to have a tough chat with my mom last month. Got things into the open, and now there is more trust.
......

If you could change something physical about yourself, what would it be and why?
My legs. I have "sturdy" legs. Wish they were thinner.
......

Besides money, what are your favorite ways to compensate people?
An activity or experience.
......

When was the last time you tried something new?
I'm going to climb a fourteener this month!
......

How would you describe yourself in three words?
Fun, positive, loving.
......

What is one thing you are not?
Negative.
......

Do you think crying is a sign of weakness or strength?
Depends on the context. I cried at my friend's wedding last weekend; I cry when I'm really angry; I once cried in my boss's

office a long time ago – he was very uncomfortable! It's a strength normally, but I know some folks who can't control their emotions whether crying or shouting.
......

What makes you angry?
Mean people.
......

What makes you laugh?
The quick-witted comebacks of my sons!
......

What are you afraid of?
Not finishing. I have lots on my to-do list!
......

What would be the first thing you would do if today was your last day?
Hug my family.
......

What's your vision of a perfect society?
Peace. True care for one another. Joy.
......

Is it possible to lie without saying a word? How?
Body language can shout sometimes. Averting the eyes.
......

What's something you check daily?
Email.
......

Are you an emotional person?
Am I female? Of course! Seriously, if you're not emotional, are you breathing? Real people are emotional.
......

What's your own definition of happiness?
Happiness depends on happenings. I prefer joy which depends on Jesus. He's more reliable.
......

Which famous person would you like to interview and which questions would you ask him/her?
Meryl Streep. She's such an amazing actress. I would like to pick her brain as to who she really is.
......

If you could choose to be born with a particular natural skill what skill would it be?
Be an auditory learner. I have to read and re-read things. I wish I could listen once!
......

What advice would you give someone who wanted to do what you do?
Start keeping a list of everyone you know, tell them what you want to do, and ask them if they can help.
......

While you are watching TV in your home a penguin walks through the door wearing a sheriff's hat and badge. What does he say?
"Howdy, Pardner. I need some deputies. You in?"
......

Do you have any secrets you want to share with the few of us reading this? We won't say anything....promise!
No secrets. Share even though people will criticize or judge you unfairly. Be you. It gets back to what we learned in kindergarten: be nice to everyone.
......

Are there any words of wisdom you'd like to pass along to us?
You are you. No one else can be you. Your responsibility is to yourself and your family, your business, your "others." Consult with those close to you, but the tough decisions are yours. Then, GO FOR IT!
......

Did you enjoy answering these questions? On a scale from 1 – 10. 1= I hated it. 10= I really enjoyed it.
10! Always good to summarize what you do, what you've done and where you are.

··········

About Lori

Website : http://www.missionroi.com

INTERVIEW 16
Madeline Hernandez

Personal Information

Full Name:
Madeline Hernandez

Age:
46

Location:
Meriden, Ct.

Relationship Status:
Separated

Number of Children:

1 boy
Educational Background:
12th grade high school

Honors & Awards:
Preceptor

Certifications:
CNA
....

General Questions

What are you known for professionally?
CNA (elderly patient care), and fitness training.
......

Tell us about how you got into your line of work.
I developed a passion for it growing up and was introduced into it by a colleague.
......

How long have you been doing what you do?
7+ years.
......

What do you enjoy most about what you do?
Obtaining results and assisting others achieve their fitness goals.
......

What are you most passionate about professionally? What most excites you about your work & the contribution you can make?

My passion is helping others reach and exceed in their fitness goals resulting in maximum results within a short period of time.

When I see the look on my trainees face as they approach their workout with me, they know they are in for hard work as I am committed and determined in assisting with their workout needs.

......

What's the single most important reason for your success?

Giving up was never an option for me as I had to learn the hard way when I injured my back and was told I would never be able to walk again? I decided to take my life back and began to take my rehabilitation into my own hands. I learned new methods to exercise and rebuild my fragile body. My desire and drive is what kept me going.

......

What do you consider to be your greatest achievement?

My greatest achievement was the day that I could walk again. It took a long time and hrs of therapy and look at me now. I'm walking and out of my deep depression.

......

How do you think women have changed over the years? Regarding business, sports and fitness.

In business women have many more opportunities, as well as challenges. Mentally, financially and physically women are under a lot more pressure to be "perfect". We have to run the household, work a 40 hour work week, and look beautiful doing it.

In fitness I see more and women competing and older women are becoming the majority. There seems to be a competition with the younger women and the mature woman. Teenagers are now becoming stage ready at an earlier time with the help of gymnastics, track and field and other sporting activities. Back in the 80's sports for women were not encouraged resulting in dismissive attitudes towards exercise and overall health.

As we get older the weight becomes harder to manage and control.
......

Do you think women are competitive with each other? Why? Regarding business, sports and fitness.
Yes women are most definitely in full competitive mode as early as childhood. In business women are not only competing with other women, they are competing against their counterparts to perform equally if not better as well as being expected to manage their household and children's lives.

In sports and fitness it seems as if the appearance becomes more important than agility, strength and overall fitness of the competitor. Women have gone to great lengths to become the best, even if it means hurting their body in the process.
......

What is the number one thing you like best about being into fitness?
Achieving my fitness goals, and proving the doctors wrong when they said I would never walk again.
......

Is there anything wrong with wanting to portray women athletes, actors, etc as feminine and physically attractive?
No, more attention should be given to portraying women athletes as feminine and physically attractive.
......

How do you deal with cravings for junk foods, sweets and salty food?

I'll have my rare moments, but if I do want something, I don't deny myself but portion control is key. If I want to fool my cravings like candy, I'll grab something hard like a carrot and of course water..or have a protein shake
......

Describe a typical day for you, starting from the moment you wake up in the morning.
I wake up early, have breakfast run errands and go about my daily routine; I then have my lunch and get ready to go to the gym to workout. After the gym, I have my dinner and begin to get ready for my evening rest/unwinding.
......

Health & Fitness Questions

What sports do you participated in for fun?
I'll participate in watching a good game of football (NYG) and baseball (NYY) but I love to bowl, kick ball, tennis, softball.
......

How long have you been playing those sports?
15+ years.
......

What got you started in that sport?
I liked to participate in social activities within my community and it became part of my lifestyle.
......

What is your biggest accomplishment in your sports? Include fun sports and any athletic career.
It helped me in my goal of staying in shape, as well as active in my social circle.
......

How do you motivate yourself and stay motivated?
I keep in mind the health benefits and when I see the results of my hard work it helps me to keep going.
......

What are some of the main foods you would include in your shopping list to maintain a lean and muscular physique?
Chicken, turkey, tuna, fish, egg whites, yogurt, cottage cheese, brown rice and vegetables.
......

What is the most challenging thing you deal with about consistently staying in top shape?
Eating every 2-3 hours. It's always the same types of food and maintaining the portions.
......

Please describe your normal diet. What do you eat in a typical day to stay in shape?
I drink a 16oz glass of cold water; I make my breakfast, four egg whites mixed with vegetables and a bowl of oatmeal. I wash that down with a hot cup of green tea.

For lunch I will have a second glass of 16 oz water. Cottage cheese, fresh fruit and tuna fish and hot green tea to wash it down.
At 2:30pm I have a protein shake and go to the gym for approximately one hour with 32 oz of cold water. After my workout I have a protein bar or fresh fruit.

For dinner I start off with 16 oz of water and beans, turkey and hot tea.
As a snack before bedtime I will have a 16 oz green glowing smoothie. Each day it varies meaning I will switch my meals around so I don't get bored of it.
......

What type of exercises do you include in your routine to stay in shape?
Cardio is a must for me, weight training and stretching, resistant bands.
......

A total beginner is about 35 pounds overweight. She doesn't really know where to start. What tips can you give her to follow the right track?
It starts with what you eat and how much you eat. Don't count calories; it is all about portion control. Water is also very important. Make sure you have clearance from your medical provider and discuss all supplements and medications. Start slow and with basic exercises. As you become more active challenge yourself and increase your exercise program.
......

What tips do you recommend for eating out at restaurants to make sure we don't gain too much weight/fat?
Don't believe what you read in the menu, stick to your knowledge of foods you know are healthy. Eliminate add-ons such as croutons, cheese, bacon...(sides) Drink water with lemon instead of alcoholic beverages and sodas.
......

What exercises do you recommend for getting a bigger, rounder and fuller butt?
The queen of all exercises is squats! Ski squats ,squat pulses, stutter step pulls, squat and front kicks, butterfly bridges or hip thrusters, static ski squat marches with weight if desired, side leg raises, stiff legged dead lifts and ,steppers. I have many other butt routines, too many mention.
......

What are your top tips for developing toned and defined arms? Specific exercises, diet advice, etc.

Stand up biceps curls with dbs and preacher curls, hammer curls, lying triceps extensions with dbs or preacher bar, over head rope extensions, db kick backs, dips, etc. I always switch up my arm routine, I would increase weight with low reps, or low weight but increase my reps..my sets varies as well 10-12 for uppers maxs 20 up to 4 sets.

Increase your HITT. You need to make your cardio workouts explosive and you need to put those underworked arms and legs under some full on stress (in a healthy way). In arms you really need to focus on losing fat. It is fat that makes arms look soft and flabby. *Remember, to tone your arms you need to remove as much fat as possible off of your entire body.* One of the best ways to kick this process along is to eat healthy and drink plenty of water.
......

What are your top tips for losing unwanted body fat? Specific exercises, diet advice, etc.
First off I always ask who I help train is their age, height, medical history, and their activity level. I'll have them ask clearance by their physician. The best way to lose any amount of weight is to have a plan in mind losing 1 -2 lbs a week is the maximum weight loss. Set a time frame when you would like to reach your goals, make a realistic goal of how much you would like to reach. For an example, My goal would be 8 lbs to lose within 4 weeks.

I'll divide 8 to the weeks, then multiply it by 1,200 calories for women and men 1,500 then divide it by six small meals per day. Cutting back on calories and smaller meals with help burn more calories then you consume on a daily basis. Exercise should be consistent and drinking plenty of water is essential. I consume ½ my body weight (70 oz. a day).

Avoid high fatty foods, processed foods, carbohydrates, salt and sugar.

Take in high in protein, simple carbs, complex carbs, fibrous carbs, and meal replacements.

Participate in yoga classes, kick boxing, zumba classes, mediation
DO NOT weigh yourself every day, remember muscle weighs more then fat. You will lose water weight first, you will notice clothes will start to feel loose , and there will be a moment where you will a plateau. Don't get discouraged , just amp up your intensity level.
......

What are your top tips for gaining lean muscle mass? Specific exercises, diet advice, etc.
High protein foods and protein shakes and slow digesting foods.
......

What are your top tips for improving breasts lift and shape? Specific exercises, diet advice, etc.
Cable crossovers, flat/incline/decline, flyes, benching and dumbbells .10-12 reps maxs 20 up to 4 sets.
......

What are your top tips for staying motivated on a fitness plan?
I create a timeline with goals that are attainable and as we reach each one, we increase/change up the plan to keep it fresh. Always go into it with a positive attitude!
......

What is your training routine like? Please include a few details.
It varies, every 6-12 weeks it includes 10 minutes of warm up/stretches and 10 minutes of cardio. Depending on the week, I will work out my chest/triceps. Back and biceps, legs and shoulders, I work on my abs twice per week.
......

Have you suffered any injuries? What injuries?
I sprained my left shoulder in one of my workouts. I injured my back while at work.
......

What things do you currently do in your training that is key to your success?
Consistency with my workout routine as well as my diet. Self motivation also plays a factor in my success.
......

Isn't it hard to stay fit? How do you manage that?!
Yes it is, because as we are getting older, our body starts to slow down and break down internally and in some cases we may have limitations due to an illness or medications that can affect our progress but you have to keep a positive attitude maintain your will power and dedication.
......

Mixed Questions

What would be your ultimate achievement in any area of your life?
My ultimate achievement would be to walk out on a fitness stage for the first time!
......

If you could be any character in fiction, who would you be?
I would be wonder woman!
......

At present, what is your biggest challenge, and what are you doing to manage this challenge?

My back injury is my biggest challenge. I maintain a routine to strengthen my back and I also incorporate core training.
......

What things do you believe differentiates you from your contemporaries?
My dedication to keep myself healthy.
......

Have you ever experienced a breakthrough, and if so, what led to it?
Oh yes! It took me approximately four years to be able to perform squats. Due to nerve damage from my back injury. I went into one of the back rooms in my gym and asked a trainer to spot me, I used a straight bar and as he guided me down, I went down as far as I could with no problems. I then continued to add some light weights and increased the tension. I cried from the accomplishment and felt a sense of pride and gratitude for myself as well as my partners.
......

Who has been the biggest influence on your life? What lessons did that person teach you?
The biggest influence in my life has been Iris Kyle. She inspired me by her determination, dedication and fighting spirit. She taught me to never give up your dream, fight for what you want, and go after your goals in life.
......

Do you have a saying or motto that you live your life by?
Don't talk about it, be about it!
......

Where do you draw your inspiration from?
Watching the upcoming events such as Arnold classics and Mr. Olympia.
......

Made any mistakes that helped or hurt you in a way that you would like to share?
Not attending the gym in over a week really hurt me.
......

What were your biggest personal battles and how did you confront them?
My abs and my back are my personal battles. I confront them every day and it is something I have to work through for the rest of my life. I also suffered from a deep depression from my debilitating injuries but this is something I overcame with hard work and dedication.
......

What were the most difficult decisions you had to make during your lifetime? Why?
I had to have 4 back surgeries and each one set me back over a year. It affected my quality of life and my first priority as a mom.
......

If you could paint a picture of any scenery you've seen before, what would you paint?
I would paint myself as the primary bodybuilder in a fitness competition.
......

What are some goals you are still trying to accomplish?
Continuing to strengthen my abs and back health as well as regain full strength of the L5 nerve damage in my ankle.
......

What are the most important lessons you've learned in life?
Never take your back for granted.
......

What are you proudest of in your life?
I am able to walk after the doctors said I wouldn't. They gave up but I pushed forward.
......

How do you set your goals?
I see the end result and develop a plan as to how I am going to get there.
......

What else would you do if you weren't in your current line of work?
I would be involved in politics or criminal justice.
......

What are your religious beliefs/spiritual beliefs?
I am Catholic, I pray to God and ask for healing and guidance.
......

What's your favorite food?
Chicken.
......

What would we find in your refrigerator right now?
Water, vegetables, brown rice, beans, cottage cheese, yogurts, and meat.
......

If you had the opportunity to get a message across to a large group of people what would your message be?
Don't listen to the negative people in your life. You have to believe in yourself, visualize yourself doing what it is everyone said you couldn't. Push forward and never give up on yourself, if you believe it you can achieve it.
......

Where do you see yourself in 5 years?

I would love to own my very own gym and clothing line (fitness gear).
......

What are you best at?
I consider myself best at my own workouts and health maintenance.
......

What books do you like to read?
James Patterson ,Stephen King, and romance novel.
......

What is your favorite type of music?
Old school freestyle and Latin music.
......

Describe your parents, what are they like?
My mother is a very compassionate, nurturing and wise woman. She is my saint! She was there when no one else was, her faith and belief in me is what kept me strong when I wanted to be weak. She was a driving force in helping me to achieve my goals when I was rehabilitating. My Dad is strict, stubborn, old school Puerto Rican. He keeps a lot inside and keeps his emotions to himself. He is strong and direct when speaking. He is sincere and caring but emotionless.
......

What were your dreams as a child and did you achieve any of them?
My dream as a young girl was to become a nurse or doctor. I was not able to achieve this dream.
......

Tell us a time in your life that was a time you'll never forget?
Giving birth to my son and getting injured at my job which changed my life forever.
......

What things do you find yourself doing that you said you'd never do?
Working out and being able to walk!
......

What are some qualities that you value in a person?
Trust, honesty, respect, dedication, loyalty and people who can be themselves and just go with the flow.

Where did you grow up and what was it like?
I grew up in Meriden, it was alive and thriving...I grew up sheltered being limited in my social life. We didn't have a lot, but we made the best with what we had. My mom was very creative with making toys for us. We were always busy and stayed out of trouble.
......

Name 5 of your favorite movies.
The Seventh Sign, The Green Mile, Life, My Sisters Keeper, and Scarface.
......

What TV shows do you like?
Seinfeld, Days of Our Lives, Friends, Everybody Loves Raymond, Good Times , The Golden Girls, and King of Queens.
......

What do you enjoy doing on a Sunday afternoon?
Staying home getting some R&R, Cleaning, and spending time with my family.
......

You are stranded in the Amazon rain forest. What 3 items would you want to have with you and why?
A man because he would keep me company, Food to eat, and a Hut in the trees to keep me out of the rain.
......

Is there anything in particular that you wish you could do over? What is it?
I wish I could go back in time and never have gotten hurt.
......

What personality traits in your mind are best suited for your job, career, etc?
I am friendly, confident and maintain an enthusiastic attitude about life!

What is your favorite drink?
Lemon Water.
......

What is your favorite color?
Blue.
......

Name a movie that touched you in some way.
Life.
......

When in life have you felt most alone? Why?
When my husband and I separated. He had to work two jobs and wasn't available for me or son. He didn't make time for his family. The hours consumed him and it affected our marriage.
......

What would be impossible for you to give up?
Working out and being advocate in what I believe in.
......

Why would someone not want to work with you?
I would push them and they would probably be sore for the following days after a workout with me!
......

What activities did you enjoy in school?

Drama and sports.
......

What kind of child were you?
Well behaved, I was quiet, shy and kept to myself. I didn't like to involve myself with people who liked to stir up trouble. It was how I was brought up.
......

If you could be a superhero, what would you want your superpowers to be?
I would be Wonder Woman and my super power would be to extract the truth from the bad guys.
......

How do you want to be remembered?
I would like to be remembered as funny, silly, compassionate, loving and understanding. Someone who goes out of their way to help out others.
......

We all have vices, what are yours?
My vices would be my temper and anxieties.
......

What is one of your favorite quotes?
If you don't hold compassion, you don't have a soul.
......

What chore do you absolutely hate doing?
I love doing my chores but dusting would be what I hate to do because I have allergies and it triggers my asthma.
......

What is your best feature?
My legs, many of my friends will tell me my arms and back are my best features.
......

What was the last experience that made you a stronger person?
My last back surgery.
......

What makes you uncomfortable, besides these questions?
What makes me uncomfortable about myself is exposing my battle wounds from having many different type of surgeries and how it looks after the out come.
......

If you could change something physical about yourself, what would it be and why?
I would change my abs because I don't feel complete. I don't like the way my stomach looks due to several surgeries and scars in and around area.
......

Besides money, what are your favorite ways to compensate people?
My ways in compensating people depending what they have done is to acknowledge and praise their work.
......

When was the last time you tried something new?
The last time I tried something new I ate something that I had on my bucket list and it was eating snails.
......

How would you describe yourself in three words?
Strong, stubborn and compassionate.
......

What is one thing you are not?
A drama queen!!
......

Do you think crying is a sign of weakness or strength?
It all depends on the situation, most likely its gives me strength because I have no control of every situation and the outcome did not start by me. I do what I can and I share what I have and if I find it isn't enough, at least I did the best that I can and I know the very next day I learn from it.
......

What makes you angry?
What makes me angry is when someone will ask me how to get into shape but is NOT willing to make change in their eating habits, always looking for a magic pill.
......

What makes you laugh?
What makes me laugh is when I go out with my cousin Mari and she end up driving somewhere else instead of going to our destination, two turns and we end up in another part of Ct. Lol.
......

What are you afraid of?
I'm afraid dying alone, losing my eye sight, losing my son and a family member and omg yes, SPIDERS lol.
......

What would be the first thing you would do if today was your last day?
I would grab my son first and give him everything else that he needs in life. I would go to church and give thanks to those who have given and done things for me and also make amends to the few people I had to let go out of my life.
......

What's your vision of a perfect society?
A world where everyone had all basic and not-so basic household needs. We all have easy access of going green (being affordable), Fundamental level of food, clothing, shelter, hygiene, health support , security which are necessary

for survival of all human being of the society . A world as well where we grew up with the basic needs of a home phone, writing letters and family values.
......

Is it possible to lie without saying a word? How?
Yes, by body language and eyes. The body will tense up and flushing of the face and you will not receive that eye to eye contact.
......

What's something you check daily?
What I check on a daily basis my intake of my meals and fluids.

Are you an emotional person?
Yes I'm very emotional.
......

What's your own definition of happiness?
Being physically and mentally healthy. Having love in my life and give love back. Being with family and friends that mean the world to me and have stood by my side in everything that I have done. Having a sense of security and humor. When you're not sad or angry. When I'm content with my life and my surroundings. Achieving goals and dreams. Knowing our loved ones are happy safe and sound.
......

Which famous person would you like to interview and which questions would you ask him/her?
It would be President Obama and I would ask him 1. What are your deepest fears that you hold about your own life? 2. If you had one wish and power, what would you do to change the world? 3. After your term is over, what would be the next thing in life that you would challenge yourself?
......

If you could choose to be born with a particular natural skill what skill would it be?
I'd be an acrobat because I would be extremely flexible.
......

What advice would you give someone who wanted to do what you do?
You have to love what you do; you have to have heart and a mind set and not to accept any failures. Keep your head up high and stay focused.
......

While you are watching TV in your home a penguin walks through the door wearing a sheriff's hat and badge. What does he say?
He says "Get dressed we are going to the club, I'm in the mood to dance salsa"
......

Do you have any secrets you want to share with the few of us reading this? We won't say anything....promise!
NO it's a secret...Just like Victoria Secret has hers, is she REALLY a she? ;).
......

Are there any words of wisdom you'd like to pass along to us?
Always over come fear let fear fear you. Fear is life's challenge and we have to learn to overcome a challenge .We learn and grow from it. Fear is the devil's work.
......

Did you enjoy answering these questions? On a scale from 1 – 10. 1= I hated it. 10= I really enjoyed it.
Yes I did I rate this as a 10.

....

About Madeline

Madeline's website :
http://bodyspace.bodybuilding.com/solidbarbie

INTERVIEW 17
Alicia Bell

Personal Information

Full Name:
Alicia Bell

Age:
29

Location:

Toronto Ontario Canada
Relationship Status:
Single

Number of Children:
0

Profession:
Personal Trainer and recreation manager

Educational Background:
BSc in Kinesiology

Certifications:
Canfit Pro NCCP Level 3
....

General Questions

What are you known for professionally?
Track and field coach and personal trainer.
......

Tell us about how you got into your line of work.
Always had a passion for sports and fitness.
......

How long have you been doing what you do?
About 10 years.
......

What do you enjoy most about what you do?
Coaching athletes to be the best that they can be and getting to see the results.
......

What are you most passionate about professionally? What most excites you about your work & the contribution you can make?
Seeing the results and improvements that all of my athletes have.
......

What's the single most important reason for your success?
Dedication and using my education and experience to give my clients programs that they wouldn't be able to get from anyone else.
......

What do you consider to be your greatest achievement?
Being chosen to coach team Canada at the World Maccabi Games in Israel this summer.
......

How do you think women have changed over the years? Regarding business, sports and fitness.
I definitely have a lot more growing to do. I think that I have become more patient with business relationships. Sports I have also worked on becoming more of a team player in business and sports.
......

Do you think women are competitive with each other? Why? Regarding business, sports and fitness.
Very competitive with each other. At least I am. I don't like to lose so everything seems like a competition to me. Women love attention and we all want to be recognized for everything that we do.
......

What memorable competitions come to mind in your career?
Running in the Canada games in 2005, playing in the LFL for the first time was pretty surreal.
......

What is the number one thing you like best about being into fitness?
That I get a lot of compliments and get to inspire many people simply from the way I look.
......

Is there anything wrong with wanting to portray women athletes, actors, etc as feminine and physically attractive?
No.
......

How do you deal with cravings for junk foods, sweets and salty food?
I give in to them most of the time if I am not training for anything specific.
......

Describe a typical day for you, starting from the moment you wake up in the morning.
Wake up, breakfast, hop on motorcycle. At first client for the day no later than 7am. Work training clients independently until 2pm then work at my recreation management job 2-10pm. Finally get home at 1040pm. Shower and sleep.
......

Health & Fitness Questions

What sports do you participated in for fun?

Football and Track and Field.
……

How long have you been playing those sports?
2 years for football and my whole life for track and field.
……

What got you started in that sport?
For football I was aggressive and like to hit and figured I was fast and I don't mind showing off my body. Track…I was faster than everyone.
……

What is your biggest accomplishment in your sports? Include fun sports and any athletic career.
Making my LFL team. Two years in a row. Competing at multiple national championships, Canada Games and Senior Nationals for track and field.
……

What competitions have you entered? What were the outcomes?
Too many to mention.
……

How do you motivate yourself and stay motivated?
Instagram photos of other inspiring women.
……

What are some of the main foods you would include in your shopping list to maintain a lean and muscular physique?
Kale, spinach, trout, salmon, chicken, almonds, promasil protein from rivals, coconut milk, eggs, bananas and pineapple.
……

What is the most challenging thing you deal with about consistently staying in top shape?
I love chips. And starbucks.
......

Please describe your normal diet. What do you eat in a typical day to stay in shape?
Lean meats and lots of green veggies. Lots of water too.
......

What type of exercises do you include in your routine to stay in shape?
Heavy weights, sprints and swimming.
......

A total beginner is about 35 pounds overweight. She doesn't really know where to start. What tips can you give her to follow the right track?
Cut out bad carbs, sugars and fats. Eat lots of lean meats and dark green veggies and don't be afraid to lift. Find a support system. Set goals. And always be doing it for a reason. Find something you love doing. If it's not lifting join rumba...etc you have to love it to stick to it.
......

What tips do you recommend for eating out at restaurants to make sure we don't gain too much weight/fat?
Don't be afraid to ask for changes to your food to include or not include certain things. If the portion is huge don't be afraid to ask for a take away.
......

What exercises do you recommend for getting a bigger, rounder and fuller butt?
Squats, step ups, lunges, dead lifts, sprints and more sprints.
......

What are your top tips for developing toned and defined arms? Specific exercises, diet advice, etc.
Diet. Eat clean. Also biceps curls into shoulder press. Lateral raises and dips dips dips.
......

What are your top tips for losing unwanted body fat? Specific exercises, diet advice, etc.
Drink lots of water, hiit training, sprints, and don't be afraid to lift heavy.
......

What are your top tips for staying motivated on a fitness plan?
DO it with a friend to keep you motivated and on track.
......

What is your training routine like? Please include a few details.
HIIT training 5-7x a week, sprints 3x a week, 3 day lifting training program.
......

What is the best way to get started in your industry?
Educate yourself, shadow someone and do it because you love it.
......

What is the best way towards becoming a personal trainer?
Make connections it's all about connecting. Also take as many educational courses for training that you can. There's so much to know.
......

Have you suffered any injuries? What injuries?
Tore my ACL and had reconstruction.
......

What things do you currently do in your training that is key to your success?
Heavy lifting.
......

Isn't it hard to stay fit? How do you manage that?!
Yes. You have to make the time and not make excuses. Always make time for training.
......

Business Questions

Tell us about your first entrepreneurial experience as a kid or older.
I was always giving away things not selling them.
......

What is the most difficult part of starting your business?
Finding clients and marketing myself.
......

How have your entrepreneurial motivations changed since you first started?
Before I was doing it because I love it and relied on word of mouth now money is always an issue. I provide for myself. So the harder I grind the better off I am.
......

What do you consider to be success as a business owner or entrepreneur?
Always continually growing, expanding and changing.
......

What's your least favorite part about being a business owner or entrepreneur?

Sometimes there are spikes in clients and sometimes everyone seems to be absent. Also always having to budget myself.
......

What's the biggest thing you struggle with as a business owner or entrepreneur?
I love to travel. Since I don't have other trainers besides myself employed its hard leaving clients for longer periods of time...or frequently. Clients don't like that.
......

How do you think running a business or being an entrepreneur has made you a better person?
It has taught me a lot about business marketing, managing and people skills. And has taught me you never know who you are meeting.
......

How did you arrive at running this business? What path brought you here?
I was tired of clients paying a gym over 100$ a session for me and me only making 40$. I realized they were paying for me not the gym.
......

What was the most difficult part of starting your business?
Finding clients and advertising.
......

What do you do on a daily basis to grow as a person/business person/entrepreneur?
Challenge to stay motivated for 12hr + days and take care of others first over myself.
......

What's unique about the service that you provide?
I train everyone as if they were an athlete. I have so much education and experience with athletes that I can transfer it very easily. I also worked injury rehabilitation so I have multiple approaches.
......

What entrepreneurial hacks have you developed to stay focused and productive in your day-to-day?
Being organized, working with schedules and I try to accommodate and be flexible for everyone.
......

Do you have any of your own branded products? If so, what are they?
Everything is TRAIN IT RIGHT. I have clothes online and an eBook.
......

Mixed Questions

What would be your ultimate achievement in any area of your life?
To own my own performance centre.
......

If you could be any character in fiction, who would you be?
Shera!
......

At present, what is your biggest challenge, and what are you doing to manage this challenge?
Financial is always an issue. I am working hard.

......

What things do you believe differentiates you from your contemporaries?
My education, experience and strife for always wanting more.
......

Who has been the biggest influence on your life? What lessons did that person teach you?
My grandmother. She is the kindest and hardest working person I know. She has taught me to always try and achieve more and to always be 15 minutes early for everything. If you are not you are late.
......

Do you have a saying or motto that you live your life by?
Train It Right.
......

Where do you draw your inspiration from?
Within. I always want more.
......

Made any mistakes that helped or hurt you in a way that you would like to share?
Don't burn bridges. Every encounter with someone could lead to great things. Also don't let anyone push you around or discourage you.
......

What were your biggest personal battles and how did you confront them?
I have an attitude and hate people telling me what to do. I have learned to be more open and listen more.
......

What were the most difficult decisions you had to make during your lifetime? Why?
To move. Sometimes it's always easy to stay comfortable but you never know what can happen if you take a chance and make a change.
......

If you could paint a picture of any scenery you've seen before, what would you paint?
River. Summer. Silence. Blue Sky.
......

What are some goals you are still trying to accomplish?
Own my own performance facility.
......

What are the most important lessons you've learned in life?
Always use every opportunity to form positive relationships and always be the best you can be.
......

What are you proudest of in your life?
My education and athletic achievements.
......

How do you set your goals?
Write them down.
......

What else would you do if you weren't in your current line of work?
Travel.
......

Do you believe in the Law of Attraction?
Yes.
......

What is your diet like?
Clean but I don't restrict my cravings.
......

What's your favorite food?
Lobster.
......

What would we find in your refrigerator right now?
Only healthy food. I don't keep junk in the house.
......

If you had the opportunity to get a message across to a large group of people what would your message be?
Never give up.
......

Where do you see yourself in 5 years?
Owning my own facility.
......

What are you best at?
Having fun.
......

What books do you like to read?
I love to read all types of books.
......

What is your favorite type of music?
Trap Music. aka Rap, hip hop.
......

Describe your parents, what are they like?
Fun.
......

What were your dreams as a child and did you achieve any of them?
To be an Olympian. No.
......

Tell us a time in your life that was a time you'll never forget?
I've had a lot of great experiences.
......

What things do you find yourself doing that you said you'd never do?
I've never said I wouldn't do anything. I want to experience life and I take all opportunities given.

What are some qualities that you value in a person?
Loyalty, honesty, sincerity.
......

Where did you grow up and what was it like?
Plaster Rock, New Brunswick, Canada.
......

Name 5 of your favorite movies.
I'm not much of a movie person. Dazed and Confused is one of my favs, Wall-e, little mermaid, Lion King, Back to the future.
......

What TV shows do you like?
Sports shows.
......

What do you enjoy doing on a Sunday afternoon?
FOOOOTBALLLLLL.
......

You are stranded in the Amazon rain forest. What 3 items would you want to have with you and why?
Cell phone, Sunglasses and a hot man.

......

Is there anything in particular that you wish you could do over? What is it?
My track career.
......

What personality traits in your mind are best suited for your job, career, etc?
People person, punctual and open minded.
......

What is your favorite drink?
Coconut anything.
......

What is your favorite color?
Pink.
......

When in life have you felt most alone? Why?
When I move to a new city by myself.
......

What would be impossible for you to give up?
Cell Phone.
......

Why would someone not want to work with you?
I am opinionated.
......

What activities did you enjoy in school?
Anything sports related.
......

What kind of child were you?
Bossy.
......

If you could be a superhero, what would you want your superpowers to be?
Teletransportation.
......

How do you want to be remembered?
As a fun person.
......

What chore do you absolutely hate doing?
Any chore.
......

What is your best feature?
Legs.

What was the last experience that made you a stronger person?
ACL reconstruction.
......

What makes you uncomfortable, besides these questions?
Not much.
......

If you could change something physical about yourself, what would it be and why?
Nose...don't like it.
......

Besides money, what are your favorite ways to compensate people?
Sessions.
......

When was the last time you tried something new?
Always try new things.

......

How would you describe yourself in three words?
Fun, Fit, Feisty.
......

What is one thing you are not?
Friendly to new ppl.
......

Do you think crying is a sign of weakness or strength?
Weakness.
......

What makes you angry?
People in my way or ppl who don't listen.
......

What makes you laugh?
Myself.
......

What are you afraid of?
The dark.
......

What would be the first thing you would do if today was your last day?
Write a letter to my grandparents while eating lobster.
......

What's your vision of a perfect society?
Where the USA and Canadian border didn't exist.
......

Is it possible to lie without saying a word? How?
Body language.
......

What's something you check daily?
Email.
......

Are you an emotional person?
Yes.
......

What's your own definition of happiness?
No worries or stress.
......

Which famous person would you like to interview and which questions would you ask him/her?
No one is famous. Were all the same. But I wouldn't mind reuniting with one athlete and ask him one question.. WHY?
......

If you could choose to be born with a particular natural skill what skill would it be?
I like mine.
......

What advice would you give someone who wanted to do what you do?
Get educated, shadow someone and get as much experience as possible.
......

While you are watching TV in your home a penguin walks through the door wearing a sheriff's hat and badge. What does he say?
Sup!
......

Do you have any secrets you want to share with the few of us reading this? We won't say anything....promise!

No.
......

Are there any words of wisdom you'd like to pass along to us?
Never give up.
......

Did you enjoy answering these questions? On a scale from 1 – 10. 1= I hated it. 10= I really enjoyed it.
5.

....

About Alicia

Alicia Bell
BSc Kin
Canfit Pro PTS
NCCP level 3 sprint and hurdle coach
http://www.trainitright.com

INTERVIEW 18
Diane Adeler

Personal Information

Full Name:
Diane Adeler

Age:
47

Location:
New Jersey

Relationship Status:
Married

Number of Children:
2

Profession:
Certified Personal Trainer

Certifications:
AAAI/ISMA, BASI Pilates, Mad Dogg Athletics
....

General Questions

What are you known for professionally?
My desire to motivate others.
......

Tell us about how you got into your line of work.
I've always been a gym rat, and always had a desire to teach fitness.
......

How long have you been doing what you do?
11 years.
......

What do you enjoy most about what you do?
Helping others achieve their fitness goals.
......

How do you think women have changed over the years? Regarding business, sports and fitness.

I think women have really stepped up their game in the fitness world. More women are out there working just as hard in the gym as men.

Do you think women are competitive with each other? Why? Regarding business, sports and fitness.
Yes to a certain extent. Coming from a figure competitor standpoint there has to be a certain level of competitiveness.
……

What memorable competitions come to mind in your career?
My 1st figure competition. October 20, 2012.
……

What is the number one thing you like best about being into fitness?
First of all for me I stay in shape and secondly I get to inspire others.
……

Is there anything wrong with wanting to portray women athletes, actors, etc as feminine and physically attractive?
Absolutely not. Women should be feminine. Feminine yet strong.
……

How do you deal with cravings for junk foods, sweets and salty food?
I limit myself. I always say you have to enjoy life but balance everything out. Life is about balance.
……

Describe a typical day for you, starting from the moment you wake up in the morning.
Wake at 5:30, have my breakfast then head to the gym to do my workout. Clients all morning. Come home to shower and have lunch. I do my house chores and errands, typical things.

My 2nd round at the gym starts at 4pm and ends around 730pm. My daughter and I most nights go and watch the sunset. I love to end my day with peace.
......

Health & Fitness Questions

What is your biggest accomplishment in your sports? Include fun sports and any athletic career.
My biggest accomplishment was training and dieting for 19 weeks to step on stage as a 1st time figure competitor.
......

How do you motivate yourself and stay motivated?
Going to the gym for me has always been looked at as "it's my job". If you don't show up you get fired. So, it's not a chore for me to get up and go. I am my own walking billboard as well. I have to do and be what I say to my clients.
......

What is the most challenging thing you deal with about consistently staying in top shape?
Well there comes a time in a woman's life when her body works against her. I am at that point but do all I can to combat that.
......

Please describe your normal diet. What do you eat in a typical day to stay in shape?
Oatmeal, egg whites, broccoli, asparagus, chicken, ground turkey, lean steak, salads, almonds, greek yogurt, whey protein powder, tuna fish, apples, bananas, blueberries, brown rice, sweet potatoes and tons of water.
......

What type of exercises do you include in your routine to stay in shape?
Leg press, squats, shoulder presses, lateral raises, lat pulldowns, deadlifts, lunges, HIIT cardio.

......

What exercises do you recommend for getting a bigger, rounder and fuller butt?
Squats all the way.
What are your top tips for developing toned and defined arms? Specific exercises, diet advice, etc.
For me, to define my shoulders I do lots of lateral raises. You also have to keep your diet relatively clean.
......

What are your top tips for losing unwanted body fat? Specific exercises, diet advice, etc.
To lose body fat you have to start in your kitchen. Keep all good wholesome clean foods in the house and avoid all processed foods. Do enough cardio training as well.
......

What are your top tips for gaining lean muscle mass? Specific exercises, diet advice, etc.
Again, for me I have to lift heavy to see any gains.
......

What is your training routine like? Please include a few details.
I do a 5 day split. Two days I train legs, 2 days back, 2 days shoulders and 1 day arms. The other days I teach spin class which is my HIIT training. I do steady state cardio on my weight training days.
......

What is the best way towards becoming a personal trainer?
Get a good certification and keep reading and learning.
......

Mixed Questions

What would be your ultimate achievement in any area of your life?
Raising my 2 children by myself the last 8 years.

Do you have a saying or motto that you live your life by?
Live, Laugh, Love.
......

What are some goals you are still trying to accomplish?
Fitness goals...having a successful off season to hit the state again as a figure competitor
......

If you had the opportunity to get a message across to a large group of people what would your message be?
To take your fitness / health journey one day at a time. To value yourself and know that you are most important and you can do whatever you set your mind to. Enjoy the journey, don't worry so much about the destination. Once you reach your destination, the journey continues on.
......

What are some qualities that you value in a person?
Honest, integrity, kindness.
......

How would you describe yourself in three words?
Humble , genuine kind.
......

What makes you angry?
People who know it all (or think they do).
......

What advice would you give someone who wanted to do what you do?

Don't do this for the money. Become a trainer because you have a passion for helping others.

About Diane

Fitness by Diane:
http://www.facebook.com/pages/Fitness-by-Diane/255811691119382

INTERVIEW 19
Lisa Moskovitz

Personal Information

Full Name:
Lisa Moskovitz

Age:
27

Location:
New York City

Relationship Status:
Single
Number of Children:
0

Profession:
Registered Dietitian

Educational Background:
Graduated Syracuse University with a B.S. in Nutrition
Dietetic Internship at New York Presbyterian Hospital

Certifications:
Certified Dietitian-Nutritionist, Certified Personal Trainer
....

General Questions

What are you known for professionally?
Private counseling for weight loss and sports nutrition.
......

Tell us about how you got into your line of work.
I always had a passion for science, fitness and food! I combined all of my passions together and found myself looking for a nutrition program during my college application process.
As soon as I graduated from college with a B.S. in nutrition I was excited as ever to start working right away. I knew private practice was where I wanted to be. I still cannot think of a more rewarding and challenging profession.
......

How long have you been doing what you do?
I have been in private practice for over 3 years.

......

What do you enjoy most about what you do?
Hearing my clients tell me how appreciative they are of my help and advice is the best feeling in the world.
......

What are you most passionate about professionally? What most excites you about your work & the contribution you can make?
I most passionate about the ability I am given to change people's lives by making them healthier and more self-confident.
......

What's the single most important reason for your success?
The single most important reason for my success is that I am always looking to grow, expand and improve. I keep my mind and heart open to new ideas which makes me a better professional.
I also try my hardest to practice what I preach!
......

What do you consider to be your greatest achievement?
My greatest achievement is that I was able follow my passion when choosing a career instead of picking a profession that would have a higher income.
......

How do you think women have changed over the years? Regarding business, sports and fitness.
Women are stronger than ever. We are not only mothers and **wives**, but now we are business owners and bread winners.
......

Do you think women are competitive with each other? Why? Regarding business, sports and fitness.
I think people are competitive with each other in general. Everyone wants to be the best at what they do!
......

What memorable competitions come to mind in your career?
Considering that I was a devoted soccer player for most of my childhood, competition comes natural to me. I think competition can be very healthy and necessary. It pushes you to be better, faster and stronger.
Having said that I am always keeping an eye out for potential competitors but only because I like to learn from them.
......

What is the number one thing you like best about being into fitness?
The number one thing I like about fitness is the high that you get from it. No matter how much of a bad day you had, exercise always seems to straighten and balance me out.
......

Is there anything wrong with wanting to portray women athletes, actors, etc as feminine and physically attractive?
No not at all. Men are portrayed the same way!
......

How do you deal with cravings for junk foods, sweets and salty food?
I give in when the craving is greater than a 5 on a scale of 1-10. I also don't deprive myself. If I want chocolate, I will have a piece but I am able to control portions by not buying a whole bag.
The less I deprive myself that more I am able to control cravings.
......

Describe a typical day for you, starting from the moment you wake up in the morning.
I get up, take a shower, go to work and on the way I grab coffee with a quick healthy breakfast such as greek yogurt with berries. I see patients in my office all day long and then by the end of the day I go right to the gym, come home have dinner watch TV for a few hours and go to bed!
......

Health & Fitness Questions

What sports do you participated in for fun?
Running, Soccer and football.
......

How long have you been playing those sports?
I have been playing soccer and running since I was able to walk!
......

What got you started in that sport?
My uncle loved soccer so one day he took me outside to play and thought I was good enough to try out for a league. He encouraged me to play and from that day on that is exactly what I did!
......

How do you motivate yourself and stay motivated?
My mantra is that everyday is a chance to start over and be better than the day before. If you're not trying to improve yourself than what are you trying to do?
......

What are some of the main foods you would include in your shopping list to maintain a lean and muscular physique?
Baby carrots, greek yogurt, turkey slices, hummus, frozen yogurt, dark chocolate, laughing cow light cheese wedges, low-carb tortillas and low-fat cottage cheese.
......

What is the most challenging thing you deal with about consistently staying in top shape?
I do not have a naturally lean or muscular shape. In fact, if I don't exercise or eat healthy I will gain body fat - TONS OF IT!
......

Please describe your normal diet. What do you eat in a typical day to stay in shape?
I eat several times per day since I do not digest big meals well. Some of my mini meals/snacks include crackers with peanut butter, salad with grilled chicken, laughing cow light cheese on a low-carb tortilla, egg-white veggie omelet, turkey slices on a low-carb tortilla, carrots with hummus.
......

What type of exercises do you include in your routine to stay in shape?
I run about 10-15 miles per week and I do circuit training 2-3 times per week.
......

A total beginner is about 35 pounds overweight. She doesn't really know where to start. What tips can you give her to follow the right track?
Start slow and take it day by day. Make a list of a few short term and long-term goals you want to accomplish. Keep track of what you eat on daily food records for accountability. Find a workout body and make sure you have support from people around you.

......

What tips do you recommend for eating out at restaurants to make sure we don't gain too much weight/fat?
Start off with an appetizer such as clear or tomato-based soup or salad with dressing on side. Always order grilled, baked or steamed fish or seafood which are naturally leanest or lowest in fat.
Get a to-go container with the meal and put half away so you can feel good about finishing your plate.
......

What exercises do you recommend for getting a bigger, rounder and fuller butt?
Squats, spin class and leg lifts.
......

What are your top tips for developing toned and defined arms? Specific exercises, diet advice, etc.
Lower weights with higher reps and cardio that incorporates arm movement (ex: running). Eat more plant-based fruits and veggies and avoid processed/refined carbohydrates.
......

What are your top tips for losing unwanted body fat? Specific exercises, diet advice, etc.
Drink plenty of water, engage in moderate exercise, eat consistently throughout the day and incorporate fiber and lean protein at every meal.
......

What are your top tips for gaining lean muscle mass? Specific exercises, diet advice, etc.
Eat protein every 2-3 hours with some complex carb. Engage in at least 1 hour of weight training 4-5 times per week. Include recovery drink with 2 to 1 carb to protein ratio.
......

What are your top tips for staying motivated on a fitness plan?
Remind yourself everyday what you are trying to achieve. Keep a pair of tight jeans or a dress hanging on your closet door or hang a picture of you when you were at your thinnest on the fridge.
......

Business Questions

What is the most difficult part of starting your business?
The most difficult part is not talking yourself out of it! It is important to stay positive and remember why you want to do this because it can be very overwhelming at first.
......

How have your entrepreneurial motivations changed since you first started?
My motivations have changed to more long-term goals rather than short-term. I used to think that I had to do everything by tomorrow but now I realize you need to slow down, think things through before you take action.
......

What do you consider to be success as a business owner or entrepreneur?
Success is being happy with what you do, reaching out to as many people as possible and not going bankrupt at the same time!
......

What's your least favorite part about being a business owner or entrepreneur?
All the responsibility and pressure can be a lot at times but it is worth it in the end.

......

How do you think running a business or being an entrepreneur has made you a better person?
I am much more responsible than ever before.
......

How is running a successful business different than what you thought it would be?
I didn't think enough about overhead expenses.
......

How did you arrive at running this business? What path brought you here?
I chalk it up to my personality. I don't perform well when I am micromanaged.
......

What do you do on a daily basis to grow as a person/business person/entrepreneur?
I listen and learn from other people including my clients!
......

Mixed Questions

What would be your ultimate achievement in any area of your life?
Feeling good about what I do on a day-to-day basis.
......

What things do you believe differentiates you from your contemporaries?
My style is constantly changing so I never get stuck in a rut.
......

Who has been the biggest influence on your life? What lessons did that person teach you?
My parents keep me the most grounded.
......

What was the best advice you were ever given?
In the end you will always get what you want and be happy, otherwise it's not the end!
......

Do you have a saying or motto that you live your life by?
You're either working on getting better or allowing yourself to get worse - there's no such thing as maintenance.
......

Where do you draw your inspiration from?
People around me.
......

What are you proudest of in your life?
Where I am today.
......

What else would you do if you weren't in your current line of work?
I like to use my creative side so probably some kind of artist.
......

What is your diet like?
Healthy but I am still human!
......

What's your favorite food?
Anything with peanut butter.
......

What would we find in your refrigerator right now?

Not much because I am rarely home!
......

What books do you like to read?
Biographies.
......

What is your favorite type of music?
Pop music or anything that keeps me energized when I exercise.
......

Describe your parents, what are they like?
Total opposites! My dad is silent and conservative and my mom will talk to anyone who will listen!
......

What were your dreams as a child and did you achieve any of them?
100%!
......

What TV shows do you like?
Shows that make you think or laugh: Game of Thrones, Modern Family, Dexter, Breaking Bad.
......

What do you enjoy doing on a Sunday afternoon?
I need time to relax and be lazy. =)
......

What is your favorite drink?
Alcohol? Dirty Martinis.
......

What is your favorite color?
Blue.
......

When in life have you felt most alone? Why?
When no one is picking up their phones!
......

Why would someone not want to work with you?
I am a major perfectionist!
......

Were you ever bullied in school?
Sadly yes!
......

What is your best feature?
My sense of humor.
......

Are you an emotional person?
Not incredibly.
......

What's your own definition of happiness?
Enjoying what you do and doing what you enjoy.
....

About Lisa

Website :http://www.yournydietitian.com

Would You Be Willing To Leave A Review?

If you would consider writing a review of this book on Amazon, I would very much appreciate it. The feedback I receive from readers will be helpful as I develop updates to this book and create other related books.

To write a review of this book, just type 'Andy Charalambous Secrets Of Successful Women in the Amazon search bar and click on reviews for the book.

If you have any comments or questions regarding anything to do with this book then please don't hesitate to send me an email at fitscribbler@gmail.com

Thank you so much,

Andy Charalambous

About the Author

Andy Charalambous

Andy Charalambous was born in London, England and has worked in a number of well-known health clubs and gyms as a fitness instructor, personal trainer and masseur.

He is not your average trainer! He has taken on fat loss experiments where he has gained weight in order to document how he will eventually lose the weight and fat. You can follow a few of his fat loss experiments by going to his website - www.fitscribbler.com - where you will find photos and images of his body transformations.

Andy also writes and creates health and fitness books and at present he has a collection of books which focus on particular areas of women's' wellbeing as well as a number of muscle building books for men. You can find these on his website too.

When he is not working he trains on the beach, cycles, swims, reads, rollerblades and does whatever he can to keep any negative thoughts at bay.

"We have more control over our lives than we think. The sooner we realize this the better the chances are of reaching our goals and fulfilling our dreams" - Andy.

Check out Andy's author website for news on newly released books and special offers:

Fit Scribbler: http://www.fitscribbler.com

Follow Andy on Pinterest:
http://www.pinterest.com/fitcribbler

Follow Andy on Twitter at:
http://twitter.com/FitScribbler

Follow Andy on Facebook:
https://www.facebook.com/fit.scribbler

Follow Andy on Linkedin:
http://www.linkedin.com/in/fitscribbler

Recommended Related Books

More Books you may like by Andy Charalambous

Just type 'Andy Charalambous' in the Amazon search bar to see all of his latest books:

Printed in Dunstable, United Kingdom